DIRE STRAITS

The Perils of Writing the Early Modern English Coastline from Leland to Milton

Dire Straits

*The Perils of Writing the Early
Modern English Coastline from
Leland to Milton*

ELIZABETH JANE BELLAMY

UNIVERSITY OF TORONTO PRESS
Toronto Buffalo London

ISBN 978-1-4426-4501-1

Library and Archives Canada Cataloguing in Publication

Bellamy, Elizabeth J. (Elizabeth Jane)
Dire straits : the perils of writing the early modern English coastline
from Leland to Milton / Elizabeth Jane Bellamy.

Includes bibliographical references and index.
ISBN 978-1-4426-4501-1

1. English poetry—Early modern, 1500–1700—History and criticism.
2. Coasts in literature.   3. Cartography in literature.   4. Landscapes in
literature.   5. England—In literature.   I. Title.

PR545.C673B44 2013   821'.30932146   C2012-907154-4

University of Toronto Press acknowledges the financial assistance
to its publishing program of the Canada Council for the Arts
and the Ontario Arts Council.

University of Toronto Press acknowledges the financial support of
the Government of Canada through the Canada Book Fund
for its publishing activities.

To my sister, Mary

Contents

Acknowledgments

I wish to thank the University of Tennessee's John C. Hodges Chair of Excellence Research Fund for financial support of this book. I would also like to take this opportunity to express my gratitude to the following for their generous support of and helpful comments on my manuscript as it was in progress: Palmira Brummett, Patrick Cheney, Dorothy Habel, Heather Hirschfeld, Theresa Krier, Joe Loewenstein, David Quint, Sandhya Shetty, Rob Stillman, Gordon Teskey, Rachel Trubowitz, Valerie Wayne, and Anthony Welch. I wish to thank the two anonymous readers for the University of Toronto Press for their helpful comments. And, finally, I am grateful to Suzanne Rancourt, Senior Humanities Editor, University of Toronto Press, for her editorial guidance and patience.

DIRE STRAITS

The Perils of Writing the Early Modern English Coastline from Leland to Milton

Chapter One

The Imperatives of Humanism: Early Modern English Shorelines under Quarantine

1. Spectral Geographies and the Coastline

Early modern English verse often depicted the coastline as a major topic of its fictions. Despite much recent compelling work on early modern English landscape (Sullivan), rivers (Herendeen, Kilgour, McRae), and cartography (Helgerson, Gillies, van Es), to date no one has studied the topic of early modern English coastlines in their own right.[1] As Helgerson's *Forms of Nationhood* has investigated, early modern English cartography enabled the land to ' "speak" ' authoritatively (to echo the resonant title of the study's third chapter, ' "The Land Speaks" '). To be sure, the mapping of coastal sites also played a crucial role in early modern English cartographical ambitions. But when early modern English verse approached the water's edge, these local coastlines sometimes 'spoke' in a more attenuated voice than did the land. In broad terms, this book argues that on those occasions when early modern English writers took their verse to the local water's edge, they did so in the fraught context of a longstanding cultural inheritance from antiquity.

1 Garrett Sullivan, *The Drama of Landscape: Land, Property, and Social Relations on the Early Modern Stage* (Stanford, CA: Stanford University Press, 1998); Wyman Herendeen, *From Landscapes to Literature: The River and the Myth of Geography* (Pittsburgh, PA: Duquesne University Press, 1986); Maggie Kilgour, 'Writing on Water,' *ELR* 29 (1999): 282–305; Andrew McCrae, 'Fluvial Nation: Mobility and Poetry in Early Modern England,' *ELR* 38 (2008): 506–34; Richard Helgerson, *Forms of Nationhood: The Writing of Elizabethan England* (Chicago: University of Chicago Press, 1992); John Gillies, *Shakespeare and the Geography of Difference* (Cambridge: Cambridge University Press, 1994); Bart van Es, *Spenser's Forms of History* (New York: Oxford University Press, 2002).

An overarching question of this book is: How did early modern English humanist verse struggle with the fact that antiquity had quarantined its maritime region's coastlines from the domain of poetry itself?

In his *Eclogues* I.66, Virgil, composing verse in the Roman *axis mundi*, described Britannia as sundered from the world ('Et penitus toto diuisos orbe Britannias').[2] Virgil's description is one of the more notable examples of antiquity's topos of *ultima Britannia*, a welter of coastlines so bleakly remote they were viewed as the last stop before *ultima Thule*, the northernmost regions of the earth.[3] Every humanist-educated early modern English versifier was familiar with antiquity's topos of *ultima Britannia*, its marginality in antiquity's *mappae mundi*. But early modern England's increasing centrality as a maritime power rendered the topos quaintly obsolete. By the reign of Charles II, the royal seal depicted the monarch as ruler of the entire sea, pointedly rephrasing Virgil to read, 'Et penitus toto regnantes orbe Brittanus.'[4] Indeed, it was not the topos of *ultima Britannia* but rather another archipelagic topos from antiquity – namely, the topos of the Atlantic's western islands as the paradisal Fortunate Isles that was ubiquitous in early modern English literature. As Josephine Waters Bennett has authoritatively demonstrated, representations of England as the Fortunate Isles were a dominant topos that appeared in a variety of verse genres encompassing pastoral, elegy, epic, tragedy, and court masque.[5] Bennett's study helps us understand how and why the topos of *ultima Britannia* withered and all but died on an island whose inhabitants were ideologically predisposed, echoing *Richard II*'s John of Gaunt, to view it as a 'precious stone set in silver sea' rather than to imagine it as lost in coastal isolation.

This book maps the lingering effects of *ultima Britannia* in the cultural consciousness of certain early modern English writers; at this juncture, I would like to contextualize my argument within (and eventually

---

2 *Virgil: The Eclogues and Georgics*, ed., intro., notes, R.D. Williams (New York: St Martin's Press, 1979).

3 A definitive twentieth-century compilation of the topos of *ultima Britannia* is included in *A Documentary History of Primitivism and Related Ideas* gen. eds. Arthur O. Lovejoy, Gilbert Chinard, George Boas, and Ronald S. Crane, vol. I (Baltimore: The Johns Hopkins University Press, 1935).

4 Aby Warburg, *Die Erneuerung der heidniscchen Antike*, quoted in Edgar Wind, *Pagan Mysteries in the Renaissance* (New York and London: W.W. Norton & Co., 1950), 226.

5 Josephine Waters Bennett, 'Britain Among the Fortunate Isles,' *Studies in Philology* 53 (1956): 114–40.

differentiate it from) the broader framework of the aims of an influential branch of scholarship in recent years, the history of cartography.
Underwriting this discipline is the study of what David Fletcher has
termed 'map consciousness,' a mode of cognition defined as 'topographical knowledge in the form of maps.'[6] Focusing on early modernity, Frank Lestringant has noted the period's 'rupture of scales that
changed people's way of viewing the world' – details gleaned from the
proliferation of charts, maps, globes, and compasses.[7] Bernhard Klein
has called valuable attention not only to early modern maps in and of
themselves but also to how these maps shaped a veritable 'culture of
mapping.'[8] Klein, picking up where Helgerson left off, has argued that
the perspectival and spatial awareness that maps fostered was as significant a factor as any in shaping the emerging early modern English
nation (as well as the larger realm of 'Britain' and the 'British Isles').
Whether the early modern Englishman gazed on the world maps of Ortelius (1570) and Mercator (1595) or on the more regional or local Tudor
and Stuart maps of Saxton, Norden, and Speed, space was persistently
measurable and visualizable. Emphasizing the characteristically ocular
power of maps to shape an early modern English sense of space, Klein
astutely quotes from Ortelius's 1606 atlas *Theatre of the Whole World* and
its description of geography as 'the eye of History' (35).

Maps of seacoasts offer a special kind of ocular pleasure, the noting
of significant coastal variations on the liminal boundaries where land
meets sea. Relevant here is a brief overview of two sub-disciplines of
the history of cartography, the new Mediterranean and the new Atlantic
studies. In the wake of Braudel's landmark work, studies of the Mediterranean from antiquity to early modernity have been reinvigorated.[9]
An influential example is Peregrine Horden and Nicholas Purcell's
The Corrupting Sea and its charting a 'new' Mediterranean divided into

6 David Fletcher, *The Emergence of Estate Maps. Christ Church, Oxford, 1600–1840* (Oxford: Clarendon Press, 1995), 1.
7 Frank Lestringant, *Mapping the Renaissance: The Geographical Imagination in the Age of
  Discovery* (Cambridge: Polity Press, 1994), 4.
8 Bernhard Klein, *Maps and the Writing of Space in Early Modern England and Ireland* (Basingstoke: Palgrave, 2001), 8. For a definitive study of the influence of cartography in
  early modern French writing, see Tom Conley, *The Self-Made Map: Cartographic Writing
  in Early Modern France* (Minneapolis: University of Minnesota Press, 1996).
9 Fernand Braudel, *The Mediterranean and the Mediterranean World in the Age of Philip II*,
  trans. Sîan Reynolds (New York: Harper & Row, 1972–3).

distinctly defined micro-regions that have rendered untenable any pre-
supposition of a 'unified' Mediterranean.[10] In a related development,
the emergent discipline of the new Atlantic studies, shifting from the
Mediterranean of the classical world to the Atlantic (and beyond to the
trans-Atlantic), has similarly charted Atlantic maritime micro-regions.
In the British Isles of early modernity, the vexed identities of 'English-
ness,' 'Welshness,' 'Scottishness,' and 'Irishness' were often bound up
with and determined by the maritime vagaries and pluralizing ambiguity of archipelagic and continental shelf formation, isthmuses, and
tidal currents.[11]

As part of its ongoing project to relocate England, Britain, and the
British Isles from the margins of the Mediterranean to a new Atlantic
perspective, the new Atlantic studies (like the history of cartography in
general) are heavily reliant on the visual and empirical data that early
modern maps and charts so abundantly provide. But the discipline's
appetite for empirical data is of limited help if we assume the task of
mapping the shorelines of the mind's eye – specifically, the impulse
of certain early modern English writers to gaze *inward* at the cognitive maps of an oceanic world still dominated by the centrality of antiquity's Mediterranean. When carefully traced, the broken coastlines
of the British Isles in fact form Europe's longest coastline. But Greco-
Roman geographic discourse, unlike the new Atlantic studies, made far
fewer distinctions among the striated coastal cliffs and tidal incursions
of the North Atlantic's elemental periphery. Antiquity's North Atlantic explorers judged all the marine region's broken coastlines – from
northern Ireland's Loch Foyle to the Shetland firths, and, for that matter, from Cornwall to Kent – as uniformly dangerous, all equidistance
from Mediterranean centrality. The local British Isles shorelines beheld
by the inward gaze of certain early modern English writers could not
be measured by chart, compass, or theolodite. Rather, their local coastal
'map' was more like a palimpsest layered by antiquity's perception of

---

10 *The Corrupting Sea: A Study of Mediterranean History* (Oxford: Blackwell, 2000).
11 Key recent historical studies of the new Atlantic are Bernard Bailyn, *Atlantic History:
   Concept and Contours* (Cambridge, MA: Harvard University Press, 2005), and *Atlantic
   History: A Critical Appraisal*, eds. Jack P. Greene and Philip D. Morgan (New York:
   Oxford University Press, 2009). A prominent volume of literary critical studies of the
   new Atlantic is *Archipelagic Identities: Literature and Identity in the Atlantic Archipelago,
   1550–1800*, ed. Philip Schwyzer and Simon Meallor (Aldershot: Ashgate, 2004).

the coastal region as *ultima Britannia*. The 'map consciousness' (to echo Fletcher) resulting from this inward gaze was necessarily implicated within the spectral geography of Mediterranean antiquity.

Scholars have long traced the powerful, intertextual currents of affinity running through the works of the canonical writers Edmund Spenser, William Shakespeare, and John Milton – namely, the poet to whom Milton biography customarily refers as the early or 'young' Milton. My book focuses on these writers – with complementary discussions of Geoffrey of Monmouth, Chaucer, Leland, Camden, Drayton, Ovid, Ariosto, Sannazaro, and many others. I do so as a means of investigating the tensions between the history of early modern English growth as a maritime presence and the literary history of early modern English humanist struggles to convert local shorelines into sites of verse inspiration commensurate with this growth – inspired sites that could once and for all render obsolete the fact that antiquity had quarantined the British Isles from the domain of poetry itself. My linkage of three figures spanning the historically and culturally disparate Elizabethan, Stuart, and Caroline periods becomes more coherent when viewed through the lens of Leicester Bradner's observation – still useful, if dated – that the young Milton was 'the last of the Elizabethans.'[12] If the young Milton indeed answered to this label, he may also have been the last of the prominent humanist-trained early modern English writers whose verse labored in the shadow of the topos of antiquity's *ultima Britannia*. To be sure, Spenser, Shakespeare, and the young Milton excelled in their deployments of the topos of England as the Fortunate Isles, and all three made significant contributions to the English genre of river verse as panegyric. All three writers were also well aware that antiquity was in ruins (poignantly noted in Spenser's *Ruines of Time*) – and that the Roman *imperium* lay in the dustbin of history. But all three were also eager to legitimate their authority via an extended mastery of classical literary traditions. And thus also haunting the 'map consciousness' of their verse (in Shakespeare's case, dramatic verse) were local shorelines as the tide-battered periphery once relegated to the margins of antiquity's *mappae mundi*.

Of Italy's Adriatic and Ligurian shores, Virgil, noted contributor to the topos of *ultima Britannia*, once wrote of his own Mediterranean

---

12 *Musae Anglicanae: A History of Anglo-Latin Poetry, 1500–1925* (London: Oxford University Press, 1940), 116.

shoreline home: 'What need I tell you of the seas that wash her shores, above and below?' (*Georgics* 2.166–7). Virgil's rhetorical question is an eloquent reminder of the link between poetry and place – a reminder, if we need one, that Mediterranean beauty-coasts were axiomatic in the poetry of antiquity.

In this context, let us turn to early modern English coastlines. If asked to think about bodies of water in early modern England, what most readily comes to mind are not shorelines but rivers, the dominant principle in early modern English topography. An early modern English verse fondness for rivers resulted in the inherently English genre of the Tudor/Stuart river poem, most notably culminating in Michael Drayton's massive, if doomed, *Polyolbion*. Geographically speaking, much of this book is located not on riverbanks but in estuarial and shoreline currents – i.e., on the material reality of the tide-ripped coves, jagged rocks, sucking sandbanks, and channel mazes that fracture and fissure Europe's longest coastline. In Greco-Roman antiquity (as will be investigated in more detail later in the chapter), these shorelines provoked a sense of dread commensurate with an otherworldly maritime region. If Mediterranean beauty-coasts were axiomatic in Roman poetry, so also was the topos of *ultima Britannia*.

Decades ago, Rosalie Colie, punning on literary 'habits' and 'habitats,' reminded us that inspired Renaissance writing was often linked to local, autobiographical sites. Colie observed expansively that, in Renaissance writing, '[g]eography counted: Boccaccio drew the Sicilian Muse from Sicily to that other Sicily, Naples, and thence to Florence in his *Ninfale Fiesolano*; Petrarch worked to endow his Helicon, the Sorge, and his Tempe, the Vaucluse, with the numen of poetic significance.'[13] Boccaccio's Naples and Florence, Petrarch's Sorge and Vaucluse all transformed local Italian and Provençal habitats into inspiration itself.

There is perhaps no more compelling portrayal of early modern English humanism's intimate linkage of poetic inspiration and Continental (particularly Mediterranean) habitats than some of the details of John Milton's tour of Italy. Milton made it a point to visit Giambattista Manso, the former patron of his epic mentor Tasso, who resided in a coastal villa by the hills of Posilipo rimming the Bay of Naples. In his venerable biography of Milton, David Masson embellished his

---

13 Rosalie Colie, *The Resources of Kind: Genre-Theory in the Renaissance* (Berkeley and Los Angeles: University of California Press, 1973), 13, 116.

account of Milton's visit by alluding to Manso's 1634 life of the brilliant if psychologically tormented Tasso, who often visited his patron in Naples: 'had there been a spot in all the world where that poet could have been at rest, Manso thinks it would surely have been Naples.'[14] Masson then narrates what Milton must have experienced as Manso reminisced about Tasso's visits:

> With none the less pleasure would Milton behold all this because Tasso had beheld it before him, or because the same Manso who now pointed out the separate beauties had pointed them out to Tasso fifty years before, and could not refrain now from mixing recollections of Tasso with them, – how here Tasso had uttered such a saying, here he had seemed suddenly moody, here he had raised his large blue eyes to heaven with that peculiar soaring look which he had seen in no man else. (814–15)

Though we cannot be certain of the truth value of Masson's narration, much can be gained by refusing to dismiss the passage as dated sentiment. In this remarkable tableau of early modern humanist habits of thought, Manso and Milton both gazed on the Mediterranean while, in their mind's eye, also envisioning Tasso as he gazed on the Mediterranean. This particular moment at Manso's Neapolitan villa thus traced a profound line of literary inheritance from antiquity to the Italian *cinquecento* to the seventeenth-century English poet whose later, magisterial *Paradise Lost* would become, arguably, the last of the line of prestigious epics deeply indebted to the poetic voices of antiquity. Presiding over this inheritance was the Mediterranean of Homer and Tasso – and now Milton, whose eyes, like Tasso's, 'soared' over the Mediterranean as he pondered his own epic future. Manso, who once watched as Tasso's eyes 'soared' over the Mediterranean, now watched as Milton's eyes also gazed at the Bay of Naples, viewing it through the mediating lens of his epic mentor. In sum, for the first time in his life, Milton gazed on what will be discussed in later detail as antiquity's *peirar*, the sacred liminality between land and sea that had nurtured centuries of Mediterranean poetry.

Masson's linkage of soaring eyes and an almost divine, vatic poetic madness inevitably reminds us of Theseus's oft-cited speech in

---

14 David Masson, *The Life of John Milton*, Vol. 1 (London: MacMillan and Co., 1881), 814.

A Midsummer Night's Dream, where the inspired poet's eye, 'in a fine frenzy rolling / . . . from heaven to earth, from earth to heaven,' succeeds in 'bod[ying] forth / The forms of things unknown,' converting 'airy nothing' into 'A local habitation and a name' (5.1.12–17). But an overarching question of this book is: when the eyes of any given early modern English poet or verse dramatist 'rolled' from, say, the boggy mudflats of Essex, to the deadly promontories of Anglesey, to the perils of the Scillies and the hazardous headlands of Portland Bill and St. David's, did these local coasts ever come into view as sites of a numinous poetics? Or rather, did the concept of a coastal poetics necessarily entail a re-envisioning of the Mediterranean? What a bystander at Manso's villa would have observed was the affective intensity with which the humanist Milton bore witness not to the 'local habitations' of British Isles coastlines, but rather to Tasso's and Manso's – and antiquity's – Mediterranean.

As mentioned earlier, the many early modern English verse representations of local coastlines were written under the banner of yet another topos, England as the Fortunate Isles. This topos had rendered antiquity's dread of *ultima Britannia* quaintly obsolete; and, these verse representations worked hand-in-glove (as will be reviewed later in this chapter) with the new university geography's proffering of these coastlines as forward-looking sites of mercantile expansion to 'brave new worlds.'[15] But this book focuses on these same coastlines as also backward-gazing tropes of humanist preservation, where one of the more intriguing tensions between early modern English continuity and change compellingly played itself out.

Earlier, I spoke of a rift between history and literary history – namely, the tension between the history of early modern English maritime growth and the literary history of early modern English humanist struggles to convert local shorelines into sites of verse inspiration commensurate with this growth. To shed further light on this rift, I turn to another sub-discipline of the history of cartography, studies that, over the last fifteen years, have focused on the 'geography of empire' in early modern English literature. The earlier-cited John Gillies, for example,

---

15 A brief list of verse renderings of the Fortunate Isles includes Thomas Blenerhasset's *Revelation of the True Minerva* (1582), Michael Drayton's *The Shepheardes Garland* (1593), Joseph Hall's *The Kings of Prophicie* (1604), and Ben Jonson's masque *The Fortunate Isles and their Union* (1624).

has demonstrated how any number of Shakespeare's plays reflect early modern England's increasing expansionist ambitions: *The Merchant of Venice* gestures in the direction of England's burgeoning trade in the Mediterranean, while *The Tempest* takes its audiences to Bermuda, a key site of England's expansion west across the Atlantic.[16] These valuable studies of the 'geography of empire' by no means assume a thorough-going demise of the old Ptolemaic universe in the early modern English verse imagination. But at the same time, their enabling assumption has been that the increasingly detailed, scientifically sophisticated maps of such continental cartographers as Ortelius and Mercator had rendered obsolete the world maps of antiquity (Strabo, Pliny, Ptolemy, among others). This assumption, in turn, has paved the way for these stud-ies' perceptions of any number of early modern English literary figures as, though hardly agents of expansionism, significantly predisposed to look at the maps of Ortelius and Mercator through the optimistic, forward-looking lens of England's growth as a maritime force to be reckoned with and of the concomitant sense of a growing 'English-ness.' But my book argues that studies of the 'geography of empire' are not complete until we examine more closely how early modern English verse gazed at the maps of the new geography through the retrospec-tive – and often melancholic – lens of what I have earlier termed the spectral geographies of an old Roman empire that managed to survive their own cartographic obsolescence.

The imperative of humanist preservations of the classical past per-sistently reminded these writers of the fact that British Isles coastlines had themselves once served as one of 'the ends of the earth' for Roman

---

16 *Shakespeare and the Geography of Difference* (Cambridge: Cambridge University Press, 1994). Other key recent studies of early modern English literary representations of the nation's maritime ascendancy are Bruce MacLeod, *The Geography of Empire in English Literature* (Cambridge: Cambridge University Press, 1999), and Andrew Gordon and Bernhard Klein, eds., *Literature, Mapping, and the Politics of Space in Early Modern Britain* (Cambridge: Cambridge University Press, 2001). For a literary his-torical study of the metaphor of the sea voyage in the genre of romance, see David Quint, 'The Boat of Romance and Renaissance Epic,' in *Romance and Generic Trans-formation from Chretien de Troyes to Cervantes*, eds. Kenneth Brownlee and Marina S. Brownlee (Hanover, NH: University Press of New England, 1985). For metaphors of the sea journey in early modern English literature, see Philip Edwards, *Sea-Mark: The Metaphorical Voyage, Spenser to Milton* (Liverpool: Liverpool University Press, 1997). For the voyage metaphor in Milton specifically, see Robert Ralston Cawley, *Milton and the Literature of Travel* (Princeton: Princeton University Press, 1951).

imperial geography. As this chapter will review in later detail, such classical geographers as Strabo, Ptolemy, and Pliny identified *ultima Britannia* as a maritime region so isolated in the North Atlantic that its coastlines were mapped as an otherworldly last stop before reaching the northwest boundaries of the earth. Even more consequential for an early modern English literary perspective was the frequency with which antiquity's almost visceral dread of the tide-ripped British Isles coastlines was, in turn, interwoven within the works of any number of the Roman empire's most prestigious poets and dramatists (Horace, Virgil, Ovid, Seneca, Catullus). As a consequence, the humanist imperatives of early modern English verse struggled to shape a local coastal poetics that ignored the accrued layers of classical perceptions of local shorelines.

Well-documented over time has been the Renaissance aesthetic imagination's sense of separation, even rupture, from antiquity – a separation that, as this book argues, drove a wedge between early modern English verse and local English coastlines as potential sites of an inspired poetics. Early modern English humanism's intimate relationship with classical models, coupled with a heightened sense of the passage of time, exacerbated a sense of belatedness vis-à-vis those same classical models. In *The Light in Troy*, a study of Renaissance Europe's central preoccupation with imitating ancient models, Thomas Greene has disclosed a pervasive Renaissance awareness of a cultural abyss, a melancholic disjuncture separating the Renaissance from antiquity. Renaissance humanism often peered into this abyss, such that, as Greene has eloquently argued, '[t]he pathos of this incomplete embrace never altogether faded from the humanist movement.'[17] An incomplete embrace across a cultural abyss cannot be mapped; and thus I suggest this concept, though grounded in Greene's scholarship in comparative literature, as a useful supplement to histories of early modern English cartography and their particular emphasis on 'map consciousness.' My book argues that when the canonical writers Spenser, Shakespeare, and Milton chose to peer into the cultural abyss between the early modern British Isles and antiquity's Mediterranean, what often came into view was the Mediterranean as the site of an inspired poetics that, almost by definition, mediated their perceptions of early modern English coastlines.

---

17 *The Light in Troy: Imitation and Discovery in Renaissance Poetry* (New Haven: Yale University Press, 1982), 6.

My next chapter, 'Lurid Shorelines: Mapping Spenser's Queen Elizabeth in Ariosto's Hebrides,' comes into view at the intersection of the burgeoning studies, over the last quarter century or so, of Spenser and the 'Irish question,' and of ongoing literary historical linkages of Ariosto and Spenser. Much recent Spenser scholarship has exposed the deteriorating bonds between Spenser and his patron-queen Elizabeth during the 1590s. I seek to further our understanding of Spenser's covert expressions of disillusionment with the Elizabethan courtly cult by investigating how he at times mapped the queen's coastline not as gateways to England's brave new world of maritime expansion, but rather as antiquity's *ultima Britannia*. If Spenser did resent writing the story of the Elizabethan *translatio imperii* while geographically and poetically isolated in Ireland, a 'salvage' island viewed by the queen's court as 'overseas,' then one safely occulted strategy for protesting her indifference was to remap her 'greatest Isle' as no less isolated than his own marginal Ireland. Not so complimentary to Elizabeth are some of Spenser's borrowings from his predecessor Ariosto's epic of the Ferrarese dynasty. Spenser explores some of the more dilatory paths of Ariosto's sprawling narrative, particularly the eighth canto, in which Ariosto temporarily abandons the high seriousness of the matter of Charlemagne to indulge in a melodrama that strands his heroine Angelica on the lonely island of 'Ebuda.' I argue that Spenser's unnamed 'Faerie' coastline of Books 3 and 4 comes into view as Ariosto's Ptolemaic Hebrides, based on the latter's familiarity with the Estense collection of Ptolemaic maps. And thus does Spenser map Elizabeth in the remote Hebrides, an *ultima Britannia* that Greco-Roman geography had located on the remote edges of the earth.

My third chapter is entitled 'Ever-Receding Shorelines: Antiquarian Poetry and Prose and the Limits of Shakespeare's Coastal Dramatic Verse.' Critics past and present have long been interested in the general topic of Shakespeare and the sea.[18] My chapter, however, ventures no farther than the shoreline. Ever since Ben Jonson's oft-cited allusion to Shakespeare's 'small Latine, and lesse Greeke,' scholars have vigorously debated the extent of the bard's humanist exposure to what has come to be called

---

18 Alexander Frederick Falconer, *Shakespeare and the Sea* (New York: Frederick Ungar Publishing Co., 1964); Steve Mentz, *At the Bottom of Shakespeare's Ocean* (London: Continuum, 2009).

'the classics.'[19] Despite the curriculum at the King's Free Grammar School at Stratford, we should not be discouraged from investigating how frequently Shakespeare may have attempted to measure the yawning gap between antiquity and early modernity, particularly if we follow him to the water's edge. A primary backdrop of my chapter is antiquarianism's intriguing ability to, as it were, act globally and think locally. Antiquarianism shuttled between continental historiographic ambition and provincial contentment, demonstrating its generic capacity to embrace both an ambitious prose agenda of inserting ancient Britain within the growing volume of world history, and an equally ambitious verse project of merging the tropes of classical poetry with the quaintness of local topography. I argue that antiquarianism's dual generic affinities for historical prose and for river poetry – and its disciplined focus on keeping the genres distinct – established early modern English protocols for how to 'write' the material reality of the East Anglian coastlines, protocols that *Cymbeline* particularly struggles to observe. My chapter reads the play with and against the grain of Leland's and Camden's verse representations of the English Channel that, unlike *Cymbeline*'s blank verse, never ceased viewing the coastline through the mediating lens of Julius Caesar.

My fourth, and most biographical, chapter is entitled 'Exiled Shorelines: Early Milton and the Rejection of the *Mare Ovidianum*.' This chapter focuses on the young Milton, identified by Leicester Bradner as 'the last of the Elizabethans': 'In the early Latin verse of John Milton we find the last and most important appearance of the all-pervading Ovidian influence in Renaissance Latin poetry.'[20] A significant body of Milton scholarship, in the wake of Bradner, has long studied Milton's humanist appropriations of Ovid. My chapter focuses in particular on the young Milton's rejection not just of the amatory elegies but also the exiled Ovid of the *Tristia* and *Epistulae ex Ponto*, written on the desolate shore where the Danube estuary flows into the Black Sea. This chapter closely examines the question: what was the young Milton's literary response to Ovid's literary response to exile? How does this question

---

19 A standard study is T.W. Baldwin, *William Shakespeare's Small Latine and Lesse Greeke*, 2 vols. (Urbana, IL: University of Illinois Press, 1944). For a cogent recent analysis of Shakespeare's successes and failures in responding to the classics, see Colin Burrow, 'Shakespeare and Humanist Culture,' in *Shakespeare and the Classics*, ed. Charles Martindale and A.B. Taylor (Cambridge: Cambridge University Press, 2004), 9–27.
20 *Musae Anglicanae*, 111.

permit us to reconfigure, or view in a different light, some of the well-established details of the young Milton's career trajectory, particularly as defined by his Italian tour (during which Milton, unlike Spenser or Shakespeare before him, viewed the *real*, not a mediated, Mediterranean)? And, finally, how might the answer to these questions provide a perspective on ongoing pressures, present well into the seventeenth century, of shaping a poetic career on an island antiquity had once banned from the domain of poetry itself? A frequent topos in Ovid's exile poetry is the waning of his poetic creativity (or *ingenium*) far from the Roman *axis mundi*. But to take his claims at face value – as Milton, despite his remarkable sensitivity to Ovidian tone, was prone to do – was to overlook how, on the shores of the Black Sea, Ovid's exile poetry set the standard for how to dictate to the muses on an estuary of the Roman empire's periphery. In the final analysis, one consequence of Milton's ambivalence toward Ovid's significant linkage of alien estuaries and poetic genre is the lengthening shadow of *ultima Britannia* over his early poems.

In the meantime, the rest of this chapter provides a fuller context for my earlier claim that antiquity had banished British Isles coastlines from the domain of poetry itself. The chapter's next section ponders the comparative chronological question of why prior medieval English depictions of the tide-assaulted coastline of the British Isles did not labor under the cultural weight of the topos of *ultima Britannia*. I will next investigate early modern English pilotage manuals and their successful – if tedious – attempts to chart the local coastlines that verse struggled to represent. I will then glance briefly at an excerpt from Lyly's *Euphues and His England* to contextualize my subsequent review of the steady evolution of the topos of *ultima Britannia* from a recurrent reference point of Greco-Roman geographical discourse to a topos of classical poetry that would end up significantly mediating early modern English verse perceptions of local coastlines. I conclude with the discourses on English poetics of William Webbe and Samuel Daniel and the insights they can offer into why early modern English verse struggled to convert the material reality of local coastlines into numinous sites of poetic inspiration that could compete with a Mediterranean sublime.

2. From Anachronism to Belatedness: Medieval English Coastlines before Humanism

Before turning to early modern English verse's shadowy inheritance of the topos of *ultima Britannia*, it may be useful to ponder the comparative, chronological question of why prior medieval English depictions of the tide-assaulted coastlines of the British Isles did not labor under the cultural weight of the topos. Though answering the question definitively is beyond the scope of this book, some at least tentative speculations are in order as to why antiquity's *ultima Britannia* had no particular power to mediate medieval England's visions of its own shorelines, why the topos was not as volatile or charged for the medieval English verse imagination.

Coastal turbulence and isolation are intimately interwoven within the fabric of Anglo-Saxon and medieval English poetry. The Anglo-Saxon *Exeter Book*'s riddle of the oyster, comically buffeted by a coastal *sundhelm*, or water-cover, nonetheless acknowledges the vulnerability of the island's otherwise lowly mollusks. Written with far more *gravitas*, the Anglo-Saxon *Seafarer* describes a lone survivor of battle, accompanied only by frost-winged seabirds, and isolated amidst the surging *stormas*, *flodwegas*, and *hrimcealde saes* of a grey marine wilderness. In the late fourteenth-century midland romance *Sir Gawain and the Green Knight*, the North Wales 'iles of Anglesay' emblematize much of the protagonist's lonely winter journey to Bercilak's castle (2.698).[21]

But these glimpses of coastal bleakness lack affective investment in antiquity's *ultima Britannia*; and to expand on this point, one can turn to the 1210 *Roman de Brut* of Wace, who explicitly identified himself not as 'English' (whatever that identification meant in thirteenth-century England) but as a Channel Islander from Jersey ('in the sea toward the west, dependent on the fief of Normandy,' 5303–4).[22] At one point, Arthur, reflecting Wace's intimate knowledge of Britain's tides, describes a deadly lake near the Severn estuary (most likely what is now known as the Severn Bore). When the tide ebbs, the lake monstrously surges and spews forth salt water that rears up in menacing waves, swallowing its banks and choking the surrounding waters with sea foam. The only escape from drowning, Arthur informs, is to hunch one's back and allow the sea foam to fly by harmlessly. Though Wace's foam-spewing Severn estuary is enfolded within Arthur's Welsh homeland, this

---

21 For a fuller context, see Robert Ashton Kissack Jr, 'The Sea in Anglo-Saxon and Middle English Poetry,' *Washington University Studies: Humanities Series* 13 (1926): 371–89.

22 *Arthurian Chronicles: Wace and Layamon*, trans. Eugene Mason (Toronto: University of Toronto Press, 1996). For a cogent account of Wace as a border writer, see Michelle Warren, *History on the Edge: Excalibur and the Border of Britain, 1100–1300* (Minneapolis: University of Minnesota Press, 2000).

spirited story seems unaware of any potential intersection between the legendary matter of Arthur and antiquity's perceptions of inhospitable British Isles coastlines.

Surely no medieval English poet was more attuned to the hazards of English coastlines than Chaucer, who, in his 'General Prologue' to *The Canterbury Tales*, makes it a point to praise the Dartmouth shipman (not to mention pirate) for his valuable skill 'to rekene wel his tydes' (104).[23] *The Man of Law's Tale*, narrating the lonely heroine Custance's exile from Syria, describes her ship's approach to 'our wilde see' (506), the North Sea, and its eventual tide-driven foundering 'Fer in Northumberlond' (508). But her running aground signals not Chaucer's distracted wandering into antiquity's *ultima Britannia* but rather his attention to the generic bounds of Christian romance: his pagan Northumberland joins a long list of Christian romance's strange coasts where lost protagonists begin the process of finding themselves. Custance's Northumberland sojourn is presided over by 'The wyl of Crist' (511), the necessary first stage of redemptive family reunion in Rome.[24]

Chaucer's *Franklin's Tale* can certainly be counted among medieval English verse's most vivid descriptions of a menacing coastline. Dorigen, longing for her husband Arveragus's safe return from his knightly adventures, promises to yield to Aurelius's seductions if he can make Pedmark's dangerous coastal rocks disappear.[25] Aurelius hires a magician whose arcane astrology conjures a kind of submerging super-tide that, in addition to being one of the tale's fictive allures, calls attention to the all-too-real marine hazards that beset the southwest Galician coast. Thus, perhaps even more gripping than this Breton lay's dazzling magical display is the lonely Dorigen's morbid fascination with Pedmark's coastal rocks. Obsessing over them daily, she roams the cliffs, 'cast[ing] hir eyen downward fro the brynke,' and staring at 'the grisly rokkes blake' at whose sight 'For verray feere so wolde hir herte quake' (859–60). At once repelled and *com*pelled by the rocks as a 'foul confusion / Of werke' (869–70), Dorigen marvels that 'An hundred thousand bodyes of mankynde / Han [these] rokkes slayn.' Though the

---

23 All references to Chaucer's *The Canterbury Tales* are from F.N. Robinson, *The Works of Geoffrey Chaucer* (Boston: Houghton Mifflin, 1957).

24 For Middle English verse depictions of the sea as a metaphor for temptation, uncertainty, and – ultimately – providence, see Sebastian Sobecki, *The Sea and Medieval English Literature* (Cambridge, UK: Brewer, 2008).

25 Robinson's editorial notes locate Arveragus and Dorigen in Pedmark (now Penmarc'h) in the southwest Finistere, on the Galician coast facing France.

jagged rocks make her 'herte quake' as she yearns for their disappearance, Dorigen is mesmerized by the sheer destructiveness of their 'foul confusion,' their potential to rip apart 'an hundred thousand bodyes.' Despite its focus on the hazards of nearby coastlines, Chaucer's exercise in a coastal pathetic fallacy takes no more note of antiquity's topos of an *ultima Britannia* than the *Gawain*-poet or Wace. His local coastlines, whether the site of Custance's romance exile or Aurelius's magical laboratory or Dorigen's psychic mirror, betray no sign of haunting by a cultural remoteness from antiquity's Mediterranean shores.

Evidence that any number of Old English and medieval English chronicles were aware of antiquity's topos of an *ultima Britannia* appears in Gildas's sixth-century *De Excidio et Conquestu Britanniae*, a history of England before the Norman conquest. That the Tudor chronicle was a highly favored mode of nationalist self-fashioning further underscores the relative absence of such a national consciousness in the medieval English chronicle. Turning to the island's jutting promontories that form impassable barriers, Gildas describes England as 'situated on almost the utmost borders of the earth,' stiff with frost. But just as Gildas seemingly echoes antiquity's topos of *ultima Britannia*, his coastal frosts quickly melt under the warming light of Christian conversion: the island 'received the beams of light, that is, the holy precepts of Christ, the true Sun.'[26] Gildas's Christian history neither evinces a national consciousness nor labors under the cultural weight of the topos of an *ultima Britannia*; rather, he perceives the island's coastal barrier – not unlike Custance's Northumberland bound to 'the wyl of Crist' – as a kind of fortunate fall awaiting Christianity's redeeming grace. In his eighth-century *History of the English Church and People*, the Venerable Bede describes England as 'an island in the ocean, lying towards the north west at a considerable distance from the coasts of Germany, Gaul, and Spain.'[27] But Bede's diligent plotting of the coordinates of England as *ultima Britannia* exposes no melancholic pondering of marine isolation from the Mediterranean.

---

26 *Six Old English Chronicles*, trans. J.A. Giles (London: Henry G. Bohn, 1891), 299, 302. For an account of medieval English cartography as more spiritually than physically preoccupied, more spatially concerned with biblical Jerusalem than with Roman antiquity, see P.D.A. Harvey's and R.A. Skelton's introduction to their edition, *Local Maps and Plans from Medieval England* (Oxford: Clarendon Press, 1986).

27 Bede, *History of the English Church and People*, trans., intro., Leo Sherley-Price (Harmondsworth, Middlesex: Penguin Books, 1955), 37.

Further speculation on why the topos of an *ultima Britannia* drove no readily perceptible wedge between medieval England and antiquity points, admittedly at the risk of some generalization, to the medieval historical imagination's well-documented rootedness in anachronism, or seamless perceptions of historical continuity. Spanning the medieval *longue durée* from Bede to the early fourteenth century, one can hear an echo of the topos in Ranulf Higden's 1327 historical geography *Polycronicon* and its quoting from Solinus's fourth-century *Polyhistor*: 'the Sea coast of Gallia had beene the end of the worlde, but that the Ile of Brytaine for the largenesse thereof euery way, deserueth the name almost of an other Worlde.'[28] But again, Higden's adducing of Solinus does not carry with it the inherited weight of a topos. To piece together how Higden read Solinus's depiction of the British Isles as 'an other Worlde,' one can turn to the historian Arthur B. Ferguson's astute account of *Polycronicon*'s temporal world-view. Ferguson argues that Higden 'still treated the classical authors as though they had written only yesterday . . . [H]e made no clear distinction between the data provided by his classical sources and those of more recent times . . . [T]he historical information tends to float in a temporal void, without fixed point of reference or a uniform medium in relation to which the flight of time might be measured.'[29] Thus, *Polycronicon* can be included among the many examples of the medieval tolerance for anachronism, and Higden's temporal world-view reveals why Solinus's observation might just as well have been written 'only yesterday.' Unfolding in a 'temporal void' without a fixed point of reference to antiquity's many other depictions of the British Isles' otherworldliness, Higden's historical imagination suggests no brooding awareness of Solinus's participation in a well-defined geographic topos consistently depicting the British Isles as a not-Mediterranean 'other Worlde.'

If the temporality of the medieval historical imagination was unselfconsciously structured on anachronism, the temporality of the humanist historical imagination was often disrupted by a sense of belatedness – what Greene has termed, as noted earlier, the 'incomplete embrace' between antiquity and early modernity. I conclude this section by briefly

---

28 *Polycronicon*, Eng. trans. John of Trevisa, ed. William Caxton (Westminster, 1482), STC 13438.
29 Arthur B. Ferguson, *Clio Unbound: Perceptions of the Social and Cultural Past in Renaissance England* (Durham, NC: Duke University Press, 1979), 92–3.

pondering Arthur Golding's 1587 English translation of Solinus, *The excellent and pleasant worke, Collectanea rerum memorabilium of Caius Julius Solinus*, as pivotal for measuring the cultural distance between early modern English humanism and antiquity. Postdating Higden by over two and a half centuries, Golding's Solinus can be included among the many translations that sustained early modern English humanism's awareness that the remoteness of the British Isles was axiomatic in Greco-Roman geography.[30] Put another way, one consequence of these translations was to awaken a topos that had remained dormant in medieval England. If Higden's adducing of Solinus's perception of the British Isles as an 'other Worlde' drifted in a temporal void, Golding's more thorough exposure to Solinus, via the massive humanist project of translation, was just one of early modern English humanism's many inescapable reminders that an *ultima Britannia*, though obsolete, might never rise above its status as the remote northwest periphery of a Mediterranean geographic imagination.

3. Philautus's Nausea

The extent to which not verse but early modern English prose was better equipped to approach the material reality of the local water's edge will be investigated in this book's third chapter. I now preview that discussion by glancing briefly at John Lyly's 1580 *Euphues and His England* – namely, its euphuistic representation of a risible English Channel, an obvious Elizabethan prose surrender to the topos of *ultima Britannia* and its cultural authority to cast a shadow on early modern English shorelines.

The contrast between the shorelines of the Mediterranean and the British Isles was succinctly summarized by the fifteenth-century Spanish traveler Don Pedro Niño. Voyaging in 1406 from the Mediterranean to the English Channel, he wrote in a later-published chronicle *El Vitorial* that '[t]he Western Sea is *not like the Mediterranean Sea*, which has

---

30 A radically abridged list of early modern English humanist translations of Greco-Roman geography would include Sir Thomas Elyot's 1530–1 Plutarch; Thomas Stocker's 1564 Diodorus Siculus; Golding's 1565 Caesar, as well as his 1587 Solinus; Sir Thomas North's 1579 Plutarch; a 1584 anonymous translation of selections from Herodotus; Sir Henry Savile's 1591 Tacitus; Philemon Holland's 1601 Pliny; and Thomas Lodge's 1602 Josephus.

neither ebb nor flow nor great currents.'[31] (The Mediterranean, topo-graphically speaking, is less a sea than a basin. And we are well re-minded here that the earliest Mediterranean navigational manual, the 1296 *Compasso da Navigare*, moving clockwise from port to port, scarcely noted tidal rhythms. Aside from the notorious Straits of Messina, only the entry into the tidal canals of Venice received any attention.)[32] The currents of the English Channel's tidal complexity that Niño observed are perhaps best charted by the maritime historian David W. Waters: the up-channel flood stream 'continues to flow in mid-Channel when inshore the tidal stream has already turned, the ebb set in . . . In the upper part of the Channel near the Dover Strait the flood continues to flow some three hours after high water, and the ebb for three hours after low-water.'[33] Prior to approaching the English coastline, Niño had never even witnessed the twin phenomena of ebb and flow – let alone the intersecting tides described so accurately by Waters.

With this context in place, let us turn to Lyly's *Euphues and His England*. Euphuism has long been recognized as a major phase in the development of English prose; and in this work worth noting is how England's coastlines provoked some of the wry humor of Lyly's dis-tinctly English prose style. Andrew Hadfield has observed that, in Ly-ly's work, 'England is forced to take a hard look at itself isolated from the rest of Europe.'[34] I would add that Lyly, not unlike Don Pedro Niño, subjected the English Channel to a particularly invidious comparison with the Mediterranean. *Euphues and His England* effectively replaced the solemn reportage of Niño's travel narrative with a satire that ex-plicitly associated the English Channel with seasickness. When Lyly brought his euphuism's formal exaggerations to the English Channel, he skewered it, inviting his readers – even, or especially, those imbued with a nationalist pride – to laugh out loud at his exposure of the strait's absurd turbulence.

---

31 Quoted in E.G.R. Taylor, *The Haven-Finding Art: A History of Navigation from Odysseus to Captain Cook*, foreword by Commodore K.St.B. Collins, R.N. (London: Hollins & Carter, 1956), 142; emphasis mine.
32 See Taylor, 104–7.
33 *The Art of Navigation in Elizabethan England and Early Stuart Times* (New Haven: Yale University Press, 1958), 34.
34 *Shakespeare, Spenser, and the Matter of Britain* (Harmondsworth: Palgrave MacMillan, 2004), 110. A seminal study of Lyly's prose style is G.K. Hunter, *John Lyly: The Humanist as Courtier* (London: Routledge, 1962).

Lyly's Athenian protagonist Euphues, sailing from Naples to London, replays not only Don Pedro Niño's but also Julius Caesar's far more storied voyage to Britannia (from Rome via Gaul) over a millennium and a half earlier. Euphues aims to entertain his fellow traveler Philautus with a reading from *The Gallic Wars* (V.12–13) and its recounting of the Roman invaders' amphibious assault on Britannia. Thus, as his own ship nears the coastline, Euphues assumes the identity of a latter-day Caesar, pompously reciting *The Gallic Wars'* vertiginous description of the British Isles' coastal geography:

> The island is in fashion three-cornered, whereof one side is toward France. The one corner of this side, which is in Kent, where for the most part ships arrive out of France, is in the east, and the other nethermore is towards the south. This side containeth about five hundred miles. Another side lieth toward Spain and the sun going down. On which side is Ireland, less than Britain, as is supposed, by the one half; but the cut between them is like the distance that is between France and Britain. In the midst of this course is an island called Man. The length of this side is seven hundred miles. The third side is northward, and against it lieth no land; but the point of that side butteth most upon Germany. This they esteem to be eight hundred miles long; and so the circuit of the whole island is two thousand miles.[35]

Caesar's Britannia, not so much a land mass as a series of erratic coastal indentations, is now 'toward France,' now 'toward Spain,' now 'butt[ing] most upon Germany.' That is to say, in whatever direction Euphues-as-Caesar turns, British Isles coastlines are a longitudinal-latitudinal confusion, rendered further disorienting by Euphues's dogged conveyance of Caesar's own determination to make sense of the topsy-turvy island's jutting promontories and scarcely charted archipelagos. Thus does Lyly transform Caesar's Britannia shores into a deft satire on early modern English pedagogy – specifically, *The Gallic Wars* as a

---

35 *Euphues: The Anatomy of Wit and Euphues and His England by John Lyly*, eds. Morris William Croll and Harry Clemens (New York: Russell & Russell, Inc., 1964), 227. In a footnote attempting to clarify but possibly further obfuscating Euphues's reference to the coast that is 'toward France,' Croll and Clemens explain: 'Lyly is speaking of the southern coast of England, and he means that the actual south-eastern corner of the island faces east, its actual south-western corner south. This false geography is due to Caesar, who had a mistaken idea of the way England lies' (229n4).

predictable staple of every early modern English schoolchild's Latin education. Euphues's ventriloquizing of Caesar is a prime example of Lyly's euphuism as a parody of antiquarian learning and a delight in language rather than knowledge or scholarship for its own sake.[36] But it also indicates the ironic extent to which the topos of an *ultima Britannia* had become a prominent Latin tutor for early modern English schoolchildren who, in effect, obediently translated an account of their island's distance from the Mediterranean *axis mundi*. Lyly's satire of *The Gallic Wars* as a standard tool of early modern English pedagogy also directly depends on a satire of the English Channel as, indeed, a dire strait in the not-Mediterranean.

Of all the events in *The Gallic Wars*, Lyly pointedly culls Caesar's first glimpse of Britannia's shoreline – particularly the English Channel – which the author exploits for his readers' further amusement. Euphues's companion, Philautus, learning the hard way the truth of Don Pedro Niño's axiom that 'the Western Sea is not like the Mediterranean Sea,' is described by Lyly as 'not accustomed to these narrow seas, [and] more ready to tell what wood the ship was made of, than to answer to Euphues's discourse' (229). Among other things, Euphues's reading is an introduction to the literal and figurative meanings of the word 'nausea.' Philautus is distressed – figuratively 'nauseated' – by Euphues's Caesarean recitations, as tedious as they are disorienting. But the fact that he is 'more ready to tell what wood the ship was made of' (i.e., he is bent double) is proof that Philautus, long suffering from lovesickness, is also literally nauseated: 'I cannot brooke these seas, which provoke my stomach sore' (229). In addition to punning on 'brooke' and 'seas,' Lyly may or may not have been indulging in further word play. One is well reminded that the Greek word for seasickness, *nausia*, derives from *naus* or ship: in Greek antiquity, nausea was, by definition, a sickness brought on by *naut*-ical voyages. To push the logic of this etymology further, one could argue that, strictly speaking, *nausia* originated in Mediterranean seas, giving rise to the possibility that for one to be 'nauseous' on the English Channel is not only to be in physical distress but also under some pressure to invent a new word for one's queasiness. Judging by the Neapolitan Philautus, 'not accustomed to these narrow seas,' Mediterranean *nausia* is not nearly as severe as English

---

36 On the importance of *The Gallic Wars* in early modern English grammar schools, see the first volume of Baldwin.

Channel seasickness. The alien nature of the English Channel sickness, moreover, has no classical etymology: proximity to the shores of *ultima Britannia* simply results in a 'sore' stomach.

Euphues's rehearsal of Caesar's past coastal disorientation and Philautus's queasy forebearance of the choppy English Channel converge as Lyly's satiric confirmation of Caesar's (and Niño's) perception of the island as distinctly not-Mediterranean. Lyly's decision to write about the English Channel in satiric prose, his blithe recasting of the cultural *gravitas* of an *ultima Britannia* as sportive frivolity, in effect surrenders to the topos's ongoing influence as a wedge between British Isles shorelines and a coastal poetics.[37] Lyly's prose achieves comic success not only by suggesting seasickness as the topos's somatic core but also by confirming that, in early modernity, one's first impression of the English Channel was always already mediated through the eyes of antiquity – in this case, Caesar's first glimpse of the waterway.

4. 'Profounde' Navigators, 'Vnlettered' Coasters, and the Fortunate Isles

I turn from Lyly's risible English Channel to what, through some eyes, could be viewed as the more serious business of early modern England's new university geography and its ambitious attempts to relocate England from the periphery of Greco-Roman *mappae mundi* to the center of a rising maritime prominence. In the last twenty years or so, burgeoning studies of early modern England's imperial cartography have demonstrated how thoroughly early modern English maps were used to legitimate power. As Lesley Cormack has shown, the discipline of geography at Oxford and Cambridge, modeled on Ortelius's 1570 *Theatrum Orbis Terrarum*, fostered an aggressive imperial worldview, remapping the British Isles for a new governing elite.[38] The hegemonic impact of the new university geography took for granted, at least theoretically, English maritime superiority over other nations and, hence,

---

37 The satiric agility of Lyly's euphuistic prose is of further note when read in the context of Bruni's praise of *The Gallic Wars'* Latinity, 'so elegant and so limpid' (quoted in F.J. Levy, *Tudor Historical Thought* [San Marino, CA: *Huntington Library Quarterly*, 1967], 37).

38 Lesley B. Cormack, *Charting an Empire: Geography of the English Universities, 1580–1620* (Chicago: University of Chicago Press, 1997).

the right to control sea passages west to the New World and east to the East Indies.[39]

As is the case with any elite discourse, what might be just as revealing is the discourse that resided in the shadows of the new university geography. I argue that marginal to the scientific and mathematical advances in navigation underwriting the new geography were early modern English pilotage manuals, committed to the task not of, echoing Cormack, 'charting an empire' but rather to the far more tedious, local task of charting the material reality of tide-ripped British Isles coastlines.

Early modern England's first navigation manual was William Bourne's *A Regiment for the Sea*, published in three editions from 1574 to 1577. Some twenty years later, in his 1593 *Pierces Supererogation*, Gabriel Harvey, a leading voice of early modern English humanism, included Bourne in a list of 'sensible industrious Practitioner[s]' deserving of note 'howsoeuer Vnlectured in Schooles, or Vnlettered in books.'[40] His nod to Bourne, though, could be read as little more than a patronizing build-up to humanist praise of his navigational heroes John Dee, educated at Harvey's Cambridge, and the Oxford-educated Thomas Hariot, both esteemed exemplars of the 'profounde Mathematician' (290), both forerunners in applying mathematics to the science of navigation.

It is worth pondering what was at stake in Harvey's damning Bourne with faint praise, his description of Bourne as a 'sensible industrious Practitioner.' Bourne's *Regiment* devoted significant attention to the local skills of pilotage, more often referred to as 'coasting,' the hard-nosed practice of negotiating the British Isles' broken coastlines. As Bourne observed, a ship-captain need not be a mathematician: 'a good

39 For a fuller context, see David M. Loades, *England's Maritime Empire: Seapower, Commerce, and Policy, 1490–1690* (New York: Longman, 2000). By 1650, England had yet to equal the Spanish and Dutch in seapower; and thus for a less-confident idea of empire, due to English failures to establish permanent settlements in the Americas, see David Armitage, 'The Elizabethan Idea of Empire,' *Transactions of the Royal Historical Society*, 14 (2004): 269–77; and Jeffrey Knapp, *An Empire Nowhere: England, America, and Literature from 'Utopia' to 'The Tempest'* (Berkeley and Los Angeles: University of California Press, 1992).

40 *Pierces Supererogation, or a New Prayse of the old Asse* (1593), in *The Works of Gabriel Harvey*, Vol. 2, ed., intro. Alexander B. Grosart (1884; rpt. New York: AMS Press, 1966), 289. Harvey owned a copy of Bourne's *Regiment*, listed in Virginia F. Stern, *Gabriel Harvey: His Life, Marginalia and Library* (Oxford: The Clarendon Press, 1979).

coaster, that is to say . . . knowe[s] every place by the sight thereof.'[41] The rudimentary skills of pilotage depended not on the increasingly sophisticated technology of the compass, chronometer, theodolite, quadrant, and astrolabe (such as those featured in Holbein's preeminently humanist painting *The Ambassadors*), but rather on the humbler, 'vnlettered' experience of the naked eye, on painstaking observation of buoys, channel markers, lighthouses, church steeples. While open-ocean mariners sailed to far-flung colonies in Virginia or Guiana, the coasters' territory remained the less-glamorous but no-less-imposing menaces of the Scillies, Lundy, or still scarcely charted Dover Straits.

Early modern English successors to Bourne improved on the *Regiment*'s charting of the material reality of England's coastlines. The year 1588, marking the defeat of the Spanish Armada, was, of course, one of the most storied years in Elizabethan England's growth as a maritime presence to be reckoned with. But also in 1588 an updated navigational manual, *The Mariner's Mirrour*, was published; and in its pragmatically technical way, this document was, among other things, a reminder that the Spanish Armada suffered defeat less because of English naval skill than because of the often storm-agitated currents of the English Channel.[42] *The Mariner's Mirrour* was itself superseded by the 1612 *Light of Navigation* of Willem Janszoon Blaeu, head of the department of hydrography in the Dutch East India Company. This document further refined the skills of pilotage by diagramming new chart-symbols for shore beacons, buoys, shoals, and partially submerged rocks. In 1623, Blaeu published *The Sea-Mirrour*, featuring such updates as more detailed charts of coastal cliff-lines and the identification of previously unknown shoals in the Thames estuary.[43]

Located at the intersection of a theoretically advanced navigation and a nascent maritime empire, Dee and Hariot, as Harvey's praise reveals, were among the prestigious cartographers ambitiously attempting

41 William Bourne, *The Regiment of the Sea* (London: Thomas Hackett, 1574); STC 3422. For a useful summary of the aims of early modern English pilotage, see Waters, 4–7.

42 *The Mariner's Mirrour*, written by Lucas Janszoon Waghenaer, was originally published in 1584 under the title *Spieghel der Zeeraerdt*. The English title was translated by Anthony Ashley. For the 1588 English translation, see *Lucas Janszoon Waghenaer, The Mariner's Mirrour*, intro. R.A. Skelton, in *Theatrum orbis terrarium: A Series of Atlases in Facsimile* (Amsterdam: World Publishing Company, 1966).

43 Willem Janszoon Blaeu, *The Light of Navigation* (Amsterdam: William Johnson, 1612).

to map England at the center of early modern maritime power. The pilotage manuals' instructions for, say, avoiding the sandbanks of Yarmouth could not compete with the broader scope and appeal generated by such documents as Dee's 1577 *General and Rare Memorials Pertayning to the Perfect Arte of Navigation*, particularly its frontispiece's visual allegory of Elizabethan coastlines as a witness to the nation's rising maritime power.[44] Queen Elizabeth is positioned, as Dee's commentary informs readers, at 'the Helm of the IMPERIALL SHIP,' proudly afloat in the English Channel. The figure of 'RES-PVBL[ica] BRYTANICA' kneels on the shore, with the figure of 'Occasion' (or Fortune) standing on a sea-cliff fortress. The frontispiece's English coast is sanctioned by the queen's ship, poised, with all the increasingly sophisticated instruments of navigation at its disposal, literally to seize the 'Occasion' to defend an autonomous England's right to maritime sovereignty. The point to emphasize here is how this emblematic frontispiece elides the pilotage manuals' quotidian emphasis on the material reality, the inconvenient truths, of England's coastlines: Dee's coastline is neither ripped by swirling tidal currents nor anxiously dotted with the buoys and channel markers so painstakingly charted by the pilotage manuals, but is rather depicted as an ideological site for the nation's maritime growth; his channel is not a mariner's trap but rather a gateway to early modern England's ongoing commitment to open-ocean navigation.

The pilotage manuals' meticulous focus on the hazards of local English coastlines was crucial for local mariners and North Atlantic merchant ships. (Indeed, Blaeu's new chart-symbol for partially submerged rocks made obvious the need for frequently updated

---

44 John Dee, *General and Rare Memorials Pertayning to the Perfect Arte of Navigation* (London, 1577); repr. Amsterdam: *Theatrum Orbis Terrarum*, 1968 [STC 6459]. For further commentary on Dee's title page, see Margery Corbett and Ronald Lightbown, *The Comely Frontispiece: The Emblematic Title-page in England, 1550–1660* (London: Routledge and Kegan Paul, 1979), 49–51; Frances A. Yates, *Astraea: The Imperial Theme in the Sixteenth Century* (London: ARK, 1985), 48–50; and John King, *Tudor Royal Iconography: Literature and Art in an Age of Religious Crisis* (Princeton: Princeton University Press, 1989), 238–41. On Dee's imperial world view, see Peter S. French, *John Dee: The World of an Elizabethan Magus* (London: Routledge & Kegan Paul, 1976). For a downplaying of overt propagandizing in Dee's role as the queen's chief maritime advisor, see William H. Sherman's chapter 'Dee and England's Maritime Empire' in his *John Dee: The Politics of Reading and Writing in the English Renaissance* (Amherst, MA: University of Massachusetts Press, 1995).

manuals, prompting the question: Amid the ever-changing contours of local shorelines, how many as-yet submerged rocks were lying in wait to crack vessels apart until final detection and charting?) But, for Harvey, 'sensible' early modern English coasters seemed scarcely to have evolved beyond Chaucer's Dartmouth shipman, trained to 'rekene wel his tydes,' but seldom gazing farther than the tide-battered coasts 'Fro Gotland to the cape of Finistere' (401, 408).

Having established this brief historical context (a context, it merits pointing out, rooted in prose), I now turn to representations of local coastlines by early modern English poets and verse dramatists. So often aware of composing on an island, many writers, as noted at the beginning of this chapter, made liberal use of the Fortunate Isles topos as perhaps the most expedient means of embellishing imperial ideology with mythopoesis. The topos originated in early Greek antiquity, when the British Isles were a scarcely known constellation of unnamed islands. The idyllic region was the presumed island home of the mythic Hyperboreans of Hesiod's *Works and Days* and the Homeric *Hymn to Dionysus*, depicting the Hyperboreans as free of disease and old age.[45] Over time, these Hyperborean islands came to be identified as the mythic *insulae fortunatae*, the source of eternal life. Although these mythic islands were, at best, vaguely located on the world's western ocean streams, opportunistic early modern English writers did not hesitate to lay claim to early antiquity's Fortunate Isles as their own British Isles, the legendary center of the world's garden paradise.

The topos of the Fortunate Isles thrived on the myth that Apollo and the Muses had abandoned the ancient world and come to England. It thus stands to reason that the varied topography – the sandbanks, scarred cliffs, sea-caves, and tidal incursions so meticulously charted by pilotage manuals – would have offered a number of sites for a capacious coastal poetics. But early modern English verse deployments of the Fortunate Isles topos did not so much engage with as abstract away from the water's edge. Insofar as this early modern island

---

45 *Works and Days*, 170–4; Hymn VII, 29, in *Hesiod, The Homeric Hymns and Homerica*, trans. H.G. Evelyn-White, The Loeb Classical Library (Cambridge, MA: Harvard University Press, 1936). The origins of the Fortunate Isles in antiquity are discussed in *A Documentary History of Primitivism and Related Ideas*, Vol. I, eds. Arthur O. Lovejoy, Gilbert Chinard, George Boas, and Ronald S. Crane (Baltimore: The Johns Hopkins University Press, 1935).

nation could lay claim to a coastal poetics, it was the ubiquitous deployments of the Fortunate Isles topos, focusing not on coastal topography but on the island as a cosmographic world paradise, bounded by the white walls that had long inspired England's venerable identity as 'Albion.' On those occasions when the topos did focus on local coastlines, never more memorably than in John of Gaunt's aforementioned salute to England as 'This precious stone set in the silver sea,' seacoasts came into focus as little more than static emblems of an integrated island nation. As often as not, this master trope indulged in 'precious' wordplays suitable for an insular 'precious stone,' as in George Peele's 1584 *Arraygnement of Paris* and its coyly circular pun on England as 'the place *Elizium* hight, and of the place, / Her name that governes there *Eliza* is.'[46] Consequently, the superficial stylistic constraints of the Fortunate Isles topos did not invite the poet or verse dramatist to linger over the intractable realities of the island's coastline. One of William Browne's 1616 *Britannia's Pastorals*, to cite another useful example, proudly narrates the muse's journey from 'the banks of Po' to 'Our alabaster rocks' (2.1.955).[47] The muse, however, does not tarry at the coastline to behold swirling tides, but rather seeks an inland *otium* and the gentler pipings of shepherds. That is, the muse is content to leave the shoreline to the labored scrutiny of the coasters' manuals.

Gerald MacLean, revisiting the topos of the Fortunate Isles with more authority than any critic since Bennett, has argued that the topos was a heady counter-discourse to Mediterranean perceptions of a remote British Isles, strategically converting English insularity into, in his words, 'a source of national pride, rather than a cause for disparagement.'[48] But a literary concern that the topos of the Fortunate Isles was irrelevant beyond English shorelines can be detected in a passage from Joshua Sylvester's 1605 translation of Du Bartas's *His Devine*

---

46 *The Araygnment of Paris* (Oxford, The Malone Society: Oxford University Press, 1910).

47 *Britannia's Pastorals* (London: John Haviland, 1625).

48 Gerald M. MacLean, *Time's Witness: Historical Representations in English Poetry, 1593–1660* (Madison: University of Wisconsin Press, 1990), 69. An early modern inferiority complex in the shadow of classical antiquity has recently been revisited by Mary Floyd-Wilson's important study of, in particular, the emergent nation's inheritance of antiquity's geohumoral discourse, briefly defined as the belief that the intemperate climates of the world's edges bred uncivil, barbarous behavior, a cause of early modern England's at-times anxious sense of its remote 'northernness' (*English*

Weekes and Workes, enjoying a considerable vogue in Jacobean England
and closely read by the young John Milton. Interestingly, Sylvester's
translation added several passages to Du Bartas's original, the longest
of which was a tribute to England-as-the-Fortunate Isles, beginning
with the apostrophe: 'all-haile (deere *Albion*), Europes Pearle of price, /
The worlds rich Garden, earths rare Paradice.'[49] This addition could be
viewed as Sylvester's energetic countering of Du Bartas's cult of French
nationalist self-consciousness (and, it should be noted, a panegyric that
imitates Virgil's praise of Italy). It could also point to the translator's
underlying concern: the fact that Sylvester felt it necessary to make this
addition at all hinted at his awareness that the topos was hardly at the
forefront of continental literary history's geo-poetic imagination, and at
his awareness that continental literary history was less invested in England as the Hesiodic Fortunate Isles than in another geographic topos,
this time from later antiquity – the topos of England as *ultima Britannia*, not an island paradise but rather the northern limit of inhabited
land before reaching *ultima Thule*. Antiquity's ethnographic discourse
on remote northern waters had also, of course, included such continental bodies of water as the Rhine and the French coastline. But Solinus's aforementioned comparative observation, in his fourth-century
Polyhistor, that 'the Seacoast of Gallia had beene the end of the worlde,
but that the Ile of Brytain for the largenesse thereof euery way, deserueth the name almost of an other Worlde' reminds us that continental
Europe could at least claim that it had remained somewhat integrated
within the bounds of antiquity's world maps.[50]

Ethnicity and Race in Early Modern Drama [Cambridge: Cambridge University Press,
2006]). But Floyd-Wilson also focuses on the adeptness with which early modern
England's own ethnographic discourse countered antiquity's geohumoral assump-
tions, finding strategies to convert the island's marginal northerness into an object
of national pride. She demonstrates, for example, how early modern England attempted to convert Mediterranean perceptions of the northerner's pale, phlegmatic
intemperance into signs of wisdom and civility. The topos of the Fortunate Isles, as
defined by MacLean, qualifies as yet another example of early modern England's
recuperative strategies vis-à-vis its 'northernness.'

49 Joshua Sylvester, *The Devine Weekes and Workes of Guillaume de Salluste, Sieur du Bartas*, ed. Susan Snyder, 2 vols. (Oxford: Clarendon Press, 1979), I.463.

50 Quoted by Ranulf Higden, *Polycronicon*, Eng. trans. John of Trevisa, 1387, printed
in Westminster in 1495 by Wynkyn de Worde. OR 1387 (Westminster: Wynkyn de
Worde, 1495).

5 Antiquity's *Apeiron*

I turn now to that 'other' topos from antiquity – the British Isles as *ultima Britannia*, a topos of later antiquity, and one far more grounded in eyewitness report. Long before Lovejoy et al.'s *Documentary History of Primitivism*, the 1607 edition of William Camden's widely read *Britannia* compiled a working list of sources for *ultima Britannia*, evidence of early modern England's widespread familiarity with this topos. With characteristic antiquarian zeal, Camden compiled the following catalogue:

Thus Virgil:

Tibi serviat ultima Thule.
While utmost Thule shall thy nod obey.

(*Georg.* 1.30)

Seneca:

terrarum ultima Thule.
Thule remotest portion of the globe.

(*Medea* 2.378)

Claudian:

Thulem procul axe remotam.
Thule most distant from the pole.

(*De Bel. Goth.* 204)

ratibusque impervia Thule.
Thule to seamen inaccessible.

(*Cons. Hon.* 3.53)

Silius Italicus:

ignotam vincere Thulam.
To conquer Thule yet unknown.

(3.597)

And Amm. Marcellinus quotes as a proverb, 'Though he lived in Thule.' (18.6.) . . . Thule is put for Britain in these lines of Silius Italicus:

Caerulus haud aliter cum dimicat incola Thule;
Agmina falcifero circumvenit acta covino.
Thus Thule's blue-stain'd native fights,
And with the scythe-arm'd car the ranks surrounds.

(17.416–17)

And so in the *Sylvae* of Statius:

refluo circumsona gurgite Thule.
Thule whom ebbing tides surround.

(5.1.91)[51]

Camden's catalogue is as diligent an example as any of one of Tudor/
Stuart antiquarianism's most cherished humanist goals –acquainting
early modern England with its historical origins in Roman antiquity.
(Of this project more will be discussed in my third chapter.) But his
citations are so spare, so lacking in context, that they offer little historical insight into why antiquity judged the waters of *ultima Britannia*
as so transgressive they deserved the ignominy of a geographic topos
of isolation. And his examples, recruited in the service of antiquarian
history, offer little insight into *literary* history – specifically, how and
why an otherwise obsolete topos continued shadowing early modern
English verse.

In order to unpack these questions, I will review the steady evolution of the topos of *ultima Britannia* from a recurring reference point of
Greco-Roman geographic discourse to a topos of classical poetry that
would end up powerfully mediating early modern English verse perceptions of local coastlines.

I turn first, not surprisingly, to the Mediterranean shorelines scarcely
mentioned thus far in this chapter, and to the affective intensity with
which antiquity viewed the Mediterranean as poetry's only sea. If it
is admissible to speak of classical antiquity as having topographical
boundaries, then they are delineated by the storied shorelines of the
Mediterranean. The sea's most ambitious historian, Fernand Braudel,
has argued with simple but resonant eloquence that '[t]he best witness to the Mediterranean's age-old past is the sea itself: This has to

---

51 *Britannia*, trans. Richard Gough, from the 1607 edition (London: Nichols and Son,
   1806), 3.726.

be said again and again.'[52] As is well known, antiquity did not hesitate to weave the Mediterranean's protected harbors into the fabric of its epic narratives. Odysseus tells Alcinous of an island near the land of the Cyclopes, 'a safe harbour, in which there is no occasion to tie up at all. You need neither cast anchor nor make fast with hawsers.'[53] Bringing Ulysses home to Ithaca, the Phaeacian sailors reach the harbor of Phorcys, an inlet so protected from the sea that, like the island near the Cyclopes, ships are not forced to tie up (13.100). Though the Troy-escaping Aeneas endures an ocean storm fueled by Aeolus, he eventually finds refuge in the tranquil waters of Dido's Carthaginian harbor, where 'no cable holds tired ships, no anchor grips them fast with curving bit' (1.170).[54] Though Dido's harbor was slated for exclusion from Roman imperial destiny, it was no less definitive of Mediterranean coastal topography. All of which is to re-emphasize that much of classical antiquity unfolded under Mediterranean eyes, and the coastline of this inland sea was, in antiquity's geographic imagination, the world's only sacred coast.

Reviewing the origins of antiquity's topos of an *ultima Britannia* as the non-Mediterranean can begin with Plato's meditation on the nature of wise rule in the *Statesman* – perhaps western history's first attempt at a *thinking* of coastal topography – and its allegory of how an heroic captain saves the ship of the Universe from being swallowed up by the watery chaos of a failure to resemble 'the boundless ocean of unlikeness.'[55] Expressing his repugnance for non-resemblance in marine terms, Plato imagined the concept of unlikeness as an *Apeiros topos anomoiotetos*, a terrifyingly boundless sea that annihilates a reassuring resemblance itself. Consequently, Greek antiquity dreaded a return to a primal *apeiron*, a boundless, oceanic void refusing to resemble – remaining always *unlike* – the protective coastal waters of the Mediterranean.[56]

---

52 Fernand Braudel. *Memory and the Mediterranean*, trans. Sîan Reynolds (New York: Alfred A. Knopf, 2001); originally published posthumously as *Les Memoires de la Mediterranée: Prehistoire et Antiquité* (Paris: Editions de Fallois, 1998).

53 *Homer: The Odyssey*, trans. E.V. Rieu (Harmondsworth: Penguin Books, 1946), 142; 9.110ff.

54 *The Aeneid of Virgil*, trans. Rolfe Humphries (New York: Bantam Books, 1982).

55 *Plato: The Sophist & The Statesman*, trans., intro. A.E. Taylor, ed. Raymond Klibansky and Elizabeth Anscombe (London: Thomas Nelson and Sons, Ltd., 1961), 273 D 6.

56 The concept of the *apeiron* is discussed in Charles E. Kahn, *Anaximander and the Origins of Greek Cosmology* (New York: Columbia University Press, 1960), 231–2, and,

The ancient Hellenic concept of the *oikoumene*, conceived by Herodotus and later adopted as a conventional term in antiquity's geographical discourse, designated the Greek homeland as an 'inhabited' or 'familiar earth' sedulously guarding its borders against the contaminating threats of the rest of the world.[57] Closely related to the *oikoumene* was Greek antiquity's privileged concept of the *peirar*, a territorial concept not nearly as familiar as the *polis*, but almost as important for structuring the lived lives of Hellenic Greeks, particularly on the western Mediterranean. Denoting a shoreline that protected the end of the land from the likes of Plato's chaotic, resemblance-annihilating marine expanses, the concept of the *peirar* resided at the core of early Greek mariners' resolve to hug the coasts, always keeping sight of land.[58] As James Romm has pointed out, 'Greek sailors and seamen felt ill at ease when surrounded by large stretches of open water.'[59] Mariners' hugging the coastline was tantamount to a symbolic tracing of the *peirar* as the preservation of a liminal boundary protecting civilization itself. And although ancient Greek mariners sailed westward to such far-flung settlements as Marseilles, they never ceased honoring the dictates of the *peirar* and its preservation of a Mediterranean coastal sacredness.

As Irad Malkin, a historian of the early Mediterranean, has argued, the ancient Greek fear of marine expanses helped cultivate the essential 'Greekness' of their otherwise-distant Mediterranean maritime colonies: the more remote these colonies' shores, the culturally closer these settlements felt to one another. Malkin goes so far as to argue that the sense of marine remoteness resulting from colonization and the concomitant need for a perceived coastal unity within the Mediterranean

---

more recently, by James Romm, *The Edges of the Earth in Ancient Thought: Geography, Exploration, and Fiction* (Princeton: Princeton University Press, 1992), 10.

57 For Herodotus on alien wastelands, see François Hartog, *The Mirror of Herodotus: The Representation of the Other in the Writing of History*, trans. Janet Lloyd (Berkeley and Los Angeles: University of California Press, 1988), 12–14.

58 The concept of the *peirar* underwrites Franco Cassano's description of the Mediterranean (reminding us of the meaning of 'Mediterranean' as a sea 'in the middle of lands') as 'a sea *between* lands, a sea that separates and links at the same time, a sea that *never becomes an abyss*, that knows the pleasure of leaving, but also that of returning' ('Southern Thought,' trans. Sandra Palaich, *Thesis Eleven*, special edition on 'The Mediterranean,' eds. Artemis Leontis and Peter Murphy, 67 [2001], 4–5); emphasis mine.

59 Romm, 16.

basin was a factor in the rise of Hellenism.[60] Marine distance from the Mediterranean 'center' was of little consequence as long as these mariners sailed in compliance with – in deference to – the *peirar* as the preservation of a liminal space along Mediterranean coasts. In sum, one manifestation of 'Greekness' was sustained contact with the sacred littorals of Mediterranean coastlines.

As the geographical limits of the Greek world continued to expand beyond the Mediterranean's original borders, the concept of the *peirar* assumed further urgency. As these borders began to stretch eastward to the Levant, south to the desert, and north to Eurasia and the Black Sea, Greco-Roman geography's well-documented perceptions of exotic peoples abounded. But as otherworldly as any – as remote as any from the sacred barrier separating Mediterranean coasts from the sea at large – were the westward Atlantic boundaries of the British Isles. By the fifth century BCE, some one hundred years after the Phoenicians had sailed as far west as Cornwall, Herodotus dwelled on this marine region's hyper-Borean location beyond the North Wind in the 'Far North' of an alien ocean.[61] Herodotus's depiction of a far northwesterly, otherworldly British Isles was the first prominent example of what in time would crystallize as Mediterranean antiquity's topos of an *ultima Britannia*, the British Isles as the last outpost before the scarcely habitable northernmost reaches of the globe.

In Greco-Roman geographic discourse, violations of the *peirar* often pointed in the direction of the North Sea in general, and the British Isles in particular; and Camden's earlier-cited catalogue of the topos of *ultima Britannia* could have drawn on any number of additional sources. In his *Germanica*, Tacitus described the North Sea as 'beyond the limits of the known world.'[62] Seneca the Elder, quoting from a poem narrating Germanicus's voyage to the North Sea, recounted that he sailed *ad rerum metas extremaque litora mundi* (to the bounds of things, to the

---

60 Irad Malkin, 'Networks and the Emergence of Greek Identity,' in *Mediterranean Paradigms and Classical Antiquity*, ed. Malkin (London and New York: Routledge, 2005), 59.

61 On Herodotus's skepticism of the Hyperborean legend, see Lovejoy et al., *A Documentary History of Primitivism*, 307.

62 *Tacitus: The Germanica*, intro. and notes Duane Reed Stuart (New York: MacMillan Co., 1923), 'Notes,' 27.

remotest shores of the world).[63] In his *Institutio Oratoria*, Quintilian described Britain as an island in a remote ocean.[64] In his *Natural History*, IV, Pliny the Elder situated the British Isles, in Philemon Holland's early modern English translation, 'as far as any land is to be seen, even to the utmost bounds of the earth; and beyond which, there is nothing to be discovered but a vast prospect of air and water.'[65] Ptolemy's *Geography*, charting this North Atlantic archipelago, claimed, 'The terminus of its [Europe's] maritime coast is located on that parallel extending through Thule, which parallel is the terminus of the sea.'[66]

Obviously, such early modern maps as the 1570 *Theatrum Orbis Terrarum* of Ortelius (Camden's mentor) rendered Greco-Roman geography's emphasis on the remoteness of the British Isles thoroughly obsolete. Less readily obsoleted, however, was the material reality of the region's periphery, antiquity's transgressive *apeiron*. The coastlines of the British Isles were not only perceived as remote, utmost, outermost, but also under siege from unrecognizably violent tides that rendered the *Odyssey*'s Phorcys a distant memory. Strabo's *De Situ Orbis*, for example, reported that in 300 BCE, Pythias of Massilia, an explorer of Europe's Atlantic coasts whose works are now lost, witnessed monstrous tides just north of Britain. Strabo also conveyed reports of British Isles' tides so formidable that the surging currents were personified as hostile armies, documenting his report by citing the legendary Cimbri tribe, inhabiting the shores of the North Sea and forced to take up arms against the flood tides that overflowed their homes. Strabo also attributed to Ephorus a report that the coastal Celts suffered more from the ravages of water than from war. When Strabo guardedly reported that Pythias sailed around Britain only 'where accessible,' he effectively identified its coastlines as shores without a *peirar*.[67]

---

63 *Suasoriae*, 1.15, in *The Elder Seneca: Declamations in Two Volumes*, ed., trans. Michael Winterbottom, The Loeb Classical Library (Cambridge, MA: Harvard University Press, 1974).

64 *The Institutio Oratoria of Quintilian*, ed., trans. H.E. Butler, The Loeb Classical Library (Cambridge, MA: Harvard University Press, 1964), 105, 7.4, 1–2.

65 *The History of the World, Commonly Called The Natural History of C. Plinius Secundus*, trans. Philemon Holland, intro. Paul Turner (Carbondale: Southern Illinois University Press, 1962), 313.

66 *Claudius Ptolemy: The Geography*, trans., ed. Edward Luther Stevenson (New York: Dover Publishing, Inc., 1991), 3.5.1.

67 *The Geography of Strabo*, ed., trans. H.L. Jones, The Loeb Classical Library (Cambridge, MA: Harvard University Press, 1917–32), II.104. For more on Pythias's

Greco-Roman geography became increasingly committed to distinguishing rumor from empirical, eyewitness accounts of the North Atlantic. But the aesthetic imagination of classical Roman poetry – picking up where Hercules's legendary warning, *Non Plus Ultra*, posted on the Pillars at the Straits of Gibraltar left off – found the rumors that fueled the topos of an *ultima Britannia* useful for shaping its topoi of nostalgia for a lost golden age; and thus, a discernible thread woven within classical Roman poetry was its abhorrence of marine transgression. According to Horace, the separation of land and ocean waters beyond the Mediterranean – the preservation of a liminal space at land's end – made possible civilization itself. Sea travel, he wrote, violated the *peirar*'s sacred littoral space: 'Vain was the purpose of the god in severing the lands by the estranging main [*Oceano dissociabili*], if in spite of him our impious ships dash across the depths he meant should not be touched' (*Odes* 1.3.21–4).[68] Horace's 'estranging main' was classical poetry's waters of transgression, never intended for 'impious' ships to sail across. Similarly, in Seneca the Younger's *Medèa*, Jason's Argonauts, pushing into the Colchian waters of a (then) distant Black Sea, are condemned for their maritime transgression: 'Too bold was he who first broke / the treacherous waves with so frail a raft.'[69] To depict the violation of this golden age sanction against wave-cleaving navigation and a loss of innocence amid marine remoteness, Ovid, as rendered in George Sandys' early modern English translation of the *Metamorphoses*, offered a mournful synecdoche: 'To visit other Worlds, no wounded Pine / Did yet from Hills to faithless Seas decline.'[70]

Atlantic voyages, see C.F.C. Hawkes, Pythias: Europe and the Greek Explorers, the Eighth J.L. Myers Memorial Lecture, Oxford University, May 20, 1975. For the ancient topos of British Isles tides as military forces, see Romm, 144.

68 All references to Horace's *Odes* are taken from *Horace: The Odes and Epodes*, trans. C.E. Bennett (Cambridge, MA: Harvard University Press, 1919).

69 *Seneca in Ten Volumes*, Vol. 8, *Tragedies*, ed. F.J. Miller (Cambridge, MA and London: Loeb Classical Books, 1917), 254–5 (II.301–5). The link between Horace's *Odes* 1.3 and Seneca's *Medea* is observed by C.D.N. Costa in his note to this passage (*Seneca's Medea* [Oxford, Clarendon Press, 1973], 99). For more on the golden-age ban on sea travel, see Harry Levin, *The Myth of the Golden Age in the Renaissance* (New York: Oxford University Press, 1969), 19–20.

70 *Ovid's Metamorphoses: Englished by George Sandys*, 5th ed. [or *Fifth Edition* if this is to be preserved as part of the title] (London: Printed by J.F. for Richard Tomlines, 1664), I.94–5.

Horace and Seneca, warning of the dangers lurking beyond the *peirar*, embodied classical poetry's authority to cordon off the *apeiron* of the British Isles from poetry. To be sure, the wintry blasts of the *mistral* and *bora* at times whipped the Mediterranean into a foamy mass. Horace was well aware that the sea could be dangerous. Again in his *Odes* 1.3, Horace marveled at the Adriatic's scouring the bays of the Calabrian shores (*fretis acrior hadriae / curvantis Calabros sinus*, 14–15); and the usually controlled poet, concerned for Virgil's safe journey to Athens, feared the *mare turbidum et / infames scopulos, Acroceraunia* (the stormy sea, and ill-famed cliffs of Acroceraunia, 19–20).[71] But later in the ode, Horace does not hesitate to identify the British Isles as engulfed by the world's most dangerous waters as he awaits not Virgil's safe return from Athens, but rather the return of Caesar, about to set sail into *ultimos / orbis Britannos* (29–30). And thus, more than the Adriatic's Calabrian gulf, the coastlines of the British Isles, swallowed up in the shadow of an utmost marine remoteness, became Roman poetry's almost catastrophic breakdown of the *peirar*.

The conceptual framework of the *peirar* presumes that a transgression, in its strictest definition, can occur only once. A fundamental premise of Hellenism's coastal topography was that once the *peirar* had been transgressed, no new sacred shoreline liminality could be declared; and thus did early modern English humanism at times inherit a British Isles as the marginal 'unthought' of Greek antiquity's thinking of the shoreline.

6. Poetry and Place, Time and Tide, and Coasts 'with no measures grac'd'

I briefly linger on antiquity's Mediterranean as among the earliest sites of Western literary history's numinous poetics. In his treatise *On the Sublime*, the late antique Greek author conventionally known as Longinus approached Mediterranean shores as potential sites for poetic inspiration. At one point he turned to the *Iliad*'s seacoasts, quoting Homer's comparison of the divine vision of the gods with the telescopic vision of mortals standing on sea cliffs: Homer's 'higher power' was able to see 'as a man with his eyes through the sea line haze may discern, / On

---

71 Even at its stormiest, antiquity's Mediterranean nourished mythopoesis – one of the more storied examples being the Straits of Messina (Scylla and Charybdis) as the playground of vengeful gods.

a cliff as he sitteth and gazeth away o'er the wine-dark deep' (5.77).[72]
Longinus adduced this analogy to expand on his concept of 'transport'
as the disappearing line of demarcation between poet and subject matter. In Homer's sublime coastal poetics, divine vision and the 'wine-
dark' depths viewed from Mediterranean sea cliffs merged as one.

I now overleap early modernity and fast-forward from Longinus's
Mediterranean sublime to English Romantic poetry's use of the sub-
lime, notably exemplified in Shelley's *Mont Blanc* and its attention
to Alpine scenes for their own sake. I particularly wish to juxtapose
Longinus's Mediterranean sublime and the not-dissimilar concept of
negative capability as it unfolded on the shores of John Keats's Isle of
Wight. In his 1817 'On the Sea,' included in a letter to John Hamilton
Reynolds written from the Isle of Wight, Keats paid homage to British
Isles coastlines as objects of poetic contemplation: the sea 'keeps eternal
whispering around / Desolate shores, and with mighty swell / Gluts
twice ten thousand caverns' (1–3).[73] In a definitive moment of Keatsian
negative capability, the pentameters of the coastal poetics maintained
a state of suspension that gave free rein to the poetic imagination as it
intersected with the action of waves upon shoreline. Though separated
by well over a millennium-and-a-half, both Longinus's 'wine-dark'
Mediterranean sublime and the negative capability of Keats's 'desolate' local Isle of Wight converted the material reality of shorelines into
a coastal poetics, initiating a poetic act of 'transport' that contemplated
the seacoast for its own sake.

The motive behind my ahistorical yoking of Longinus and Keats
is to underscore what, from an early modern English verse perspective, might have been most remarkable about Keats's shoreline negative capability – its refusal to bear any cultural burden from antiquity's
Mediterranean: Keats conducted no internal debate as to whether the
often bleak and patently not-Mediterranean Isle of Wight could ever
be as inherently poetic as antiquity's storied, 'wine-dark' sea. Keats's
English Romantic sensibilities effortlessly brought a sublime poetry
to local shorelines. Absent from 'On the Sea' is early modern English
humanism's preoccupation with *ultima Britannia*.

---

72 Longinus, *On the Sublime*, in *Critical Theory Since Plato*, rev. ed., Hazard Adams
    (New York: Harcourt Brace Jovanovich, Inc., 1992), 82.
73 *John Keats: Selected Poems and Letters*, ed., intro., Douglas Bush (Boston: Houghton
    Mifflin, 1959).

To turn, finally, to early modern English verse, the popularity of the epyllion is just one of many examples of how frequently and effortlessly humanist-educated early modern English poets and verse dramatists turned to antiquity's Mediterranean for an inspired poetics. In *Hero and Leander* (1593–8), to cite one such instance, Christopher Marlowe, under the spell of Musaeus, situated his poem on the coastlines of an Ovidian Hellespont, whose waves he described as

> playing on yellow sand,
> Send[ing] foorth a ratling murmure to the land,
> Whose sound allures the golden *Morpheus*,
> In silence of the night to visite us.
>
> (347–50)[74]

In these lines, (verse) sound and (coastal) sounding merge seamlessly in the somnambulant 'murmure' of the surf, the waves curling on the Mediterranean's golden sand serving as Morpheus's marine cue to induce mortals to yield to deep sleep. Throughout Marlowe's tale, the language of eros is spoken by and through Mediterranean shorelines. We might be tempted to imagine Marlowe's 'murmuring' waves as anticipating Keats's 'eternally whispering' waves of the Isle of Wight's shore – until we remind ourselves of the simple cartographic fact that Marlowe's coastal poetics remained firmly rooted in antiquity's Mediterranean.[75]

This chapter's third section concluded by observing that antiquity's perception of the British Isles, where land was brought into unnatural contact with the sea, was the marginal 'unthought' of antiquity's thinking of the coastline. In this context, provisional examples of a seeming early modern English reluctance to bring verse to the local waters' edge are two passages spoken by Salerio in Shakespeare's *Merchant of Venice*, the first of which is often regarded as one of the bard's most lyrical blank verse passages. In a play prominently featuring early modern maritime trade routes, Salerio is convinced that the cause of his friend Antonio's melancholia is the vulnerability of his far-flung merchant

---

74 Roma Gill, ed., *The Complete Works of Christopher Marlowe*, 4 vols. (Oxford: Clarendon Press, 1987).
75 Technically, Leander swims across the channel that leads to the Black Sea, slightly in from the Mediterrannean.

ships, and he seeks to reassure his friend that he too would be anxious – that the mere sight of a stone church would be sufficient to remind him of imperiled ships:

> [I would] bethink me straight of dangerous rocks
> Which, touching but my gentle vessel's side,
> Would scatter all her spices on the stream,
> Enrobe the roaring waters with my silks.

(1.1.31–4)

As long as Salerio's blank verse is free to linger on open seas, it exquisitely converts the realities of coastal danger into a lyrical eroticism: his dangerous rocks 'touch' the sides of 'gentle vessels,' scattering their hulls' sensuous wealth amidst silk-robed waters. What one might customarily picture as the grinding collision of rock and ship is transmuted into a seductive caress that results in the scattering of seed-like spices and silks amidst fecund waves. But later in the play, when he must report that one of Antonio's ships may have foundered on the Goodwins, a sandbar near the Thames estuary and a notorious graveyard for merchant ships, Salerio tellingly shifts from blank verse to prose: the Goodwins are a 'very dangerous flat, and fatal, where the carcasses of many a tall ship lie buried' (3.1.4–5).[76] Put another way, when Salerio's dreamy blank verse reaches the turbulent English Channel, his poetry, like Antonio's ship, also shatters and disintegrates – as if conceding that only the more pragmatic medium of prose (such as the prose of the coasters' manuals) can negotiate the treacherous Goodwins.

In his 1586 *Apology for Poetry*, Philip Sidney voiced a recurrent sixteenth-century concern that England was infertile ground for poetry, at one point asking why 'poesy, thus embraced in all other places, should only find in our time a hard welcome, in England.'[77] Sidney, George Puttenham, William Webbe, and others all followed the lead of Scaliger's 1561 *Poetices* and its depiction of the poet as maker.[78] In the process, they may, however inadvertently, have pointed in the direction of local coastlines as the source of English poetry's efforts to probe the

---

76 In *King John*, the Goodwins wreck the Dauphin's supply ships.
77 *An Apology for Poetry*, ed. Geoffrey Shepherd (London: T. Nelson, 1965).
78 For a more detailed discussion, see S.K. Heninger Jr's chapter 'Poet as Maker' in his *Touches of Sweet Harmony: Pythagorean Cosmology and Renaissance Poetics* (San Marino, CA: The Huntington Library, 1974).

mysterious core of what Webbe termed 'writing Poetically.'[79] Repeating
the frequent gesture of deriving poetry's roots from the Greek *poiein*
and the Latin *facere*, Webbe defined poetry as a fundamentally *made*
thing, the 'arte of making,' suggesting that poetry originated not so
much from Theseus's 'airy nothing' as from the 'makeable' materials –
and, by extension, 'local habitations' – already at one's disposal: for
Webbe, the poet's hand appropriated what was *at hand* to achieve the
union of cadence and idea, just as Orpheus's hand-strummed lyre
tamed the wild solitudes of Thrace.[80] Webbe's discourse on poetry as
'making' was written amid the controversy surrounding whether English vernacular verse could ever imitate the quantitative meters of classical prosody (briefly defined as an aural basis for poetic meter); and
it called attention not only to the etymological link between 'making'
and 'poetry,' but also punned that British poetry, 'pitifully mangled and
defaced by rude smatterers,' was '[t]his brutish poetry' (29).[81] Although
by the latter decades of the sixteenth century Webbe's pun had become
overworked, it could still resonate with readers particularly invested in
his etymology of poetry as a 'made' thing. Could British poetry 'make'
something from 'brutish' coastlines – a verse that, unlike the Fortunate
Isles topos, elected not to abstract away from coastlines?

On Mediterranean seacoasts, what Webbe referred to as 'writing
Poetically' depended on a link between poetry and place, particularly
reinforced by the synchronicity of time and tide, the intimately inter-
locked causality between (lunar) time and tidal ebb and flow.[82] To sail,
however, from the Mediterranean to, say, Salerio's English Channel is to
confront Greco-Roman geography's marine regions of non-resemblance,

---

79 William Webbe, *A Discourse of English Poetry*, in *The Renaissance in England: Non-
    Dramatic Prose and Verse of the Sixteenth Century*, eds. Hyder E. Rollins and Herschel
    Baker (Lexington, MA: D.C. Heath and Company, 1954).
80 William Webbe, *A Discourse of Englishe Poetrie*, in *Elizabethan Critical Essays*, 2 vols.,
    ed. G. Gregory Smith (Oxford: Oxford University Press, 1904). On representations of
    Orpheus in English Renaissance poetry, see Sean Keilen, *Vulgar Eloquence: On the Re-
    naissance Invention of English Literature* (New Haven: Yale University Press, 2006).
81 For a detailed study of the quantitative verse movement in Elizabethan England,
    see Derek Attridge, *Well-Weighed Syllables: Elizabethan Verse in Classical Metres* (Cam-
    bridge: Cambridge University Press, 1974), and, more recently, the first chapter of
    Helgerson, *Forms of Nationhood*.
82 Within the generic bounds of the English river poem, Spenser's *Prothalamion* empha-
    sizes the synchronicity between riverine water and time by punning on 'Themmes'
    and time.

the disturbance of nature's synchronicity between time and tide. Here, tidal ebb and flow do not participate in rhythmic alternation but rather force their interrupted currents into a competitive collision, engorging the concept of 'time' itself. To approach land's end almost anywhere along British Isles shorelines is to confront turbulent zones where tidal rhythms, punished for naturally swelling in response to lunar time, are not permitted to play themselves out in curling murmurs, but are rather left to disintegrate randomly amidst jagged rocks. On these shorelines, the numinous link between poetry and place is parodied by a shredded tide whose otherwise predictable rhythms of ebb and flow are disrupted, forced into mistiming, on a broken coastal topography.

In his 1603 *Defence of Ryme*, Samuel Daniel, unlike Webbe, defended English verse against the frequent charge that it was inferior to both classical verse and continental vernaculars: 'all our vnderstandings are not to be built by the square of *Greece* and *Italie*.'[83] The immediate context of Daniel's commingling of national pride and defensiveness was an investment in the future of English poetry, specifically a call for his native poetry to end its fealty to the constraints of classical prosody's quantitative verse – the effort to accommodate its native vernacular's rhythms, rhymes, and syllabic counts to the 'long' and 'short' syllables of classical prosody.

Daniel's support for easing the restrictions of classical poetry's quantitative verse revealed his awareness of vernacular poetry's potential to shape an emergent national consciousness. But he was also shadowed by an awareness that, on the Continent, the Italian vernacular had enjoyed a relatively seamless inheritance from Latin, as discussed in Book 2 of Bembo's *Prose della vulgar lingua* (1525), maintaining that the Italian vernacular was a natural continuation of Latin.

Two of Daniel's dedicatory poems reflect early modern England's notoriously conflicted attitude toward Italy; and the poet's ambivalence toward Italy also eventually intersects with his ambivalence about English coastlines and their role in the island's poetic isolation from the Mediterranean. In the dedicatory poem to his 1594 closet drama *The Tragedy of Cleopatra*, addressed to the Countess of Pembroke, Daniel called for an English verse literally at home with its own rhymes and

---

83 *Poems and a Defence of Ryme*, ed. Arthur Colby Sprague (Cambridge, MA: Harvard University Press, 1930), 139.

syllable counts. In this poem, Daniel anticipated the nationalist optimism of his *Defence of Ryme*, turning to the genre of the river poem – specifically the Thames – to consolidate the prestige of English vernacular poetry. (I will discuss the genre of the English river poem in greater detail in my second and third chapters.) Daniel announced his hope that the examples of Sidney and Spenser would show the world 'how far Thames doth out-go / The Musike of declined *Italy*.' Here, Daniel's typically humanist goal of recapturing the ancient union of music and poetry via a new national verse joined hands with his *Defence of Ryme*'s refusal of exile in the aesthetic margins of Mediterranean poetics. To seal his argument, Daniel countered antiquity's perception of a remote England with the emergent nation's own topos of a degenerate contemporary Italy, a frequent topos effectively ameliorating a cultural envy of Mediterranean antiquity. In the process, English waters proved crucial to Daniel's call for a new national poetry: his tribute to tributaries, as it were, proffered the Thames as the embodiment of English poetry itself. Though a 'northern' river, the Thames sounded the poetic notes that promised to drown out 'The Musike of declined *Italy*.' For Daniel, it was not quantitative verse but rather the riverine rhythms of the Thames that served as topographic inspiration for the kind of aural basis of poetic meter so prized by the ancients.

But Daniel's confidence in the English vernacular is not so evident in a 1602 sonnet written to his patron Sir Edward Dymoke, with whom he had traveled in Italy in the early 1590s.[84] While in Italy, he and Dymoke had met Giambattista Guarini, renowned author of *Il pastor fido*, ranked with Tasso's *Aminta* as *cinquecento* Italy's most widely acclaimed pastoral romance. Dymoke received the 1602 sonnet from Daniel as part of a dedication of the latter's translation of Guarini's romance from an anonymous rendering. In his sonnet, Daniel speaks not as the poetic supplanter of a declining Italy, but rather as a tentative, apprentice poet who has yet to master the voice of the great Italian vernacular poets, let alone antiquity's quantitative verse. In one of the sonnet's personal reminiscences, Daniel was compelled to remind Dymoke that his Continental mentor

---

84 For Daniel's travels in Italy, see Marc Eccles, 'Samuel Daniel in France and Italy,' *Studies in Philology* 34:2 (1937): 148–67.

. . . hath oft imbas'd
Vnto us both the vertues of the North,
Saying, our costes were with no measures grac'd,
Nor barbarous tongues could any verse bring forth.

(16–19)[85]

In his criticism of coasts 'with no measures grac'd,' Guarini likely did not intend a literal reference to England's coastlines but rather appropriated them as expedient metaphors for the true object of his critique, England's 'barbarous' verses. Nor need we take too seriously Daniel's stylized deference to the geohumoral stereotypes of Guarini's disdain for 'the vertues of the North.' But Guarini's focus on coastlines, as conveyed in Daniel's reminiscence, nonetheless uncannily voices antiquity's quarantining of British Isles coastlines from the domain of poetry itself. His coastal metaphors posed the urgent concern of supporters and opponents alike of English quantitative verse – i.e., whether authentic English vernacular poetry, either bound by or freed from classical constraints, could be nurtured within such 'brutish' coastal boundaries. Daniel's recall of Guarini's English coasts 'with no measures grac'd' laid bare a question of whether Daniel's humanist goal of recapturing the ancient union of music and poetry via a new national verse could seduce the muses to abandon Mediterranean beauty-coasts and inspire poetic song amidst English tidal chaos. These are some of the questions the following chapters of this book will attempt to answer.

---

85 Samuel Daniel, dedicatory poem to Sir Edward Dymoke accompanying his translation of Guarini's *Il pastor fido*, in *The Complete Works in Verse and Prose of Samuel Daniel*, Vol. I, ed. Alexander B. Grossart (London: Spenser Society, 1885–96).

Chapter Two

Lurid Shorelines: Mapping Spenser's Queen Elizabeth in Ariosto's Hebrides

1. 'compassed with one Sea'

In 1601, near the end of Queen Elizabeth's reign, the Scottish cartographer Timothy Pont finally completed a long-term project, begun in 1583, to draw the first topographical survey of Scotland, including the Orkneys, Shetlands, and Uist in the South Hebrides.[1] In all probability Elizabeth's Scottish successor King James had consulted Pont's detailed surveys as further impetus for his projected union of England and Scotland. In 1603, the king's geo-prophetic vision viewed the British Isles not only as binding one realm but also as surrounded by one ocean, encouraging Parliament to view the region as 'one Island, compassed with one Sea.'[2] The king's vision of national maritime unity apparently insured that even the isolated archipelagos off the northern coast of Scotland (far from James's native Edinburgh) were geographically part of 'one Sea,' their coastlines as inherently 'British' as, say, the Thames estuary.

Some thirty-five years after James's proclamation of a coast 'compassed with one Sea,' John Milton's famous elegy *Lycidas*, as part of its mapping of the Irish Sea and the North Atlantic where Edward King drowned, alluded to 'the stormy *Hebrides*' (156, italics in text) that might have glimpsed King's wave-swept body.[3] (Milton's elegy will be

---

1 Pont's original maps are housed in the map collection of Edinburgh's National Library of Scotland.
2 'Speech of 1603,' in *The Political Works of James I*, ed. Charles Howard McIlwain (New York: Russell and Russell, 1965), 271.
3 Milton alludes to the Orkneys in *Epitaphium Damonis*, 178.

discussed in detail in my fourth chapter.) To be sure, Milton's Hebrides are a bleak, *unheimlich* archipelago. But the allusion is also evidence of early modern England's increasing familiarity with the formerly remote Scottish islands, now brought into closer perspective by the maps of the well-known Ortelius and Mercator as well as the local surveys of such lesser lights as Pont.

In 1654, the Dutch cartographer Johan Blaeu collected and published Pont's maps in his widely circulated *Atlas Novus*, which, among other developments, granted Scotland's western islands an unprecedented visibility in the mid-seventeenth-century European cartographic imagination. But much earlier, at about the time Spenser published the first installment of *The Faerie Queene*, an epic celebration of Elizabeth's 'greatest Isle' (1.Proem.1), Pont had barely completed his travels in Scotland's western islands.[4] The point I wish to emphasize here is that James's telescopic vision of an island 'compassed with one Sea,' the visibility of 'the stormy *Hebrides*' in an elegy playing a major role in Milton's laureate ambition, and the mid-century publication of Pont's maps all countered an earlier Elizabethan reluctance to map these North Atlantic archipelagos as part of England's sovereign coastlines. In *The Faerie Queene* Book 3.3, the prophet Merlin, during his account of the Briton-Saxon wars gleaned from Geoffrey of Monmouth's *Historia regum Britanniae* (c. 1136), catalogues a series of ancient regional monarchs ethnically cut off from the line of 'Renowned kings' who will be Arthegall's and Britomart's descendants. To cite one example, Merlin pointedly narrates Cadwallin's slaying of the unnamed 'king of *Orkeny*' (3.37), insuring that the isolated island, one of 'six Islands comprouinciall' (32), lay well beyond the bounds of Briton destiny, beyond the island nation's eventual emergence as a New Troy.[5] Merlin's marginalized '*Orkeny*' is one outcome of the epic's calculated plan to

4 All references to *The Faerie Queene* are taken from *Edmund Spenser: The Faerie Queene*, ed. A.C. Hamilton, text edited by Hiroshi Yamashita and Toshiyuki Suzuki (London: Longman, 2001).

5 Harry Berger Jr has identified the other five islands/coastlines 'comprouinciall' as Norway, Denmark, Ireland, Iceland, and Gotland ('The Structure of Merlin's Chronicle in *The Faerie Queene* III.iii,' in his *Revisionary Play: Studies in the Spenserian Dynamic*, intro. Louis Montrose [Berkeley and Los Angeles: University of California Press, 1988], 123–4). As reported in Tacitus's *Agricola*, 27, in 83 AD, Agricola was intent on advancing north into the Scottish Highlands, but he never reached the outlying islands. The Hebrides were under Norwegian control until 1262.

define the integrity of Britain's coastal boundaries via a Briton politico-ethnicity authoritatively cordoned off from the remote islands of the North Atlantic.

But in *The Faerie Queene*, poetry and prophecy do not always merge so seamlessly. Later in the epic, as I will argue, a marginalized Hebrides haunts the narrative, suggesting that Elizabeth's England and Scotland are, indeed, one coastline – unified not, however, under the anticipatory banner of James's 'one Sea' of a 'Great British' empire, but rather in the retroactive shadow of the spectral geography of an 'older' empire. Specifically, *The Faerie Queene* revisits the Roman empire's obsolete – but, for Spenser, still culturally charged – geography of *ultima Britannia*. Unlike Merlin's prophecy, this cartographic topos, to repeat a point brought up in my first chapter, made no distinctions among the striated coastal cliffs and tidal incursions of the marine region's elemental periphery. North Atlantic explorers perceived all the region's coastlines as equidistant from the Roman *axis mundi*.

A brief, bird's-eye view of the locales, both geographic and literary historical, visited in this chapter might seem as roundabout as the meanderings of the *Orlando furioso*'s hippogriff. The itinerary begins in Spenser's Ireland, then moves to the poet's presumably 'fictive' Faerie strand, to Sannazaro's Bay of Naples, back to Colin's Irish Sea, further east to Britomart's Thames, northwest to Ariosto's Hebrides (via the maps of the Estensi), and, finally, back to the Faerie strand as Spenser's version of antiquity's Hebrides. Obviously, there are no empirical data by which the coordinates of this seemingly improbable coastal itinerary can be plotted. But if we connect the dots of these locales, then what emerges are Spenser's pseudo-Hebrides, the result of his persistent, inward gazing on North Atlantic coastlines through the lens of the Mediterranean. Seeking to further our understanding of the scope of Spenser's well-documented discontents with his royal patron Elizabeth, I investigate how the poet sets up antiquity's isolated Hebrides as the cartographic stage for acting out his ambivalence toward the queen's at-best uneven patronage.

2. Poet, Royal Patron, *Ultima Britannia*

The link between maps and the legitimating of state power is nowhere better revealed, as we saw in the previous chapter, than in Lesley Cormack's studies of the ambitions of such Elizabethan geographers and cartographers as John Dee and Richard Hakluyt to map (or at least

attempt to map) England as a new imperial world center. In their imperial vision, maps were crucial to the nation's self-definition. Hence, un-
mediated iconographic links between maps and English *imperium* are
obvious in Queen Elizabeth's oft-discussed portraiture.[6] In her 1588 Armada portrait, for example, the queen's right hand rests gently, but no
less authoritatively, on a small globe, her royal navy (not yet an official
'Royal Navy') in full view through the window behind her. In her famous 1592 Ditchley portrait, the queen stands on a map of England that
also embodies her rule over the nation's rise to early maritime prominence. Her white shoes rest delicately on her island's southern half,
close to the map's representation of her London epicenter. The portrait
is a fitting companion to the allegorical title page of Dee's 1577 *General
and Rare Memorials Pertayning to the Perfect Arte of Navigation* (discussed
in my first chapter), where the figure of 'Britannia,' kneeling on the
shoreline, urges Elizabeth to seize Occasion by the forelock – that is,
to seize the moment to usher in the nation's era of imperial centrality.

On a more dissonant note from the literary front, recent studies have
exposed the deteriorating bonds between Spenser and his patron-
queen Elizabeth during the 1590s.[7] I seek to further our understanding
of Spenser's covert expressions of disillusionment with the Elizabethan
courtly cult by investigating some of the ways in which he maps the
queen's coastlines not as Dee's Britannia, gateway to England's maritime expansion, but rather as antiquity's *ultima Britannia*, located on the
extreme northwest edges of the world.

It may seem irrelevant to dwell on what is cartographically absent
from the Ditchley portrait. Specifically, it may seem beside the point to
observe that Elizabeth's imperial stance blocks from view the island's
North Atlantic archipelagos, once identified by Ptolemy as the tide-
ripped, northernmost final stop before emptying into antiquity's 'Hyperborean ocean.'[8] But I hope to show that Books 3 and 4 of *The Faerie*

---

6 The definitive study of Elizabeth's portraiture is Roy Strong, *Portraits of Queen Elizabeth* (Oxford, Clarendon Press, 1963).
7 Catherine Bates, *The Rhetoric of Courtship in Elizabethan Language and Literature* (Cambridge: Cambridge University Press, 1992), and Jane Tylus, *Writing and Vulnerability
in the Late Renaissance* (Stanford University Press, 1993). For the general decline of the
patronage system under Elizabeth, see *The Reign of Elizabeth I: Court and Culture in the
Last Decade*, ed. John Guy (Cambridge: Cambridge University Press, 1995).
8 *Claudius Ptolemy: The Geography*, trans., ed. Edward Luther Stevenson (New York:
Dover Publishing, 1991), 46. As late as 1699, an anonymous author, commenting on

Queene use the brush strokes of poetry in effect to paint Ptolemy's isolated Hebrides (the 'Haiboudai') onto the Ditchley portrait's canvas –
the Hebrides, that is, as the coastal map of his discontents with the
queen.

In 'mirrors more than one' (Britomart, Belphoebe, Amoret) does *The
Faerie Queene* reflect Elizabeth's chastity. Spenser's *Letter to Raleigh* that
accompanies the 1590 *Faerie Queene* is at best a sketchy summary of his
epic tribute to Elizabeth. It is all the more noteworthy, therefore, when
the poet alerts his readers to the future 'misery of Florimell,' whose
virginity includes her in the virgin cult of Elizabeth/Gloriana as the epic's 'most excellent and glorious person of our soueraine the Queene.'
Spenser addresses the potential indecorum of associating the preservation of chastity with 'misery' by pointedly including Florimell's vicis-
situdes among several episodes that are not so-termed 'intendments'
but rather 'Accidents,' events driven less by the engines of epic destiny
than by chance and happenstance, the staples of the romance genre. In
so doing, the poet seemingly compliments his queen by casting her as
that most alluringly feminine of literary heroines, the romance damsel
in distress.[9]

Florimell is memorably portrayed as fleeing a 'grisly Foster' through
the woods of Faerie land, her 'faire yellow locks' trailing behind her
(3.1.16). But the fact remains that many of Florimell's perils take place
on an unmapped, menacing seacoast where readers with more time
than Elizabeth had to sift through *The Faerie Queene*'s complexly layered narrative can begin to speculate on just how disingenuous the *Letter to Raleigh*'s distinction between 'intendments' and 'Accidents' may
be. It may be no 'Accident' that this virginal heroine is stranded on a
remote coastline (and one that appears in both the 1590 ad1596 editions
of the poem). This coastline may be a covertly disguised 'intendment'
that relocates the queen from the Ditchley portrait's imperial center
to an obsolete but, for such humanist poets as Spenser, still culturally
charged cartography of the topos of an *ultima Britannia*.

Scottish coastlines, compared them to a louse, 'whose legs and engrained edges representing the Promontories and Buttings out into the sea: nor does the comparison
determine there . . . [it] has calved those nitty Islands called the Orcades, and the
Shetlands (quasi Shite-Land) islands . . . ' (*The Character of Scotland* [London, 1699]:
sig. A2r).

9 The vulnerable Florimell opposes her to *The Faerie Queene*'s martial virgins, Belphoebe
   and Britomart.

Antiquity's geographic topos of an *ultima Britannia* is more than implicit in Spenser's *The View of the State of Ireland*, where the author's
stand-in Irenius observes that Ireland 'is by Diodorus Siculus, and by
Strabo, called Britannia, and a part of Great Britaine.'[10] Irenius recruits
these ancient geographers in the service of early modern New English
politics, offering their perception of Ireland as a territory within a larger
Britain as political justification for England's colonial mapping of Ireland under the name of a sovereign 'Great Britaine.' But Spenser knew
that underwriting Diodorus Siculus's and Strabo's discourse on Britain
was not politics but geography – namely, classical geography's topos of
an *ultima Britannia*. Spenser's rigorous humanist education had taught
him that these geographers' mapping of Ireland as 'a part of Great Britaine' confirmed antiquity's few if any distinctions among the coastlines
of the elemental periphery it identified as Britannia.

Such early modern continental cartographers as Ortelius and Dee's
mentor Mercator had long since rendered the topos of *ultima Britannia* obsolete; and one can safely conclude that Elizabeth, for one, was
hardly under pressure to lay aside matters of state to preoccupy herself
with the topos' cultural and geographical distancing of the British Isles
from an earlier Mediterranean *axis mundi*. But Spenser composed much
of *The Faerie Queene* as a civil servant in colonial Ireland; and, residing
on the margins of the queen's 'greatest Isle,' he had more occasions to
contemplate the lingering relevance of this otherwise obsolete topos
for his version of a *translatio imperii*.[11] Unlike the cartographers of the
new British history, antiquity's North Atlantic explorers, as mentioned
in my previous chapter, did not divide what is known as the British

---

10 *Edmund Spenser: A View of the State of Ireland*, eds. Andrew Hadfield and Willy Maley
(Oxford: Blackwell Publishers, 1997), 52.

11 Influential book-length studies of the vexed question of Spenser in/and Ireland
include (and are by no means limited to) Richard Rambuss, *Spenser's Secret Career*
(Cambridge: Cambridge University Press, 1993); Andrew Hadfield, *Edmund Spenser's
Irish Experience: Wilde Fruit and Salvage Soyl* (Oxford: Clarendon Press, 1997); Willy
Maley, *Salvaging Spenser: Colonialism, Culture and Identity* (London: Palgrave MacMillan, 1997); Richard A. McCabe, *Spenser's Monstrous Regiment: Elizabethan Ireland and
the Poetics of Difference* (New York: Oxford University Press, 2002); Thomas Herron,
Spenser's Irish Work: Plantation and Colonial Reform (Aldershot: Ashgate, 2007). For
the gender politics shadowing the subject of Spenser in/and Ireland, see Clare Carroll, 'The Construction of Gender and the Cultural and Political Other in *The Faerie
Queene* 5 and *A View of the Present State of Ireland*: The Critics, the Context, and the
Case of Radigund,' *Criticism* 32 (1990): 163–91.

Isles into distinctive micro-regions. From a Hibernian vantage point, Spenser would have been all the more aware that these explorers had judged all the archipelago's broken coastlines as uniformly dangerous, all equidistant from the liminality of the Mediterranean *peirar*.

Spenser's poetic isolation on a 'salvage' island distanced from London's network of court patronage was exacerbated by his patron-queen's inconsistent support of his well-documented career ambitions. If Spenser did at times resent writing the story of the Elizabethan *translatio imperii* in geographic isolation on an island viewed by the queen's court as 'overseas,' then one safely occulted strategy for protesting her indifference was to remap her 'greatest Isle' as no less isolated than his own marginal Ireland. Writing in England's colonial periphery, Spenser remaps the queen's realm as itself peripheral – not an increasingly metropolitan center but antiquity's *ultima Britannia*. And thus readers are presented with the irony of Spenser, attempting to fashion himself as 'England's Virgil,' even as he permits antiquity's spectral geography to exert its regressive pull on visions of England's imperial future.

3. The Turn to Literary History: Mapping Spenser's Faerie Seacoast via Ariosto

Key episodes in Books 3 and 4 of *The Faerie Queene* render the aforementioned Florimell 'chaste' but also perpetually 'chased' by male predators, even more vulnerable by stranding her amidst 'the surges hore' and 'craggy clifts' (3.4.7) of the baleful Faerie seacoast. My as-yet far-from-self-evident mapping of this surrogate for the queen in a Hebridean terror-coast entails a number of steps that it will be this chapter's task to disclose. A point of origin for my argument is the possibility that the poet's imaginary Faerie world, so often presumed unmappable, can at times be plausibly charted somewhere other than in a fictive not-Britain.

Put another way, the argument begins with a resistance to Samuel Taylor Coleridge's oft-cited conclusion that Faerie land 'is in the domains neither of history or geography . . . it is truly in the land of Faery, that is, of mental space.'[12] More recently, Spenser scholarship has been inclined to peel away the layers of the poet's studied vagueness

---

12 Samuel Taylor Coleridge, *Miscellaneous Criticism*, ed. T.M. Raysor (Cambridge: Harvard University Press, 1936), 37.

('where is that happy land of Faery, / which I so much do vaunt yet no where show') to map actual portions of Faerie land.[13] Though cagey about Faerie's not-British whereabouts, Spenser does, after all, offer an orienteering challenge to his readers to search for 'certain signes here sett in sondrie place' (2.Proem.4). Perhaps, he slyly hints, parts of Faerie land can even be mapped across the Atlantic in 'fruitfullest Virginia' (2.Proem.2).

Or, perhaps the Faerie seacoast can be mapped, via the literary history of dynastic epic, back across the ocean in the North Atlantic's Hebrides. A reliable 'sondrie place' for locating the Faerie seacoast – and, as I will eventually argue, a key if covert influence on Spenser's mapping of England in *ultima Britannia* – is the eighth canto of the *Orlando furioso*, the 1532 Ferrarese dynastic epic written by Ludovico Ariosto, one of several esteemed 'Poets historicall' singled out for praise in the *Letter to Raleigh*.

Ariosto's epic was often on Spenser's mind as the latter mapped the dynastic coordinates of his own epic.[14] In fact, his programmatic surpassing of Ariosto's version of the *translatio imperii* results in, arguably, *The Faerie Queene*'s most successful merging of poetic ambition and deference to his queen, converting British provinciality into imperial centrality. Relevant here is Spenser's aforementioned prophet Merlin. Elizabeth was undoubtedly pleased with one of *The Faerie Queene*'s more authoritative remappings of Ariosto's Ferrarese New Troy: its relocation of the *Orlando*'s Merlin to the British Isles.[15] In Canto 3.16–60,

---

13 Michael Murrin has argued that much of Faerie land, following the examples of the thirteenth-century *Huon of Bordeaux* and Jean of Arras's late fourteenth-century *Melusine*, can be located in Southeast Asia ('Spenser's Fairyland,' in *The Allegorical Epic: Essays in Its Rise and Decline* [Chicago: University of Chicago Press, 1980]). More recently, Wayne Erickson has investigated similarities between Faerie land and England in his *Mapping the Faerie Queene: Quest Structure and the World of the Poem* (New York: Garland Press, 1996).

14 A list of the earliest pathbreaking studies of Ariosto's influence on Spenser includes R.E. Neil Dodge, 'Spenser's Imitations from Ariosto,' *PMLA* 12 (1897); Susannah McMurphy, *Spenser's Use of Ariosto* (Seattle: University of Washington Press, 1924); Thomas Greene, *The Descent from Heaven: A Study of Epic Continuity* (New Haven: Yale University Press, 1963); chapter 6 of Paul Alpers's *The Poetry of the 'Faerie Queene'* (Princeton: Princeton University Press, 1967); Robert M. Durling, *The Figure of the Poet in Renaissance Epic* (Cambridge, MA: Harvard University Press, 1967).

15 A study of Elizabeth as *The Faerie Queene*'s 'most actively signaled' reader is Maureen Quiilligan, *Milton's Spenser: The Politics of Reading* (Ithaca: Cornell University Press, 1983).

Ariosto's Merlin prophesies the ancestral glory of the Estensi, culminating in the poet's patron Ippolito as a new Augustus. This Merlin, however, derives not from Welsh tradition but rather from the poet's familiarity with continental disseminations of the matter of Arthur as it intersected with the matter of Charlemagne. Spenser, reading Ariosto closer to the geographical origin of the matter of Arthur, counters by restoring an authentically Welsh Merlin whose delve, not just a romance locale, is pointedly located in 'Maridunum, that is now by chaunge / Of name Cayr-Merdin cald' (3.3.7).[16] Exploiting the Tudor myth of Welsh descent from Arthur, Spenser strategically remaps Cayr-Merdin's provinciality as nothing less than the center of Tudor England as a Trojan renovatio.

Less flattering to Elizabeth are those moments when Spenser strays from the structure of epic prophecy to explore some of the more dilatory paths of Ariosto's sprawling narrative. In his epic's eighth canto, Ariosto temporarily abandons the high seriousness of the matter of Charlemagne in favor of a melodrama that strands his hermit-chased heroine Angelica on the lonely, orc-patrolled island of 'Ebuda' (a location most likely stemming from his familiarity with the Estense collection of Ptolemaic maps to be discussed later in this chapter). This episode, in turn, provides proleptic clues that the bleak Faerie seacoast where Elizabeth's rape-threatened surrogate Florimell is stranded is also identifiably Hebridean.

For two days in 1507, Ariosto read his as-yet unfinished epic to a convalescent, and deeply appreciative, Isabella Gonzaga d'Este. Ariosto's patroness, her name echoing the Orlando's own pirate-kidnapped 'Isabella' (3.30–1), apparently enjoyed the tales of the epic's many imperiled heroines, including the eighth canto's stranding of Angelica in the Hebrides. But Spenser's patroness Elizabeth read portions of his epic not within the protective, continental confines of the duchy of Ferrara, but rather on an island whose north-by-northwest coast was the Hebrides; and thus, much more was at geographic stake in The Faerie Queene's adaptation of the Ebuda episode. Depending on the care with which she read the episode, the queen was, at least implicitly, induced to gaze northwestward to picture herself as shadowed by the cultural threat of being stranded on antiquity's edges of the earth.

---

16 For attention to Cayr-Merdin as Spenser's exercise in antiquarian discourse, see Andrew Fichter, Poets Historical: Dynastic Epic in the Renaissance (New Haven: Yale University Press, 1982), 172; and Bart van Es, Spenser's Forms of History (New York: Oxford University Press, 2002), 52–8.

4. Cymoent's Lyrical Mediterranean, Marinell's Terror-Coast

Homeric hymn and Florentine vernacular poetry merge eloquently on Mediterranean shores in Angelo Poliziano's 1475–8 *Giostra di Giuliano de' Medici* and its account of the birth of Venus, driven ashore by zephyrs:

> E dentro nata in atti vaghi e lieti
> una donzella non con uman volto,
> da' Zefiri lascivi spinta a proda,
> gir sopra un nicchio . . .

$$(\text{I.xcix})^{17}$$

Spenser, too, takes his vernacular English poetry to Poliziano's hymnic Mediterranean in his account of the birth of Venus in Book 4 of *The Faerie Queene*. The goddess was bred 'of the fomy sea,' born when Saturn's genitals were thrown into the ocean (12.2.2). Spenser's Mediterranean is as fertile for poets as for engendered goddesses. But one wonders if, in his return to the birth of Venus, Spenser pondered something Poliziano did not have to – i.e., his poetic distance from an ancient, hymnic Mediterranean. When an early modern English poet took his poetry to the Mediterranean, was the gesture necessarily derivative? Did images of more proximate English shores inevitably intervene?

This chapter will culminate in a detailed examination of how Ariosto's Hebridean *ultima Britannia* becomes mapped within the gender politics of *The Faerie Queene*. But over the course of the next three sections, I seek a richer context for this conclusion by probing the extent to which England's Virgil often took pains to depict his Faerie seacoast as patently not-Mediterranean. Spenser's stranding of portions of his narrative in Ariosto's Hebrides becomes all the more noteworthy if we consider his intimate familiarity with Mediterranean shorelines as antiquity's privileged training ground for poets. His refusal to assign a precise location to his Faerie seacoast, as we shall see, breaks rank with what he knew was Mediterranean poetry's custom of laying autobiographical claim to the local shores that nourished it.

In the introductory chapter, I highlighted Rosalie Colie's reminder that, in Italian Renaissance writing, '[g]eography counted,' with such

---

17 *Stanze cominciate per la giostra del Magnifico Giuliano de Medici*, trans. David Quint (Amherst, MA: University of Massachusetts Press, 1979).

local habitats as Boccaccio's Florence endowing his writing with what she termed 'the numen of poetic significance.' I would add that an intimate link between Italian Renaissance genre and Mediterranean coastal habitats was forged in Jacopo Sannazaro's piscatory eclogues, his site of a numinous poetics being the deep blue Bay of Naples in view of the Villa Mergellina where he wrote (not far from Manso's villa, visited decades later by Milton). When his five neo-Latin eclogues were published in 1526, they inspired an immediate Renaissance Italian vogue for an idealized seacoast.

Sannazaro's piscatory eclogues are deeply rooted in a venerable Mediterranean coastal poetics with a powerful sense of place.[18] The genre originated with Theocritus's *Idylls*, set in the poet's native Sicily, where shepherds batten their flocks while stealing glimpses of the sea and overhearing the distant surf – or where forsaken lovers sing to their lost beloveds as waves reflect the moonlight, as the sea-breezes themselves breathe sighs of lament. Almost a century ago, Henry Hall, reviving Sannazaro for English audiences, captured the dreamy charm of the Theocritean shoreline-pastoral in ways that virtually define antiquity's Mediterranean-caressed *peirar*: 'In a land of islets, islands and promontories many a youth drove his flock afield on hillsides whence he could look down on the blue shield of the sea, rimmed with white surf . . . '[19] Theocritus's idylls were imitated by Virgil, whose celebrated fourth *Georgic* features such charming vignettes as the sea-god Proteus taking shelter in a coastal cave on a hot day, while his companionate sea-creatures gambol in the waves.[20]

Sannazaro's eclogues also transport ancient pastoral's mix of rustic naivety and cultivated sophistication to the seashore. In his first eclogue, 'Phyllis,' Mediterranean shores resonate with the sympathetic plaints of sea-birds mourning the anniversary of the death of the fisherlass Phyllis. Her grieving lover Lycidas visits her coastal tomb and erot-

---

18 Sannazaro's echoes of, in particular, classical Roman models were refined in the Neapolitan academy of Pontano. On his eclogues as a revival of the Latin language at the roots of ancient pastoral, see William J. Kennedy, *Jacopo Sannazaro and the Uses of Pastoral* (Hanover and London: University Press of New England, 1983).

19 Henry Hall, *Idylls of Fishermen: A History of the Literary Species* (New York: Columbia University Press, 1914), 1.

20 For a brief discussion of Sannazaro's figure of Proteus, see A. Bartlett Giamatti's chapter 'Proteus Unbound: Some Versions of the Sea God in the Renaissance,' in his *Exile and Change in Renaissance Literature* (New Haven: Yale University Press, 1984), 125–6.

ically stretches out on the kelp-bedded shore (*proiectus in alga*, 54).[21] In Sannazaro's second eclogue, 'Galatea,' coastal tropes inspire the fisher-youth Lycon's lament for his absent beloved Galatea: in vain, he offers her wool 'softer than froth from the sea' (*lana maris spumis quae mollior*, 41). The sea-loving Lycon chides the ungrateful Galatea for deserting the seacoast's bounty:

> I have sent you a thousand oysters wrested from the hanging rocks of Miseno. Posillipo harbors the same under her broad flood; the same, Euploea under her shimmering waves. Nesis harbors for me a multitude of sea-urchins . . . Furthermore, my hand is skilled at plucking murex under the water . . . (*Ostrea misens, pendentibus eruta saxis / mille tibi misi, totidem gurgita vasto / Pausilypus, totidem vitreis Euploea sub undis / servat adhuc; Plures Nesis mihi servat echinos . . . / Praeterea mihi Sub pelago manus aftis legendis muricibus*, 30–7).

Loyal to Lycon is the mythic Glaucus, a once-humble fisherman transformed into a sea-deity. In sympathy with Lycon, Glaucus becomes a poignant 'divinity of the swelling waters' (*aequoreae Glaucus scrutator harenae*, 54), the Bay of Naples' presiding genius.

Spenser's familiarity with Sannazaro is evident in E.K.'s preface to *The Shepheardes Calender*, where the Neapolitan poet is praised as one of the 'divers other excellent both Italian and French poetes whose foting this Author euery where followeth.'[22] Poetic traces of Sannazaro's 'foting' are particularly observable in the pseudo-Mediterranean depths of *The Faerie Queene*'s sea-nymph Cymoent, mother of the Faerie knight Marinell. Though her marine world is reflected in any number of Elizabethan venues (emblems, maps, iconographies, court festivities, pageants, entertainments), Cymoent's balmy seas and quaint sea-shell treasures seem particularly indebted to the elegant detail of Sannazaro's eclogues.[23]

---

21 All references to the original neo-Latin and English translation of Sannazaro's eclogues are from *Jacopo Sannazaro: Latin Poetry*, trans. Michael C.J. Putnam (Cambridge, MA: Harvard University Press, 2009).

22 All references to Spenser's shorter poems are from *The Yale Edition of the Shorter Poems of Edmund Spenser*, eds. W.A. Oram, E. Bjorvand, R. Bond, T.H. Cain, and R. Schell (New Haven: Yale University Press, 1989).

23 At the sea-gods' banquet before the marriage ceremony of the Thames and Medway, Spenser renames the sea-nymph Cymoent 'Cymodoce,' a figure appearing in Sannazaro's 'Proteus' eclogue. The only other noteworthy early modern English experiment with Sannazaro's piscatorials is Phineas Fletcher's 1637 *Piscatorie Eclogues*.

'Deuoyd of mortal slime,' Cymoent dwells in a protective realm of mythic marine plenitude (3.4.35). Intercourse with Marinell's father Dumarin is elliptically described as his 'by her closely lay[ing]' while she slumbers (3.4.19) – perhaps the only way to limn the consummated love of 'mortal sire' and 'immortal wombe' (4.12.4). As the daughter of Nereus, Cymoent possesses arcane marine powers (as do all the Nereids): 'with her least word [she] can assuage / The surging seas, when they do sorest rage' (4.11.52). The poet also singles out her capacity 'To rule his [Nereus's] tides, and surges to vprere' (4.12.52). Cymoent lives an idyllic life of marine-pastoral bliss. In Book 4, in gratitude to Tryphon (quaintly dubbed 'the seagods surgeon') for healing her son's wound, she gives the god a whistle 'of a fishes shell . . . wrought with rare delight' (4.11.6).

The neo-Latinate charm of Cymoent's domain is never so cloying as when she and her sisters summon sea-chariots to carry them to the wounded Marinell, smeared 'all in gore / And cruddy bloud' (3.4.34) on the Faerie strand. Neptune responds to her maternal crisis by calming his 'mightie waters' for the sea-nymphs' train of chariots:

> The waves obedient to their beheast,
> Them yielded readie passage, and their rage surceast.
> Great *Neptune* stood amazd at their sight,
> Whiles on his broad round back they softly slid
> And eke himself mournd at their mournfull plight . . .
> For great compassion of their sorrow, bid
> His mightie waters to them buxome bee.

(3.4.31–2)

A school of graceful dolphins, 'raunged in array,' draws Cymoent's chariot, amidst some of *The Faerie Queene*'s most self-consciously mannered poetry:

> As swift as swallowes, on the waues they went,
> That their broad flaggie fins no fome did reare,
> Ne bubbling roundel they behind them sent,
> The rest of other fishes drawen weare,
> Which with their finny oars the swelling sea did sheare.

(3.4.33)

For Sannazaro's influence on Fletcher, see Lee Piepho, 'The Latin and English Eclogues,' *Studies in Philology* 81 (1984): 461–72.

Cymoent's chariot gliding softly on Neptune's back, her graceful, broad-finned dolphins so delicately propelling their way through the ocean they leave 'ne bubbling roundel' in their wakes, the other char- iot-drawing fish 'shear[ing]' the sea-swells with their 'finny oars,' are all images so exquisite in their piscine perfection that, at this moment, readers are altogether seduced into neglecting the fate of Cymoent's wounded son. For six carefully crafted stanzas, Cymoent's grief is the poetic occasion for a synchronized marine ballet distracting readers from Marinell's coastal misery.

All of which serves as Spenser's virtuosic tribute to Sannazaro's Nea- politan poetics. But, borrowing from E.K., the 'foting' of Sannazaro's piscatorials also takes the poet briefly to *ultima Britannia*. In 'Galatea,' the despondent Lycon wonders whether or not he should go into exile in foreign lands: 'Shall I go in search of sluggish [ice-clogged] waters consigned beneath the farthest pole of Boreas, eternally white with stiffening chill?' (*Boreae extremo damnata sub axe / stagna petam et rigidis*, 64–5). Sannazaro's topos of *ultima Britannia* is conventional enough (a *cinquecento* echo of Virgil, Juvenal, Catullus, etc.). But England's Virgil, residing not all that far from Lycon's imagined exile in hyperborean waters, was forced to confront antiquity's *ultima Britannia* as his own exile from a Mediterranean erotic *pietas*. As if compulsively following Sannazaro's 'foting' to *ultima Britannnia*, Spenser's Cymoent-narrative also finds itself drifting amidst the maritime region of the topos.

Thus, as *The Faerie Queene*'s narrative approaches the shallower wa- ters of the Faerie strand, it founders on a tide-ripped coastline at odds with Sannazaro's invoking of Theocritean and Virgilian shores as ideal training grounds for aspiring poets. When the nymphs dismount their chariots near the shoreline, Spenser ceases mapping Marinell's coast in his mother's pseudo-Mediterranean. As Cymoent's dolphins sequester themselves in safer waters well shy of the coastline,

> their temed fishes softly swim
> Along the margent of the fomy shore,
> Least they their fines should bruze, and surbate sore
> Their tender feet vpon the stony ground.

> (3.4.34)

In Poliziano's *Giostro*, as mentioned earlier, zephyrs accompany Venus to Mediterranean shorelines. At this stage in *The Faerie Queene*, how- ever, the poet pointedly notes that the sea-nymphs' dolphins and other 'temed' fish steer clear of the shoreline, protecting their delicate fins from the 'surbat[ing]' perils of Marinell's dwelling. No longer the 'bux-ome' waters of Cymoent's depths, Marinell's strand does not nurture but 'bruze[s]'; and here exist no exquisitely intact 'fishes shells wrought with rare delight' – only whatever primal marine life can survive the wave-scoured rocks. At Marinell's coast, the plenitude of his mother's Sannazaran depths ends and the tidal violence of a different coastal topography begins.

Spenser does not disclose the location of Marinell's 'margent.' But Cymoent's sea-creatures, prudently halting their shoreward progress, offer a clue: they effectively mime antiquity's dread of the breakdown of a protective liminality between land and sea. Put another way, Mari-nell dwells in an *apeiron* that the poet refuses to claim as the site of a numinous poetics.

Relevant here is a brief digression on Marinell's literary historical an-tecedents. *The Faerie Queene*'s third and fourth books present readers with three largely unrelated Marinells: Book 3's 'doughty, rich young man,' in the words of Thomas Roche (184); the same book's maternally overprotected adolescent reluctant to fall in love; and Book 4's pin-ing lover of Florimell, whom he did 'learne to loue, by learning louers paines to rew' (4.12.13). The latter two Marinells, despite their differ-ences, sustain ongoing associations with the Faerie seacoast, prompting a consideration of their literary historical prototypes. Of Book 3's over-protected Marinell, one can recognize two key classical antecedents, the narcissistic Achilles and Adonis who are, at times, explicitly shoreline precursors of Marinell.[24] The epic's second Marinell, Florimell's pining coastal beloved, also has a literary history at least superficially trace-able to the piscatory eclogue's Lycidas and Lycon.

---

24 For more on Marinell as a type of the 'reluctant' Achilles, see Isabel E. Rathborne, *The Meaning of Spenser's Fairyland* (New York: Columbia University Press, 1945), 279–89, and Thomas P. Roche Jr, who also observes that Marinell's parentage, like Achilles's, is half mortal, half immortal (*The Kindly Flame: A Study of the Third and Fourth Books of 'The Faerie Queene'* [Princeton: Princeton University Press, 1964], 185–6). In his discussion of Marinell, James Nohrnberg calls attention to Silius Itali-cus's first-century *Punica*, where Achilles, the overprotected son of the sea-nymph Thetis, is explicitly associated with the seacoast (*The Analogy of 'The Faerie Queene'* [Princeton: Princeton University Press, 1976]). In this work, the sea-nymph Cymo-doce asks Proteus to prophesy the future of the Italian shore; and in order to do so, he must tell a story that includes Achilles (VII.409ff.). (Interestingly, the *Punica*'s Cy-modoce, hearing the future of the seacoast, resurfaces – almost literally – in Book 3 of

But Marinell dwells on a seacoast exiled from Mediterranean literary history. Though the knight is recognizably archetypal, Spenser pointedly foregrounds the dangerous reality of his lived life on the Faerie strand. In Marinell's coastal domain, from which Cymoent's dolphins keep their distance, the echoes of a Mediterranean literary history become fainter – drowned out, as it were, by

> the surges hore,
> That against the craggy clifts did loudly rore,
> And in their raging surquedry disdaynd,
> That the fast earth affronted them so sore,
> And their deuouring couetize restrained.

(3.4.7)[25]

On this coast, where breakers smash against defiant rocks, it is impossible to speak of a region where land 'meets' sea; and Spenser's poetry is as cacophonous as his earlier depictions of Cymoent's depths were elegant and sonorous. Spenser's nineteenth-century readers (such as Keats who, as mentioned in my previous chapter, lyrically noted the 'twice ten thousand' sea caverns of the Isle of Wight coast) might have been tempted to place the Faerie seacoast within an aesthetics of the sublime. But for early modern readers accustomed to viewing poetic seacoasts through a Sannazaran lens, this shoreline utterly mocks the Neapolitan poet's sequestering *peirar*. The Faerie seacoast is, rather,

---

The Faerie Queene as the Thetis-like mother of Marinell, determined to shield him from woman's love by confining him to the seacoast.) Another obvious classical antecedent of Marinell is Adonis, doted on by Venus – and, at times, an explicitly coastal figure. In Ovid's *Metamorphoses*, Adonis's body is laid out on the shore (10.716); and Theocritus describes Adonis's mourners as carrying the dead god forth 'among the waves that break upon the beach' (*Idylls* XV.132–6). Marinell's other possible Virgilian-Ovidian source may be the Trojan Polydorus, whose wounded body is lamented on the shore by the Trojan women in both the *Aeneid* (6.536–46) and the *Metamorphoses*.

25 Two cantos earlier, readers catch their first glimpse of Marinell's seacoast through the eyes of Britomart, for whom the rock-strewn shore is less real than psychological, mirroring the dynastic heroine's adolescent pining for Arthegall. For an account of Britomart's coastal lament for Arthegall as unfolding on the boundary between narrative and allegory, see Susanne Lindgren Wofford, 'Britomart's Petrarchan Lament: Allegory and Narrative in *The Faerie Queene* III.iv,' *Comparative Literature* 39, no. 1 [1987]: 53).

the graveyard of any attempt to accommodate a Mediterranean poetics within its tides.[26] In contrast to E.R. Curtius's poignant vision of the *Odyssey's* many 'blessed shores . . . free from ills and where the pains of death are unknown,' Marinell's inaccessible domain presents an increasing threat of drowning.[27] His past defeats of 'An hundred knights' have contributed to his putative 'noble fame' throughout Faerie land (3.4.21); but the knight, displaced from the Mediterranean's tide-caressed shores, has also been displaced from a numinous poetics to the Faerie coast's 'raging' asynchrony of time and tide.

Of Marinell's mortal father Dumarin one knows nothing, except for his name's etymology as 'of the sea.' Further probing the watery mysteries of Marinell's genealogy, his liminal status as neither human nor deity, can shed light on one of *The Faerie Queene's* many oddities – why Marinell is never as compatible with water as his name signifies. Though 'half mortall' (4.12.4), Marinell strikes readers as ontologically distinct from, say, Sannazaro's Glaucus, a mortal fisherman turned sea-deity—as if the dalliance between Marinell's father and mother, Dumarin and Cymoent, had not been fully endorsed by Nereus, Neptune, and his mother's other sea-chaperones. Given the twin etymologies of his parents' names (Dumarin as 'of the sea,' and Cymoent as a 'wave-tamer'), one would anticipate that the happy result of their union would be a water-baby at home on land or sea, a child ordained into a life of marine fulfillment. But Marinell, as Dumarin and Cymoent's half-mortal son, is neither secure in the waves of his mother's 'buxome'

---

26 To be sure, one might argue that Marinell's domain possesses at least some measure of beauty, 'bestrowed,' as it is, 'all with rich aray / Of pearles and pretious stones of great assay' (3.4.18). But these 'pretious stones,' anticipatory parodies of John of Gaunt's famous depiction of England, in *Richard II*, as 'a precious stone,' have been cast ashore by the sea-god Nereus as the lost treasure of shipwrecks. They do not so much adorn as litter the coast, transforming it into the sea-gods' designated dumping ground for the plundered 'spoyle of all the world,' a graveyard of doomed cargo (4.18). Leonard Barkan has described these coastal gems as 'multiple, cold, and infertile' (*Nature's Work of Art: The Human Body as Image of the World* [New Haven: Yale University Press, 1975], 271). Readers' final glimpses of the tide-raked Faerie coast are early in Book 5, where its erosive force particularly asserts itself. The Egalitarian Giant lectures Arthegall: 'the sea it selfe does thou not plainly see / Encroch vpon the land there vnder thee?' (2.37). Two cantos later, the brothers Amidas and Bracidas feud bitterly over who gains and who loses in the battle between 'deuouring Sea' and 'lands decay' (4.8–9).

27 E.R. Curtius, *European Literature and the Latin Middle Ages*, trans. Willard R. Trask (New York, 1953), 186.

ocean nor at home at the battering, battered Faerie seacoast—in Marinell's own words, 'this forbidden way' where he must live out his days
(3.4.14); and although raised in a coastal 'rocky caue as wighte forlorne'
(3.4.20), he never swims. (In this regard, Marinell presents a curious
contrast to the dynastic hero Arthegall who, even when fully armed,
'in swimming skilful was, / And durst the depth of any water sownd'
[5.2.16].) And even on the coast, he is always susceptible to drowning, a
real (or satirically comic?) danger at odds with antiquity's topos of the
Achillean, protected youth.

Marinell's marine limitations are exposed in Book 4, where he accompanies his mother to the Thames and Medway's river-wedding
festivities 'to learne and see / The manner of the Gods, when they
at banquet be' (4.12.3). In attendance are mythology's renowned sea-
gods, including Neptune, who 'rules the Seas, and makes them rise or
fall'; Eurypulus, who 'calmes the waters wroth'; and Alebius, who
'know'th / The waters depth, and doth their bottome tread' (3.11.11–
14). All three sea-gods dwell, literally, in their element. But Marinell is
unable to join his mother (now renamed Cymodoce) at the sea-gods'
banquet:

> He might not with immortal food be fed,
> Ne with th'eternall Gods to bancket come;
> But walkt abrode, and round about did rome,
> To view the building of that vncouth place.

(4.12.4)

Marinell's exile from Mediterranean antiquity is all the more obvious
upon recalling that in Virgil's celebrated fourth *Georgic*, Aristaeus, son
of the sea-nymph Cyrene, is wondrously conveyed by a mountain-
wave beneath the ocean to visit the source of all the rivers.[28] But Marinell, though also at the confluence of the world's seas, is strangely
hydrophobic: readers are told that Cymoent 'of his father Marinell did
name' (3.4.20), but the *marin* of Du-*marin* has not been fully enfolded
into the *marin* of *Marin*-ell. Or, perhaps Mari-*nell*, though Dumarin and
Cymoent's son, is the negation of the sea, exiled on the Faerie strand's
grievous 'margent.'

---

28 For more on Cyrene's cave as the origin of the world's rivers, see David Quint's
    chapter 'The Virgilian Source,' in his *Origin and Originality in Renaissance Literature:
    Versions of the Source* (New Haven: Yale University Press, 1983), 32–42.

Marinell's marine discontents extend beyond his role as overprotected son to his other role in *The Faerie Queene* as the lamenting coastal
lover of Florimell, imprisoned in the sea-god Proteus's bower. (How
the imperiled heroine gets there will be discussed in this chapter's
final section.) Spenser locates the god's dwelling 'at the bottome of the
maine,' tracing the boundaries of Marinell's strand. Forcing the knight
to cling to the coastal rocks 'Vnder the hanging of an hideous clieffe,'
Proteus's bower is Spenser's Faerie strand at its most bone-crushing,
located

> Vnder a mightie rocke, gainst which do raue
> The roaring billowes in their proud disdaine,
> That with the angry working of the waue,
> Therein is eaten out a hollow caue
> That seems rough Masons hand with engines keene
> Had long while labored it to engraue.

> (3.8.270)

Lest his readers forget the dangers of the coastline, Spenser reminds
them, in Book 4, that Proteus's dungeon is 'Deepe in the bottome of an
huge great rock' and 'wall'd . . . with waues, which rag'd and ror'd / As
they the cliffe in peeces would haue cleft' (4.11.3–4). Perhaps anticipated
by the 'rocky caue' where Marinell was raised as a child, Proteus's sea-
dungeon is a zone of precipitous drop-offs and high tides disguising
undersea turbulence where land and sea fight to establish dominance.
Wave-smacked rocks shatter the walls of water, and with each impact,
the rocks themselves lose mass, resulting in caves 'engraue[d]' by the
'Masons hand' of erosion. The imprisoned Florimell's pleas for help are
lost amidst the pounding, cliff-cleaving waves that 'pearce the rockes,
and hardest marble weare' (4.12.7).

In an attempt to preserve Spenser's allegorical voice, critics have
tended to gloss over the all-too-real dangers of the Faerie strand, customarily identifying Marinell and Florimell's eventual betrothal as
the poet's allegorical unity of water and earth.[29] But Marinell's marine
exile undermines this anticipated elemental *discordia concors*. Despite
the promise of his watery name, Marinell cannot approach Proteus's

---

29 Northrop Frye interprets them as Proserpina-Adonis or Ishtar-Tammuz, myths of
    vegetative decay and renewal (*Anatomy of Criticism* [Princeton: Princeton University
    Press, 1957], 153). See also Roche, 185.

cave to rescue Florimell: 'he found no way / To enter in, or issue forth below: / For all about that rocke the sea did flow' (4.12.15). Unlike the sea-god Alebius, whose marine agility enables him to explore watery depths, Marinell is confined within his own coastal rocks, on the brink of being dashed to bits should he seek to 'issue forth below.' Unable to swim, dive, or hold his breath while submerged, 'In this sad plight he walked here and there, / And romed round about the rocke in vaine, / As he had lost him selfe, he wist not where' (4.12.17). Even when he is at home (either on the coast or accompanying his sea-nymph mother), Marinell is in exile – a 'walker abrode' amidst 'vncouth' marine realms, a lonely coastal roamer 'round about' the breakers, and 'lost . . . he wist not where.'

The piscatory eclogue, as we have seen, lingers on Mediterranean seacoasts as perhaps nature's most protective havens for bereaved lovers. So attuned to lovers' plaintive sadnesses are the genre's wave-resounding waters (i.e., Glaucus as 'a watcher of the watery strand') that rocky shores and ocean waves work in tandem to create a coastline more seductive than threatening. The eclogue's 'vasty deep' rhythmically merges with the shore-lovers' laments, and the breakers' pounding energy erotically intensifies in response to their pathos. Marinell's Faerie 'margent,' however does not sequester him within an erotic solipsism but rather exposes the knight to coastal exile.

Before this chapter returns to the Hebrides with which it began, the next two sections will investigate two privileged Spenserian poetic genres, pastoral and verse prophecy, respectively. In these genres, Spenser's poetry further reveals its ongoing resistance to viewing British Isles coastlines through any lens other than *ultima Britannia*.

5. Local Rivers, Local Shores in *Colin Clouts Come Home Againe*

Although the similarities between Marinell's strand and the rugged coastlines of the British Isles are obvious, Spenser does not specify the shore's 'Faerie' location. In contrast, significant portions of his pastoral *Colin Clouts Come Home Againe*, written in the early 1590s, unfold in view of Elizabeth's coastlines. Richard McCabe has inserted Spenser's pastoral within a tension 'as to whether monarchs are beholden to poets or poets to monarchs' (174). I would add that this tension can be placed in sharper relief if we focus on the poem's coastal topography. Cynthia-as-Elizabeth presumably resides in (England as a) pastoral Arcadia, free from 'grisly famine' and 'ravenous wolves' (316, 320), far

removed from the 'barrein soyle' (656) of Colin's Irish homeland. Even
so, Spenser-as-Colin, unlike Sannazaro, shapes his pastoral persona
by *refusing* to lay claim to local coastlines, and by mapping not only
his provincial Ireland but also the queen's 'greatest Isle' as equidistant
from antiquity's *axis mundi*.

   Colin Clout is an often thinly disguised autobiography of Spenser's
1589 journey from Ireland to England to present the first three books
of *The Faerie Queene* to his printer William Ponsonby – and to seek an
audience from Elizabeth.[30] Written between the two installments of
Spenser's epic, *Colin Clout* also briefly positions readers between Ireland and England on the Irish Sea. Colin / Spenser's pastoral voice at
times sounds a generically conventional note of worldly disillusionment, never so audible as when Colin approaches Cynthia's coastline.
If, like pastoral in general, *Colin Clout* is an extended meditation about
poetry itself, then it is also a poem about how Spenser declines an
opportunity to transform local English coastlines into a green world
where pastoral verse can flourish.

   To unpack this argument, I begin not with seacoasts but with rivers – that is, the probability that if asked to recall local bodies of water
in Spenser's poetry, one will turn not, as in Sannazaro's eclogues, to
coastlines but to rivers. In his 1596 betrothal poem, the *Prothalamion*,
the synergy between riverine flow and poetic eloquence comprises
Spenser's refrain, 'Sweete *Themmes* runne softly, till I end my Song.'
Rivers, of course, are lavishly celebrated in the fourth book of *The Faerie Queene* and its marriage of the Thames and Medway. Much has
been written about Spenser's riverine imagination, how it places such
world-renowned rivers as 'the fertile Nile,' the 'Great Ganges,' and the
'immortall Euphrates' in proximity with such quaintly provincial English tributaries as the 'chaulky Kenet,' the 'soft sliding Breane,' and
the 'wanton Lee.'[31] Of the wedding ceremony's incantatory roll call of

---

30 For some of the parallels between Spenser and the pastoral persona in *Colin Clout*,
    see Nancy Jo Hoffman, *Spenser's Pastorals: 'The Shepheardes Calender' and 'Colin Clout'*
    (Baltimore: The Johns Hopkins University Press, 1977).
31 Key studies of the Thames and Medway episode include Charles G. Osgood,
    'Spenser's English Rivers,' *Transactions of the Connecticut Academy of Arts and Sciences*
    23 (1920); Roche, *The Kindly Flame*; Gordon Braden, 'river-run: An Epic Catalogue
    in *The Faerie Queene*,' *ELR* 5 (1975): 25–48; Jack B. Oruch, 'Spenser, Camden, and the
    Poetic Marriage of Rivers,' *Studies in Philology* 64 (1967): 606–24; and Wyman H. Her-
    endeen, *From Landscape to Literature: The River and the Myth of Geography* (Pittsburgh:
    Duquesne University Press, 1986).

British rivers, Coleridge once observed that 'the mere names constitute half the pleasure we receive.'[32]

Venerating the Tudors' Welsh roots, the marriage ceremony showcases the rivers Severn and Dee, the latter 'which Britons long ygone / Did call diuine' (39). But just when readers might conclude that Spenser's exhaustive catalogue of English and Welsh rivers has spent its chorographic energy, the poet announces that 'Ne thence the Irishe Riuers absent were' (40). As if to remind the queen where so much of Spenser's epic was written, such rivers as the Liffy, Slane, Aubrian, Boyne, Trowis, and Allo sustain another five stanzas of poetry.[33] It should be noted that of all the guests in attendance at this river marriage, the poet reserves his most deeply personal chorographic praise for the beloved river flowing through his Kilcolman estate, the 'Mulla mine, whose waues I whilom taught to weep' (4.11.41). And thus Spenser's autobiographical counterpart to Sannazaro's Bay of Naples is not a Mediterranean seacoast but Ireland's far less-storied but no less inherently poetic river Mulla.

Eight cantos earlier, 'Ne thence' were the Irish rivers absent from Cambell and Triamond's chivalric combat; and at this point, we can make the transition from local rivers to local shorelines. Spenser's chorographic glimpse of the Shannon, Ireland's (and, in fact, the British Isles') longest river, idly interrupts the knights' combat and anticipates the eleventh canto's river poetry. Flowing into the Atlantic near Limerick, this river, the same 'spacious Shenan' attending the wedding ceremony, becomes the vehicle of an extended epic simile bolstering the poet's observation that neither combatant can establish dominance:

Like as the tide that comes fro th'Ocean mayne,
Flowes vp the Shenan with contrarie forse,
And ouerruling him in his own rayne,
Driues back the current of his kindly course,

---

32 Quoted in Raysor, 36.

33 In *A View of the State of Ireland*, New English colonial politics briefly cedes place to Irenius's reflection on 'beautifull and sweet' Ireland – particularly its 'many goodly rivers, replenished with all sort of fish more abundantly' (27). In the wake of scholarship on the question of Spenser in/and Ireland, recent studies have focused on the colonial politics embedded in the marriage ceremony's Irish rivers (Hadfield, *Edmund Spenser's Irish Experience*; McCabe, *Spenser's Monstrous Regiment*; van Es, *Spenser's Forms of History*; and Joan Fitzpatrick, *Shakespeare, Spenser and the Contours of Britain* [Hertfordshire: University of Hertfordshire Press, 2004]).

> And makes it seems to haue some other sourse:
> But when the floud is spent, then backe againe
> His borrowed waters forst to redisbourse,
> He sends the sea his owne double gaine,
> And tribute eke withal, as to his Soueraine.

(4.3.27)

The simile takes on a poignant autobiographical life of its own, reflecting the poet's keen observation of the 'double gaine,' the commingled fresh and salt waters of Irish estuaries. Temporarily freeing himself from the demands of chivalric narrative, the poet shares his observations of Irish tidal bores, courses, and 'redisbours[ings].'

Among other things, the simile reminds us it is a topographical necessity that estuaries eventually debouch into seas; and local seas comprise a zone that, in the wedding ceremony of the Thames and Medway, Spenser declares off limits to a Mediterranean poetics. Although seventeen sea gods from mythic antiquity are summoned to attend the ceremony, conspicuously absent are any presiding deities of local English seacoasts – as if Spenser judged the sea caves eating into the chalky headlands of Flamborough, or the steep escarpments of the North and South Downs, or the tide-shredded coasts of Lulworth Cove as lacking the incantatory magic of a riverine mythpoesis. Irish coastlines, unlike Irish rivers, are indeed 'absent thence': the Shannon has been invited to the wedding ceremony, but the same local seas that trade tidal flow with the estuary's 'redisbourse[d]' waters never make the guest list.

Before turning to *Colin Clout*, we should not overlook the asynchrony of (poetic) time and (salt water) tide that opens the *Amoretti* 75, perhaps Spenser's most widely admired sonnet. The poet writes the name of his beloved Elizabeth Boyle not on a riverbank but 'vpon the strand' (1), only to have the script washed away by the tide. Determined that his sonnet poetry achieve eternal fame, the poet then announces his ambition to inscribe her name 'in the heuens' (12). Here, the sonnet tropes away from a mutable, tide-scoured coastline to a celestial home for celebrating his beloved. But the tide that, in the *Amoretti* 75, once 'made my paynes his pray' (4) threatens again to wash over his poetry – this time as *Colin Clout* approaches the shoreline realm of another Elizabeth, Spenser's royal patroness. Here, Colin gives the *Amoretti* 75's unmapped tide a local habitation and a name – the churning waters between Ireland and England.

Hobbinol's inviting Colin to narrate his far-flung journeys is a recognizably pastoral convention. And thus Colin narrates the Shepherd of the Ocean's (Raleigh's) passage from Irish to English shores. But less conventional to the pastoral is Colin's alarm at how quickly local estuarial 'redisbours[ings]' become the depths of dangerous straits:

> So to the sea we came; *the sea?* That is
> A world of waters heaped vp on hie,
> Rolling like mountains in wide wildernesse,
> Horrible, hideous, roaring with hoarse crie.
>
> (196–9; emphasis mine)

'The sea?' Colin's question indicates that Hobbinol, Cuddie, and the other members of the rural rout to whom he narrates need a further context for envisioning this alien body of water. The local 'greene alders by the *Mullaes* shore' (59) apparently comprised the only 'shore' they had ever seen. From Spenser's more sophisticated humanist perspective, Colin's description of the Irish Sea's '[h]orrible' waves may be a retroactive glance back to antiquity's *ultima Britannia*, as in Catullus's description of *horribilesque ultimosque Britannos*, 11.11–12).[34] For that matter, *Colin Clout*'s autobiographical impulses might have drawn upon Spenser's own memory of how the sea's shoreward-racing 'wide wildernesse' toyed with the vessel carrying the precious manuscript intended for his queen – the Irish Sea, that is, as yet another threat to the fragile bond between epic poet and patron.

Much recent scholarship has thoroughly documented Elizabethan England's and Ireland's widely divergent histories of the colonizer and colonized. But *Colin Clout*'s water-'heaped' Irish Sea makes no coastal distinction between the two islands. The waters that assault both coasts with indiscriminate force are neither inherently Irish nor English. Elizabethan courtiers may have often regarded Ireland as 'overseas,' but *Colin Clout* reminds us that the two islands' coastal borders share the topography of antiquity's *apeiron*. Typically, Elizabethan pastoral engages in a richly intertextual dialogue with its classical sources. But as Colin records his visceral fear of the Irish Sea, the strains of Mediterranean pastoral – Sannazaran echoes of the shores of Miseno, Posillipo, Euploea, and Nesis – are no longer audible.

---

34 *Catullus*, Eng. trans. Francis Warre Cornish (Cambridge, MA: Harvard University Press, 1962).

Gone from Colin/Spenser's account of Cynthia's looming shoreline is the chorographic eye once so tenderly cast on England's local rivers – as if, unlike the 'soft runnings' of the *Prothalamion*'s Thames, the Irish Sea's 'hoarse crie' resists transposing into poetic song. The Shepherd of the Ocean, in his role as guardian of Virgilian pastoral innocence, attempts to reassure Colin that he is sailing not on a 'wide wildernesse' but rather on the idyllic pseudo-classical shores of the shepherdess Cynthia's flocks: her 'heards be thousand fishes with their frie, / Which in the bosome of the billowes breed' (242–3). Worth remembering at this point is how, some thirty lines earlier, Colin had achieved his own far more graceful synthesis of local (Irish) place and classical (Ovidian) myth, interweaving the *Metamorphoses*' story of Arethusa flowing through the subterranean caves of Sicily (5.577–641) into his own account of the deceitful river Bregog's erotic underground mingling with the Mulla (104–55). All of which is to argue that the otherwise provincial Colin can indeed recognize a successful merging of local place and classical myth when he sees one.[35]

But on the Irish Sea, Colin is scarcely distracted by the Shepherd's idealized, mythopoeic waters, and focuses warily on the all too real topography of England's southwest-facing coastline. He narrates that after passing Lundy on the north coast of Devon,

> From thence another world of land we kend,
> Floting amid the sea in ieopardie,
> And round about with mightie white rocks hemd
> Against the seas encroaching crueltie.
> Those same the shepheard told me, were the fields
> In which dame *Cynthia* her landheards fed.
>
>   (272–7)[36]

The last two lines of this passage comprise the Shepherd of the Ocean's second go at reassuring Colin that they are not 'amid the sea in ieopardie' but rather entering Cynthia's white-rocked Fortunate Isle.

---

35 For a rich reading of Spenser's Irish rivers through the lens of what he terms Ovidian and Italianate 'myths of locality,' see Rudolf B. Gottfried, 'Spenser and the Italian Myth of Locality,' *Studies in Philology* 34, no. 2 (1937): 107–25.

36 In *Polyolbion*, Drayton's art of personification portrays Lundy as considerably more seductive: she appears as 'a Nymph to idle toyes inclin'd... / A lusty black-brow'd Girle, with forehead broad and hie / That often had bewitched the sea-gods with her eye' (IV.23–4).

But again, Colin resists viewing the scene through the Shepherd's eyes. As the ship nears the coastline, Colin spots the headlands of Cornwall: 'a stately heape of stones [did] upreare, / That seemd amid the surges for to fleet, / Much greater then that frame, which us did beare' (185–7). The Cornish headlands viewed by Colin are at once Albion's 'stately' sentinel and a tidal assailant, 'Floting amid the sea in ieopardie,' an unpromising port for *The Faerie Queene*'s landfall on Elizabeth's shores.

To return briefly to the marriage of the Thames and Medway, the river guests, as they make their entrance into Proteus's hall, flow in a stately dignity inherited from Hesiodic, Homeric, Ovidian, and Virgilian rivers. If the local coastal waters smashing against *Colin Clout*'s Lundy and Cornwall had instead curled with Mediterranean gentleness, then they too might have been invited. Idle speculation, perhaps. But it is a fact that Spenser's aesthetic imagination forecloses on any accommodation of the British Isles' *apeiron* within his poetics of the river marriage. And even his favored pastoral mode – from *The Shepheardes Calender* to the Mount Acidale episode of his epic's sixth book, so crucial to the shaping of his poetic career – refuses to transform local English coastlines into the pastoral green world of Mulla's 'greene alder[ed]' banks. Though Colin's poetry once taught the Mulla's waves to weep, the shepherd spurns any ambition to become the Irish Sea's Orpheus, calming its 'hoarse crie.' Though Colin seemingly leaves banishment behind, his otherwise autobiographical pastoral refuses to imitate Sannnazaro's fondness for his local coastlines (the numinous Misenum, Eupleoa, Nisis), sites of the latter's autobiographical poetics.

Colin's fear of the Irish Sea prompts the question: If, in 1589, this strait had swallowed his ship and, along with it, his epic manuscript, how deeply would Elizabeth have mourned the loss of the poem that was dedicated to her? However one ponders this question, Spenser exposes the futility of the Shepherd of the Ocean's effort to depict Cynthia's realm as a pastoral paradise: the very fact of Colin's sea-voyage reminds his readers that in the golden age, sea travel had yet to be invented. Inconceivable was the prospect of a poet having to brave the *apeiron*'s dangerous seas only to gain access to a potentially indifferent patron.

6. Prophecy as Slander: Britomart's Thames, Paridell's Briton Seacoast

Before returning full circle to the Hebrides with which this chapter began, we can travel eastward, from Cynthia's (would-be) pastoral

Cornish coast to Elizabeth's storied Thames, where epic prophecy is no more effective than pastoral in approaching the material reality of British Isles coastlines. The fairy queen's estuary is both a clichéd emblem of her imperial realm and alien waters that not even the authority of Spenserian prophetic verse, with its patient investment in early Briton history, can rescue from the shadow of antiquity's *ultima Britannia*.

The Faerie Queene features several key prophetic voices (Contemplation, Eumnestes, Merlin) who are the building blocks of Spenser's rhetoric of praise for Elizabeth's Trojan ancestry. But the echoes of slander's rhetoric of blame and accusation also resonate, most audibly in the obnoxious barking of the Blatant Beast that entangles both poet and queen in a web of mutual distrust and culminates in the epic's abandonment before completion.[37] A dominant prophetic thread woven throughout *The Faerie Queene* – what Angus Fletcher years ago termed the 'Galfridian matrix' – is the epic's many ambitious genealogical linkages of Brutus's ancient Britain and Elizabeth's Tudor empire, culled from Geoffrey of Monmouth's *Historia regum Britanniae*.[38] In the stanzas leading up to Merlin's prophecy, Spenser celebrates 'The fatall purpose of diuine foresight' (3.3.2). But two stanzas later, the temporality of prophecy oscillates between 'dew degrees and long protense' (3.3.4). That is to say, Spenser implies that prophecy can narrate national history and imperial genealogy as either the timely unfolding of 'dew degrees' or the indefinite deferrals of 'long protense' during which destiny's 'fatall purpose' can become unpredictable fate – or can become truly 'fatall,' shadowed by untimely death. This section investigates slander and/ as an act of 'bad timing' that relocates Galfridian prophecy within the shadow of *ultima Britannia*.

Elizabeth would most certainly have been pleased with Merlin's aforementioned marginalizing of the isolated Orkneys from her imperial epicenter. (See this chapter's first section.) But less pleasing might have been a passage at the outset of *The Faerie Queene*'s earlier prophetic history, the *Briton moniments*, whose heavy borrowing from Geoffrey to narrate British history from Brutus to Uther explicitly maps the queen's

---

37 On the Blatant Beast as the extension of the poet's own voice, see Kenneth Gross, 'Reflections on the Blatant Beast,' *Spenser Studies* 13 (1999): 101–23. For the general topic of slander in *The Faerie Queene*, see M. Lindsay Kaplan, *The Culture of Slander in Early Modern England* (Cambridge: Cambridge University Press, 1997).

38 Angus Fletcher, *The Prophetic Moment: An Essay on Spenser* (Chicago: University of Chicago Press, 1971), 106–21.

shorelines within *ultima Britannia*. Here, Spenser digresses from Geoffrey to ponder the ancient Mediterranean sailors who first espied Britain's south-facing coastlines. The poet revisits not the exhilaration of
discovering the Fortunate Isles but rather antiquity's fear of the region's
coastal hazards: an anonymous 'venturous Mariner' struggles 'his ship
from those white rocks to saue, / Which all along the Southerne seacoast lay, / Threatning vnheedy wrecke and rash decay' (2.10.6). Early
Greek mariners, as mentioned in the previous chapter, customarily
chose to hug the Mediterranean coastline in deference to the concept
of the *peirar*. But Spenser's 'venturous Mariner' learns a hard lesson
in the coastal topography of *ultima Britannia*: to hug the transgressive
waters of the British Isles' coastlines is to forfeit the protections of the
Mediterrranean's tide-caressed shoreline. In this digression, Spenser is
less invested in Geoffrey's fertile Albion than in the region's daunting
white cliffs as the bane of Mediterranean sailors exhausting their nauti-
cal skills to avoid 'vnheedy wrecke and rash decay.'

This inhospitable coastline is the object of outright slander in Book 3.9,
where Spenser revives the Galfridian matrix in the form of an exchange
between Elizabeth's surrogate, the martial but often naive Britomart,
and the jaded knight Paridell, more often viewed as a voluptuary than
a slanderer. This Aegean-born knight sets his own genealogy in competition with Britomart's right to recruit Geoffrey in the service of British
history.[39] To be sure, this descendant of the Helen-abducting Paris is an
obsolete vestige of Homeric epic. And true to his notorious ancestry,
he later initiates a tawdry seduction of Hellenore ('Helen-whore') – but
not before he degrades Elizabeth's elite Trojan descent by stranding it
on the shores of an *ultima Britannia*.

Promoting the prestige of his upbringing on the pseudo-mythic
Aegean island of Paros – from an Elizabethan perspective, a geographically perverse *eastering* of empire—Paridell undermines the aims of
dynastic epic itself by exposing the vanity of any attempt to found

---

39 Key studies of their exchange include Roche, *The Kindly Flame*; Michael O'Connell,
    Mirror and Veil: The Historical Dimension of Spenser's 'Faerie Queene' (Chapel Hill:
    University of North Carolina Press, 1977); Mihoko Suzuki, *Metamorphoses of Helen:
    Authority, Difference, and the Epic* (Ithaca: Cornell University Press, 1989); Heather
    Dubrow, 'The Arraignment of Paridell: Tudor Historiography in *The Faerie Queene*,
    III.ix,' *Studies in Philology* 87 (1990): 312–28. For Paridell as embodying 'cultural ex-
    haustion,' see Harry Berger Jr's chapter 'The Discarding of Malbecco in *The Faerie
    Queene* III.ix–x,' in his *Revisionary Play*, 1988.

New Troys: Troy is 'now nought, but an idle name,' 'buried low' in its own ashes, punished by a 'direfull destinie,' its 'worthy prayses being blent' by a disgraceful and 'embaste ofspring' (3.9.33). Britain's coastal boundaries structure their exchange when Britomart diverts attention from Paridell's doomed version of the *fata Troiana* to recall the rich history of the Thames, the riverine apotheosis of the New Troy. At this juncture, *The Faerie Queene*'s contemporary readership might have rehearsed this preeminently nationalist river's role in Tudor court ceremonies – for example, Elizabeth's travelling upriver from Greenwich to the Tower of London for her 1558 coronation.

But Britomart invokes not the stately dignity of the inland Thames (the gently flowing waters of Spenser's *Prothalamion*, for example) but rather the river's estuarial turbulence as it approaches an inhospitable tidewater:

> It *Troynouant* is hight, that with the waues
> Of wealthy *Thamis* washed is along,
> Vpon whose stubborne neck whereat he raues
> With roring rage, and sore him selfe does throng,
> That all men feare to tempt his billowes strong,
> She fastned hath her foot, which standes so hy,
> That it a wonder of the world is song
> In forreine landes, and all which passen by,
> Beholding it from farre, doe thinke it threates the skye.
>
> (3.9.45)

From one perspective, Britomart's iconographic depiction of Troynovant's foot on the neck of the Thames is a robust tribute to Brutus's nation-founding heroism, exemplifying how, in Fletcher's apt reading of the image, 'heroes create a *civitas* to harness brute energy' (136). The foot of Brutus's London Bridge attempts a 'brutal' mastery of the Thames, rendering the estuary a gateway to an emergent maritime power, heir to imperial Rome as history's New Troy.

But from another perspective, Britomart's salute to the Thames's 'billowes strong' threatens to drown in a poetics of marine turbulence.[40] Her Thames is both symbolic of a Galfridian Lud's town, and also the

---

40 Even the inexhaustible riverine imagination of Michael Drayton's *Polyolbion* became more tentative at the Thames estuary. Of Brutus's choice of location for Lud's town, Drayton noted

estuary whose dangers were so assiduously charted by late sixteenth and early seventeenth-century coasters' manuals. Seeking a poetic harnessing of the river's escalating energy that eventually hurls it toward the English Channel, she struggles to contain the waters within a static emblem of imperial glory; and her salute is evidence that any description of the estuary's undisciplined hydraulics is itself subject to assault by the currents under the London Bridge. Her noting the Thames's reputation 'In forreine lands' also inadvertently reminds readers that the estuary is, in fact, the same hazardous tidewater necessitating Britain's long-overdue first tide-table.[41] The estuary both anticipates the nation's imperial future and recedes into the past to revisit antiquity's seemingly obsolete maps of the British Isles as not a *civitas* but a shoreline swallowed up in the 'brute energy' of a marine remoteness.

Paridell seizes on Britomart's Thames as an opening to turn *The Faerie Queene*'s Galfridian matrix against itself.[42] He counters Britomart's panegyric by turning not to Brutus the nation founder, but to Brutus the patricidal son. To echo Arthur's response to reading the *Briton moniments* (2.10.64), Paridell seemingly suggests to Britomart 'How brutish is it not to vnderstand' Britain's origins as *ultima Britannia*. As a result,

---

Where fair *Thames* has course into a crescent casts
(That forced by his tides, as still by her he hasts,
He might his surging waves into her bosom send)
Because too far in length, his Town should not extend.

(16:325–8)

Here, Drayton fashions an etiological myth of why the Thames is crescent-shaped – a personification suggesting the river's fear of its own tidal bores. Avoiding the 'surging' tides that threatened to annihilate its status as a river, Drayton's Thames (and, by extension, his river poetry) refused to extend 'too far in length' – too far, that is, into the churning ocean that exposed the waters of the New Troy as antiquity's waters of non-resemblance.

41 This chart was found among some manuscripts written at St Albans in the twelfth century. It unceremoniously described the estuary as 'a Flod at London Bridge' (quoted by Taylor, 135).

42 In the final analysis, Paridell may be doing little more than what Spenser himself did in his prose *View of the Present State of Ireland*, which offers a far blunter critique of the Brutus myth than we find in *The Faerie Queene*'s Galfridian prophecies. For a valuable perspective on the differences between mythic and historical truth in Spenser's poetry and prose, see Judith H. Anderson, 'The Antiquities of Fairyland and Ireland,' *JEGP* (1987): 199–214.

the knight's revisionist early Briton history rewrites Britomart's 'roring' estuary as the curse of an isolated coastal periphery.

If Britomart's Geoffrey inspires her praise of Brutus's founding of London ('so huge a mind could not in lesser rest' [46.7]), Paridell adduces Geoffrey to remind his interlocutor of the island's more dubious pseudo-mythic origins – namely, why Brutus sailed to Albion in the first place. Brutus fled 'for feare . . . / Or els for shame' after accidentally slaying his father Sylvius 'through luckles arrowes glaunce.' And thus does Paridell dredge up Geoffrey's own initial portrayal of Brutus as doomed to a marine 'wearie wandring' and 'fatall course' (48) that swept him away to an isolated coastline. Prophecy's 'fatall purpose of diuine foresight,' highlighted in Spenser's earlier invocation to Merlin's narrative, has now deteriorated into Paridell's exposure of Brutus's 'fatall course,' resulting from, as it were, the 'fatall' bad timing of Brutus's 'luckless' arrow. Epic destiny temporarily cedes place to the vagaries of ocean currents as Paridell pointedly revisits Geoffrey's account of Brutus's protracted western wanderings from Rome to the island of Loegecia to Aquitaine and, finally, to an island 'wholly waste, and void of peoples trode, / Saue an huge nation of the Geaunts broode' (3.10.49). Paridell's Brutus is not so much a new Aeneas as, echoing *Othello*, an 'extravagant and wheeling stranger' (1.1.138) cut loose from Rome's imperial moorings. And if Geoffrey's Briton coast eventually becomes the heroic site of Corineus's defeat of indigenous giants, Paridell's Briton coast is little more than an island prison for patricidal Mediterranean vagabonds.

No 'wealthy *Thamis*' in Brutus's Albion – just exile 'Into the vtmost Angle of the world he knew,' driven to an island 'The furthest North, that did to them appear' (3.9.47). The knight's locating of Britain as 'the vtmost Angle of the world' is strategically double-edged. On the one hand, it gestures in the direction of England's Saxon lineage, particularly Bede's well-known story of Bishop Gregory's word play on 'Angleshmen' as heavenly 'angels.'[43] But on the other hand, Paridell's hinting at England's Saxon ethnicity sounds a discordant, ill-timed note within the manifestly Briton context of Britomart's praise of the Thames.

---

43 In his 1605 *Remains Concerning Britain* (1605), William Camden summarizes Bede's story of how Gregory recognized the 'Angleshmen . . . for they have Angelike faces, and seeme meete to be made coheires with the Angells in heaven' (ed. D.R. Dunn [Toronto, 1984], 16).

He implies that in antiquity's geography, Briton coastlines – including the estuary presumably leading inland to Brutus's New Troy – were considered no less-marginal than the marginalized 'Orkeny' of Merlin's chronicle; and he implies that the Britons, far from 'angelic,' were 'angled,' unmistakably echoing Ptolemy's designation of the British Isles as an 'unknown land'; or Tacitus's depiction of the British Isles as 'far away'; or Pliny's British Isles as positioned 'even to the utmost bounds of the earth.'[44]

At this point Paridell, '[P]erceiuing, euer priuily' that Hellenore is smitten with him, abruptly concludes the Galfridian history he has just begun – not with slander but with inaccurate praise for Brutus's 'worke great Troynovant, his worke is eke / Fair *Lincolne* . . . so heard I say old *Mnemon*' (51). As noted in Hamilton's edition, there is no chronicle source for Brutus's founding of Lincoln; and thus does Paridell's revisionist history further deteriorate into patent inaccuracy or, at best, recycled half-remembrances from the dusty archives of 'old *Mnemon*.' 'So ended Paridell' (51): the lustful knight has become bored with his own slander. He turns his attention from Britomart to Hellenore and to what he knows best, Ovidian pursuit of the *ars amatoria*—and eventual rape. Meanwhile, Britomart, we can imagine, retires to her bedchamber to replay, in solitude, the 'end' of Paridell's locating Brutus in the shadow of *ultima Britannia*.

Readers wholly invested in the authenticity of Britain as a New Troy (most notably, Elizabeth) had the option of dismissing Paridell's 'Angle[d]' Britain as the jaded cant of Paris's descendant, himself a vagabond as estranged from Britain's imperial future as Brutus was from Rome's. By way of linking Paridell to his creator's intentions, one could argue that the knight is as obsolete as Spenser was marginal in his 'overseas' Ireland. But Paridell (Spenser-as-Paridell?) does successfully demonstrate that no British version of the westering of empire could render obsolete the far more venerable history of a geographical topos originating in antiquity. In the final analysis, Paridell, reviving antiquity's original slandering of British coastlines, strives to inflict as much damage to the epic's prophetic structure as the Blatant Beast.

---

44 In his 1327 *Polychronicon*, Higden writes: 'Anglia hath that name as it were an angle and a corner of the world' (22–5), in *The English Translation of John Trevisa and of an Unknown Writer of the Fifteenth Century*, ed. Churchill Babington et al., 9 vols. (London, 1865–86).

7. North by Northwest: Ariosto's Ptolemaic Hebrides

After visiting Colin's tide-scarred Devon coastline and Paridell's 'angled' early Briton coastline, we are well-positioned to return to Marinell's Faerie strand, where no Theocritean shepherds catch seductive
glimpses of the sea, and no Sannazaran Lycons pause to observe delicate urchins. This shoreline comes into focus not as a 'Faerie' seacoast
but rather as a shoreline somewhere in the British Isles; and final evidence for this mapping may be found in Spenser's borrowings from
Ariosto's *Orlando furioso*, whose heroine Angelica is terrorized on a
coastline so oddly located one has to resort to the maps of antiquity to
find it. And where one finally locates it is in *ultima Britannia* – namely,
Ptolemy's Hebrides.

The *Orlando* comprises a vast *mappa mundi*, enfolding several detailed
itineraries into its sprawling narrative. Ruggiero, soaring on his wayward hippogriff, travels from Cathay to the south of France to the West
Indies to the East Pacific. Astolfo's journeys on the hippogriff take him
from Asia to North Africa to the straits of Gibraltar.[45] The recovery of
the world maps of Ptolemy was undoubtedly one of humanism's great
triumphs; and these maps particularly captured Ariosto's attention.
Luciano Serra has demonstrated that the *cinquecento* city-state of Ferrara was an important European center of cartographical study, and the
Estense library housed a large collection of the maps of Pliny, Strabo,
and – particularly significant, as will become clear – Ptolemy.[46]

In his epic's final canto, Ariosto offers his own tribute to Sannazaro
as luring poetic song from the mountains to the shores (*ch'alle Camenae /
lasciar fa i monti et arbitar l'arene*, 46.17).[47] But twice, Ariosto isolates imperiled heroines not on the Neapolitan beauty-coasts of his admired
contemporary, but on the muse-abandoned islands just off the Scottish
coastline. Compared to his epic's other far-flung locations (such as Al-

---

45 For Ruggiero's tracing of three-quarters of the world of Ptolemy's *Geography*, see
    Douglas Biow, *'Mirabile Dictu': Representations of the Marvelous in Medieval and Renais-
    sance Epic* (Ann Arbor: University of Michigan Press, 1996), 108.
46 On early modern Ferrara as a center of cartography, see Luciano Serra, 'Da Tolomeo
    alla Garfagnana: La Geografia dell'Ariosto,' in *Ludovico Ariosto: Il suo tempo, la sua
    terra, la sua gemte* (Regio Emilia, A. Manzoni, 1974), 153–6. Ariosto had probably
    consulted a map on which the definitive 1482 Ulm edition was based. Editions of
    Ptolemy were published in Rome in 1478, 1490, 1507, and 1508.
47 All references to the *Orlando furioso* are from *Ludovico Ariosto: Orlando Furioso*, ed.
    Lanfranco Caretti (Torino: Giulio Einaudi, 1966).

cina's enchanted isle), these islands are not that distant from continental Europe; but the poet suggests they might as well lie on the earth's remote edges. In the eighth canto, Angelica is stranded on the lonely shore of Ebuda where, naked and chained to a rock, she is preyed upon by hungry orcs. Two cantos later, the poet, still indulging his sado-comic impulse to map female vulnerability on a forbidden coastline, locates his narrative off the northeast coast of Scotland (*vers Scozia*), where Olimpia, sailing northeast from Holland to Zealand, is stranded after her ship, tacking sharply left (*alla sinistra banda*), is blown off-course by a North Atlantic storm (10.15). Replaying Angelica's tribulation, Ariosto's improbably felicitous geography strands Olimpia on yet another bleak, orc-patrolled coastline.

As the almost ridiculously lurid model for the perils of Spenser's Florimell (to be discussed in this chapter's final section), Angelica's coastal ordeal warrants a brief summary.[48] The heroine, fleeing Europe to return to her native Cathay, is pursued by a lecherous but impotent hermit. He conjures a demon that frightens her horse into bolting out to sea, eventually carrying her to a remote island (6.37–49). On this harsh and lonely (*aspro et ermo*) coast, Angelica is trapped among dark rocks (*scuri sassi*) and sea-caves (*spaventose grotte*), reduced to praying that she will drown amidst protruding rock (*rilevato sasso*) and horrid reef (*scoglio*). When the hermit overtakes her, readers discover that the heroine is destined not for rape but rather for a fate almost as miserable – an even more distant coastal exile. The inhabitants of the remote island of Ebuda, scouring the coastal waters in search of women to sacrifice to the sea-god Proteus's monstrous orc, capture her and chain her naked body to Ebuda's coastal rocks. (To put this low comedy in further perspective, one can pause to note that in Sannazaro's 'Galatea,' by contrast, the Mediterranean's coastal orcs do not demand sacrificial victims, but rather slumber in sympathy with grieving lovers.) Awaiting sacrifice to Proteus's orc, Angelica is eventually rescued by Ruggiero, traversing Europe on his hippogriff.

It is worth speculating on the extent to which this episode may have contributed to Ariosto's well-documented dubious reputation among certain *cinquecento* literary critics for violating the decorum of epic high

---

48 On Ariosto's imperiled heroines, see Valeria Finucci, *The Lady Vanishes: Subjectivity and Representation in Castiglione and Ariosto* (Stanford, CA: Stanford University Press, 1992).

seriousness. Inherited from Boiardo, Ariosto's interweaving of epic and romance was reviled by, among many others, the epic theorist Antonio Minturno for generating page-filler plots where 'many things mingle neither according to verisimilitude nor necessity.'[49] Minturno undoubtedly read Ariosto's chaining of Angelica's naked body to a coastal rock as just such a page-filler lacking any epic 'necessity' within the *Orlando*'s dynastic matter of Charlemagne.

At the same time, Ariosto's lurid breach of epic high seriousness gains momentum from the *gravitas* of ancient geography's aversion to the world's northwest edges. Though lacking epic 'necessity,' the Ebudan episode charts Angelica's vulnerability as directly proportionate to antiquity's perceptions of this archipelago's remoteness. As if the towering rocks and craggy reefs where Angelica's horse initially strands her are not alien enough, Ariosto's narrative sweeps his heroine further westward to the Ebudan coast. For that matter, Angelica is swept away from the genre of dynastic epic – literary history's *medius mundi locus* – to what antiquity judged the edge of the world.[50]

A Mediterranean source for Ariosto's explicit association of female terror with coastal remoteness could well have been Ovid's myth of Europa, seized by Jove and carried off to Crete. But Ariosto escalates this Ovidian representation by sweeping a distressed damsel from the Mediterranean to the North Atlantic. And thus a visual source for his North Atlantic might have been a 1498 Dürer engraving, *Das Meerwunder* (fig. 1), that depicts a grisly merman abducting a mermaid from a churning surf; and on the sea-bluffs in the background, coastal rocks ward off the city's inhabitants from the scene of her abduction.[51] Ariosto seemingly gives Dürer's otherwise-unidentifiable coast, conceived

---

49 *L'Arte Poetica*, quoted in Allan Gilbert, *Literary Criticism, Plato to Dryden* (New York: American Book Company, 1940), 276. For the authoritative summary of *cinquecento* critical controversies concerning the *Orlando*'s generic status, see Bernard Weinberg, *A History of Literary Criticism in the Italian Renaissance*, 2 vols. (Chicago: University of Chicago Press, 1961).

50 Noting Ruggiero's lack of control over the hippogriff, Albert Ascoli ponders Ebuda's remoteness by observing that the paladin is swept 'beyond the long-established limits of human experience' (*Ariosto's Bitter Harmony: Crisis and Evasion in the Italian Renaissance* [Princeton: Princeton University Press, 1987], 136).

51 It might be worth noting that when Ariosto was twenty-three, Dürer made two enthusiastically received trips to Venice.

Figure 1 *Das Meerwunder* Albrecht Dürer engraving c.1498 © The Trustees of the British Museum

within a northern European imagination, a local (or, more accurately, remote) habitation and a name in antiquity's extreme North Atlantic periphery.

At this point in the narrative, the *Orlando*'s readers cannot be blamed for their uncertainty as to exactly where, on the world map, Angelica's fate further unfolds. The islands off Scotland where Olimpia is abandoned are *alla sinistra banda* ('on the left tack'), perhaps in the vicinity of the Orkneys. Ebuda, the poet informs us, is in the Hebrides; but the question arises: where is *Ariosto*'s Hebrides? The poet narrates that Ruggiero spots Angelica while gliding north-by-northwest beyond the straits of Hercules, beyond the *ultima terra* of England, arriving at Ebuda, which lies *nel mar di tramontana inver l'occaso, / oltre l'Irlanda* ('in the great northern sea, toward the west, beyond Ireland' [8.51]). And thus particularly relevant here is Ariosto's access to the maps of Ptolemy that were housed in the Estense collection. In his *Geography*, Ptolemy writes: 'Above Hibernia are the Ebudan islands five in number, the largest of which toward the west is called Ebuda . . . ' (II.i; p. 49).[52] As the historian O.A.W. Dilke usefully points out, Ptolemy's Ireland is six degrees too far north, occupying the same latitudes as north Britain; and the extreme northern region of mainland Scotland is, in Dilke's words, a 'conspicuous deformation,' jutting far out to the northeast (fig. 2).[53] As a result, Ptolemy's Hebrides are stranded in the remotest northwest boundaries of his world map. They seemingly drift away from Scotland, which turns its 'deformed' back on its own longitudinally skewed archipelago.

Ptolemy's cartographic error, then, marks the 'truth' of Angelica's Hebrides as located in antiquity's otherwise obsolete topos of an *ultima Britannia*. When Ariosto chose to (dis)locate Ebuda beyond Ireland in the extreme northwest corner of the globe, he also introduced this geographical topos into the literary history of dynastic epic. Like Angelica's refractory horse, or Ruggiero's uncontrollable hippogriff, the

---

52 In the third century A.D., Solinus reported that the Ebudan islands were separated by narrow, dangerous straits (*angusta interluvie*), and that agriculture was unknown to the island's primitive inhabitants (Solinus, *Collectanea rerum memorabilium*, quoted in Lovejoy et al., 367).

53 O.A.W. Dilke, *Greek and Roman Maps* (Baltimore: The Johns Hopkins University Press, 1998), 82. At the same time, Dilke also gives Ptolemy credit for being generally recognized as the first cartographer to develop a coordinated, more mathematically precise system of latitudes and longitudes.

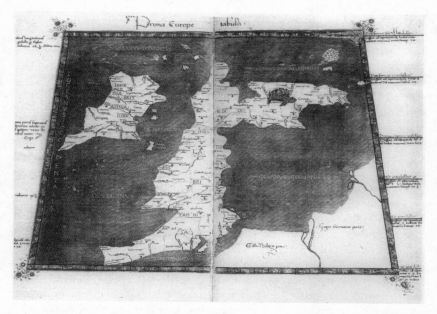

Figure 2 Map of the British Isles from Ptolemy's 'Geography,' Ebner collection (1460)

Orlando's urbane westering of empire goes momentarily berserk, hurling the narrative *too* far northwest, warped into an improbably remote Hebrides geo-culturally estranged from the more serious epic matter of Charlemagne. But the sportive frivolity of Ariosto's Ebuda does have the more serious consequence of offering a useful literary historical clue that the coordinates of Marinell and Florimell's terror-strand can be plotted not in the fictive space of 'Faerie' but rather in the maps of antiquity's *ultima Britannia*.

8. Reading Spenser Reading Ariosto's Hebrides

Spenser likely pegged the *Orlando*'s eighth canto as introducing a different kind of coastline into both the geography and the gender politics of epic literary history: in Homeric epic, men are tragically seduced by the blandishments of Circean, Mediterranean beauty-coasts, but in Ariostan epic, women such as Angelica (and Olimpia) are subjected to prolonged, lurid torture on northern British Isles coasts. For *cinquecento* literary critics, as we have seen, Ariosto's coastal stranding of Angelica was likely one of the *Orlando*'s many eminently dispensable episodes. But Spenser might have perceived a larger significance in Ariosto's toying with the British Isles as a cartographic extremity in the top-left corner of the Ferrarese geo-literary imagination. Ariosto's lurid coastal comedy may have presented Spenser with a strategy for acting out his discontents with the queen by remapping her courtly epicenter in the remote northern islands of Ariosto's Ptolemaic Hebrides.

Whereas Ariosto comically exploited what his Ferrarese perspective viewed as the Hebrides' remoteness, the *Orlando*'s Elizabethan readers would have been hard-pressed to ignore the eighth canto's persistent drift to the north-northwest boundaries of their own British Isles, described two cantos later as *ultima Inghilterra* (10.72). But if, as is likely, many of these readers turned instead to the *Orlando*'s 1591 English translation by Elizabeth's godson Sir John Harington, then they were taken on a detour of Ariosto's Hebrides.[54] In Canto 10.60 of his translation (verse 72 of the original), the epic's protagonist (anglicized as Rogero), traversing Europe on his hippogriff, briefly lands in England, just prior to his rescue (and own decidedly unheroic attempted rape) of Angelica. In his translation's margins, Harington briefly nods to his Italian original, noting that 'Ariosto cals us ultima Ingleterra, the uttermost country. So in time past the old Romans wrate.'[55] The tone of Harington's marginal note on a once-'marginal' England is casually informative, even patronizing: he reduces antiquity's venerable geographic imagination to the writings of 'old Romans' – a demystification of *ultima Britannia* as an obsolete holdover from 'time past.'

Though Harington includes the lurid comedy of Ariosto's impotent hermit, he abstracts away from the geographical specificity of the eighth canto's coastline, perhaps the devoted godson's recognition of the original episode as all too proximate to his monarch and godmother. Harington's Angelica is stranded on 'a solitarie place' (40.2) vaguely located (not unlike the mythic Fortunate Isles) 'about the setting of the sonne' (45.4). But he never identifies the coastline as the Hebrides; and Angelica's translated terror-coast lacks the original coast's

---

54 It should be noted here that in light of the queen's impeccable mastery of Italian, she likely read at least selected portions of the original.

55 All references to Harington's translation are taken from *Ludovico Ariosto's 'Orlando Furioso,' translated into English Heroical Verse by Sir John Harington*, ed., intro. Robert McNulty (Oxford: Clarendon Press, 1972), 117.

telltale cartographic detail, its attention to the all-too-real dangers of
the Ebudan straits. Absent from his translation are the island's protruding rocks, dark sea-caves, and jagged reefs that, for antiquity, traced a
dreaded *apeiron*. As if apologizing for dwelling on the hermit's lurid de-
sires, Harington appends a compensatory 'Moral' to Angelica's perils:
'In the hard adventures of *Angelica* we may note how perilous a thing
beautie is if it be not especially garded with the grace of God and with
virtue of the mynde, being continually assayld with enemies spirituall
and temporall' (99). Pedantically forcing a moral from an episode that
Minturno likely judged unnecessary to the epic plot, Harington's moral
glosses over Ariosto's compulsively low comic triangulation of male
impotence, female vulnerability, and coastal remoteness.

   Spenser also chooses not to identify as the Hebrides the coastline
where his heroine Florimell is stranded. But as my earlier discussion
of Marinell argued, the topographic specificity of the Faerie coast is a
convincing facsimile of Ariosto's *ultima Britannia*. On Spenser's Faerie
seacoast, female vulnerability on a menacing shoreline is also sado-
comically showcased; and Florimell's imprisonment in Proteus's sea-
walled dungeon closely mirrors Angelica's imprisonment amidst the
Ebudan rocks. So extensive, in fact, were Spenser's borrowings from
Ebuda that Florimell, unlike Angelica, is almost exclusively a coastal
heroine.[56]

   As critics have often noted, Florimell is *The Faerie Queene*'s paradigmatic 'fearefull damzell' – all the more desirable for being perpetually
chased by male pursuers; and on Spenser's Faerie coast, Florimell becomes allegorized as fear itself. As she flees from 'the griesly Forster'
and the witch's hyena-monster that craves 'feed[ing] on womens flesh'
(3.7.22), the poet depicts her escape route topographically: she is 'com-
peld to change / The land for sea, at randon there to raunge' (3.8.20).
Though wandering 'at randon' is romance's definitive itinerary, Florimell's 'randon' wandering leads her specifically to Marinell's seacoast, where she endures – literally and metaphorically – 'new waues
of weary wretchednesse' (3.8.20). When Spenser narrates that 'now she
gan approach to the sea shore' (3.7.25), he might as well have alerted
readers that his heroine has wandered into the low-comic genre he inherited from Ariosto's Ebuda. The poet pauses to compare Florimell to

---

56 William Blissett notes Angelica's influence on Florimell ('Florimell and Marinell,'
    SEL 5 [1965]: 91).

Ovid's Daphne fleeing Apollo 'on th'*Aegean* strond' (3.7.26), but this comparative nod toward antiquity's Mediterranean proves cynical. Whereas Daphne is saved by her father Peneus via transformation into a laurel tree, Florimell must endure a lonely struggle for survival on her Faerie strand, its terror absurdly heightened when the witch's hyena-monster disembowels her horse. The Ovidian exoticism of Daphne's '*Aegean* strond' is replaced by Florimell's arrival at a 'roring shore' (3.7.27), bowel-strewn by a roving hyena – a shoreline all the more distant from the mythic shores of an Ovidian Mediterranean where a wondrous metamorphosis saves Daphne from rape.

Spenser never so mimetically aspires to Ariosto's characteristic mix of debased sexuality and threatened virginity as when Florimell, seeking refuge in a fishing boat, 'with the tide droue forward careleslie' into the ocean – only to encounter a lecherous but impotent fisherman, 'droncke with drowsinesse' but lust-incited when he awakens and gazes upon her (3.8.21–2). Crudely responding to her pleas to return to shore, the fisherman 'threw her downe, ne car'd to spill / Her garments gay with scales of fish that all did fill' (3.8.26), reducing Sannazaro's piscine pathos to fishy bathos. The sea-god Proteus eventually rescues the heroine from the fisherman, only to imprison her in his coastal dungeon when she spurns his own attempts to seduce her.[57] Florimell, like Angelica, is not rescued but displaced – 'chaung'd from one to other feare' (3.8.33) – from peril in the coastal fishing waters to even greater peril amidst Proteus's 'roaring billowes,' raging as if 'they the cliffe in peeces would haue cleft.' And thus does Spenser relocate Proteus, 'Shepherd of the seas of yore' (3.8.30), from the Mediterranean to the Hebrides, where he is transformed into a sadistic warden of an Ariostan marine-prison. (Here, one is well-reminded that Proteus was not in attendance at the marriage of the Thames and the Medway.)

Like Angelica, Florimell is also eventually rescued. But her impending marriage to Marinell is deferred, left 'to another place to be perfected' (4.12). Marinell's strand all but disappears from Spenser's narrative – but not until the poet has stranded the virgin Florimell, a high-profile participant in *The Faerie Queene*'s fictive representations of the courtly cult of Elizabeth's virginity, amidst a number of irresolutions. How can

---

57 For Spenser's imitations of Ariosto's Proteus, see Alpers, 195; Roche, 11–14; and A. Bartlett Giamatti, *Play of Double Senses: Spenser's Faerie Queene* (Prentice-Hall, 1975). Pamela J. Benson reads Florimell's rescue by Proteus as an act of Grace ('Florimell at Sea,' *Spenser Studies* 6 [1985]).

Elizabeth expect her Trojan *renovatio* to overgo the *Orlando*'s strategic encoding of any further westering of empire beyond Charlemagne's court (or the Ferrara of Ariosto's patron Ippolito) as lost in antiquity's remote edges of the world? How can an epic poet residing in a marginal Ireland be expected to surpass a continental predecessor who has succeeded in transporting antiquity's topos of an *ultima Britannia* into the literary history of dynastic epic? How can Spenser prevent the queen's coastal 'envy of less happier lands,' echoing *Richard II*'s John of Gaunt, from becoming an unenviable literary historical joke whose recondite punch line originates in Ariosto's lurid deployments of an *ultima Britannia*? Finally, how can we return to the Ditchley portrait without discerning the spectral geography of a Ptolemaic Hebrides that lurks behind the queen's profile of imperial authority?

This chapter has charted a roundabout, improbable itinerary that eludes the visual space of conventional cartography. But this circuitous, unmappable itinerary best illustrates Spenser's message to Elizabeth, otherwise securely positioned in her London epicenter, that North Atlantic explorers had once perceived all the regions of the British Isles (from the English Channel to the Hebrides) as equidistant from the Roman *axis mundi*. When viewed through Spenser's Hebridean 'map consciousness,' the queen's empire is not Dee's Britannia, gateway to an era of maritime expansion, but is rather Ptolemy's *ultima Britannia*, stranded not only in the extreme northwest edges of the world, but stranded far from the Mediterranean's venerable literary history.

The early modern Ireland where Spenser labored as both civil servant and, presumably, England's Virgil, was eminently mappable in the sixteenth century (i.e., John Goghe's 1567 *Hibernia*, Baptista Boazio's 1599 map of Ireland). Not so mappable was the Ireland where Spenser's fictive Hebrides become a palimpsestic layering of Ariosto and Ptolemy. The origin of this unmappable Hebrides lay somewhere between the fanciful cartography of an epic poet writing not all that far from the Mediterranean and a classical geographer highly influential in relegating the Hebrides to the margins of the *axis mundi*.

Chapter Three

Ever-Receding Shorelines: Antiquarian Poetry and Prose and the Limits of Shakespeare's Coastal Dramatic Verse

1. Antiquarianism at the Water's Edge

To its considerable methodological advantage, Tudor/Stuart antiquarianism, as will be discussed in later detail, frankly acknowledged – indeed thoroughly embraced – the historical validity of antiquity's topos of *ultima Britannia*. Phrased in broad terms, this chapter will culminate in a reassessment of some of the crucial differences in the generic aims of antiquarian chorographic verse and antiquarian prose as these modes endeavored to represent England's local shorelines. Relevant here is what I will discuss as antiquarianism's intriguing ability to, as it were, act globally and think locally, shuttling with equal ease between continental historiographical ambition and provincial contentment. And thus did antiquarianism demonstrate a generic capacity to embrace both an ambitious prose agenda of inserting ancient Britain within the growing historical interest in Northern Europe's indigenous inhabitants prior to the Roman invasion, and an equally ambitious verse project of merging tropes of classical poetry with the quaintness of inland riverbanks. John Leland's and William Camden's dual generic affinities for prose history and for river poetry – and their immaculate distinction between the two genres – established well-defined protocols for how to 'write' the material reality of East Anglian coastlines and, finally, how to avoid unwitting entrapment within the shadow of *ultima Britania*.

The capaciousness of these dual generic affinities places in sharper relief my chapter's related goal of investigating the obstacles Shakespeare encountered in attempting to craft a North Atlantic coastal dramatic verse that could replace the venerable verse tradition of a Mediterranean sublime and, once and for all, exit the shadow of *ultima*

Britannia. I will look at two of the better-known plays of the *Henriad*, as well as *King Lear* and, in greatest detail, *Cymbeline*, both written during James's reign within six years of one another, both located in ancient Britain, and both revealing characters who struggle to orient themselves on an ever-receding East Anglian coastline. In the case of *Cymbeline*, the ever-receding coastline is a Galfridian coastline, both rejecting and entrapped within Galfridian history. At the vanishing point of this ever-receding coastline, what does come into focus is how antiquarian chorography, unencumbered by the fictive requirements of Galfridian pseudo-history and openly acknowledging the historical validity of *ultima Britannia*, set the standard for how early modern English verse should attempt to 'write' local coastlines.

2. Shakespeare's Coastal Legerdemain

Throughout his history plays, Shakespeare's blank verse often turned to local tidal rhythms for nationalist inspiration, resonant reminders of the fact that Shakespeare lived much of his adult life exposed to the sensory stimuli of the Thames' tidal currents, winds, and waves, as well as to the ships, both royal and merchant, anchored in the Thames. Thus, in his nationalist history plays, fully in step with the post-Armada times, Shakespeare was under no pressure to engage with antiquity's topos of an *ultima Britannia*; and he did not hesitate to convert the churning tides of England's east-facing coastlines into nationalist emblems. In *1 Henry VI*, King Henry depicts his swelling passion for Margaret 'like as rigor of tempests and gusts / Provok[ing] the mightiest hulk against the tide' (5.5.5–6).[1] In *3 Henry VI*, the king's recounting of the uncertain outcome of a recent battle against the York faction merges with tidal rhythms:

> Now sways it this way, like a mighty sea
> Forced by the tide to combat with the wind;
> Now sways it that way, like the selfsame sea
> Forced to retire by fury of the wind.

> (2.5.8)

These and many similar images rendered the history plays' local tides integral to how the emergent nation thought about itself; and these tidal

---

1 All references to Shakespeare's plays are taken from *The Norton Shakespeare*, gen. ed. Stephen Greenblatt (New York and London: W.W. Norton & Company, 1997).

images scripted Shakespeare's signature in the ongoing early modern English project, echoing Helgerson, to 'write' the nation.

But it is also the case that, at key moments, Shakespeare struggled to represent local coastlines. Of note here is John of Gaunt's praise of England in *Richard II*. As critics have pointed out, his speech is structured on the fallacy of England as an island.[2] Gillian Beer cogently observes that, in general, 'the word 'island' has a peculiar force in English which emphasizes its connection to individualism. The sound 'I' at the beginning of the word creates a habituating consonance between the ego and the island.'[3] With Beer's observation in mind, we can look more closely at Gaunt's speech, which is not only one of early modern English literature's most quoted speeches but also one of its most conflicted. Gaunt envisions England as 'This little world / This precious stone set in silver sea' (2.1.45–6), while also describing the island as 'a moat defensive to a house' (48). Gaunt strives to depict England as an isolated, protected island-refuge, but he inversely concedes that it is a kind of prison vulnerable to invasion. We could say that, rephrasing Beer, Gaunt's England exposes a 'habituating *dissonance*' between (early modern) ego and island; and Gaunt's island fallacy is fully exposed if we turn to the new British history and its complicating of any attempt at mapping an 'England' separate from 'Britain' or the 'British Isles.'

In addition to being structured on an island fallacy, Gaunt's speech cannot adequately account for coastlines, in particular. The same smashing waves that carve out an island-paradise also transform the island into a 'moated' prison. Gaunt's images fall into a representational gap as he attempts the impossible task of envisioning an island, an insular integrity, *without* coastlines.

In *King John*, the Duke of Austria plays with the etymology of England-as-Albion, proffering Dover as an already clichéd 'pale, white-faced shore, / Whose foot spurns back the ocean's roaring tides' (2.1.23–4). The Duke's static Fortunate Isle is typical of how the topos expeditiously tropes away from an *apeiron* in order to summon an ideal,

---

2 Lisa Hopkins, *Shakespeare on the Edge: Border-crossing in the Tragedies and the* Henriad (Aldershot: Ashgate, 2005), 1. On the island fallacy in general, see Gilliam Beer, 'The Island and the Aeroplane,' in *Nation and Narration*, Homi K. Bhabha, ed. (London: Routledge, 1990), and Robert Shannan Peckham, 'The Uncertain State of Islands: National Identity and the Discourse of Islands in Nineteenth-century Britain and Greece,' *Journal of Historical Geography* 29, no. 4 (2003): 499–515.

3 'Discourse of an Island,' in *Literature and Science as Modes of Expression*, ed. Fredrick Amrine (Dordrecht and Boston: Kluwer Academic Publishing, 1989).

emblematic nationalist island.[4] We can thus observe with particular interest that in *King Lear*, a 'history' play only insofar as its backdrop is ancient Britain, Shakespeare more earnestly tests his verse's evocative power at a topographically specific Dover. A shamed Lear, having prematurely parceled his island realm, eventually seeks redemption for his cartographic violence by making his way to Dover; and audiences viewing this play for the first time might have reasonably anticipated the aged king's journey to the coast as culminating in an operatic lament to Dover as a kind of North Atlantic sublime, a Shakespearean response to the venerable verse tradition of a Mediterranean sublime. But a North Atlantic coastal poetics never coheres, and, within the bounds of *Lear*, Dover never comes into view.

Between Regan and Cornwall, the question 'Wherefore to Dover?' is repeated three times (3.7.55–9).[5] Uttered in the midst of their sadistic blinding of Gloucester, their repetitive queries seem oddly aphasic, amnesic – as if to signal that Shakespeare's dramatic verse has itself forgotten how to locate the water's edge.[6] Thus a key scene in *Lear* (ironically, a scene of attempted suicide) is born prematurely, just prior to its reaching the coast – namely, in the fields near Dover. Abandoned by Regan to 'smell / His way to Dover' (92–3), Gloucester heads to the coast as the site of his self-annihilation; and he directs the disguised Edgar to lead him to 'a cliff, whose high and bending head / Looks fearfully in the confined deep: / Bring me to the very brim of it' (4.1.73–5). But (for reasons that Shakespeare criticism has long debated) Edgar oddly deceives his father into believing they have reached what the son describes as the 'fearful / And dizzy' Dover 'brim' between headland and surf. I will not quote this familiar deception in full; but worth briefly rehearsing is how Edgar, picking up where Regan's visceral, primal salt-water smell leaves off, enhances Gloucester's sensory experience on this pseudo-'brim' by

---

4 Presumably the mariners of Mediterranean antiquity named the island 'Albion' after its white cliffs (*albis rupibus*). For more on this etymology, see Carrie Anne Harper, *The Sources of the British Chronicle History in Spenser's 'Faerie Queene'* (Philadelphia: University of Pennsylvania Press, 1964).

5 In *Cymbeline*, Imogen refers to the Welsh coast's Milford Haven as 'blessed,' only to be faced with the uncertainty of its location and having to instruct Pisanio to 'tell me / How far'tis thither?' (3.2.49–50). For an important topographical account of how Imogen misjudges the distance between Lud's town and Milford Haven, see Sullivan, *The Drama of Landscape*.

6 In this context it is worth noting that the figures of 'Kent' and 'Cornwall' echo the names of local coastlines; but their names seem almost arbitrary, empty ciphers that carry no particular topographical weight.

appealing also to hearing and sight – a coastline for the mind's eye of his blind father. Thus, Edgar elegantly observes the cliff-clinging, herbal samphires; the crows 'that wing the midway air'; and the tidal surge 'That on th'unnumbered idle pebble chafes' (4.6.11–21).

If we ponder the simple fact that Edgar guides both his father and *Lear*'s audience so near to, yet so far from the coastline, then we have an example of a Shakespearean coastal legerdemain – a seacoast that now we see, and now we don't. For that matter, the audience is twice removed from the real Dover Cliff, left to envision merely a representation of what – at its most immediate – would still have been an already-mediated, theatrical representation of a coastline. In a cogent commentary on this passage, Stephen Orgel has argued that from the scene's outset the audience most likely knows it is being lied to by Edgar, but it still 'wants the scene to work' – not only for Gloucester's sake (his anguish deserves the 'truth' of a suicide-cliff) but also for poetry's sake: Edgar's imagistic lies comprise, in Orgel's assessment, 'some of the best poetry in the play.'[7]

Any number of passages from this most operatic of Shakespeare's plays are eminently quotable, such as Lear's rage amidst the heath's howling winds, capturing Shakespeare's sublime probing of evil and cruelty. Edgar's description of the Dover Cliff, on the other hand, makes no inherently thematic contribution to the play. But if we agree with Orgel that Edgar's lines are also the play's most inherently *poetic* passage, then a number of questions arise – namely, the question of why Shakespeare did not take his dramatic verse to the real Dover Cliff to craft what might inevitably have become his canon's most eloquent North Atlantic response to Longinus's Mediterranean sublime; and the question lingers as to why he invested so much energy in poetry for its own sake on a coastline that does not even exist in the space of theatrical representation, much less in reality. Now we see the Dover Cliff – and now we don't; and audiences are left to 'smell' their own way to Dover's saltwater.

3. From *Henry IV* to *Henry V*: Chorographic Nationalism and Coastal Provinciality

I now glance back a decade or so before *Lear*'s first performance at two of Shakespeare's most popular history plays, particularly the moments

---

7 Stephen Orgel, 'Shakespeare Imagines a Theater,' *Poetics Today* 5 (1984): 557.

that, when viewed in hindsight, anticipate *Lear*'s difficulty in representing local coastlines. Much of this book's previous chapter could be summarized as the ways in which Spenserian verse thrived less on brackish estuaries and salty coastlines than on freshwater rivers. In a similar vein, I begin my discussion of two plays from the *Henriad* not on the coastline, but further inland, with a focus on the tensions inherent in Shakespeare's river chorography, revealing, as it shifts from blank verse to prose, his inconclusive efforts to remove local coastlines from the specter of provinciality and, hence, the shadow of *ultima Britannia*.

In his 1623 ode to Shakespeare, Ben Jonson praised 'the sweet swan of *Avon*! What a sight it were / To see thee in our waters yet appear, and make those flights upon the bankes of Thames, / That so did take *Eliza*, and our *James*' (71–4). Jonson could accord the bard no higher praise than to place him within the literary historical line of the beloved river poets who converted otherwise provincial rivers into preeminently nationalist emblems.

Shakespeare was not the committed champion of chorographic verse that his friend Michael Drayton was. But Jonson's 'swan of Avon' sings sweetly of local rivers early in *1 Henry IV*, prior to Glendower's and Hotspur's tense land grab. The play was performed at the height of the English history play's nationalist appeal, and Shakespeare masterfully deploys the river topos's unique alliance of local geography and history to celebrate Elizabeth's realm. The tensions between the king's antagonists Hotspur and Glendower can be placed in even sharper relief by examining how they invoke the river topos, a chorographic – if, within the temporality of the play itself, anachronistic – fondness that surely resonated with the play's Elizabethan audiences. Hotspur, not yet committed to a regional apportioning of the island, recounts for the king Mortimer's courage in opposing Glendower: the Severn, 'affrighted with their bloody looks, / Ran fearfully among the trembling reeds / And hid his crisp head in the hollow bank' (1.3.104–6).[8] Here, Hotspur is not the rash youth who will later strive to bend the 'cranking' Trent to his territorial will (3.11.5–6), but is rather an anticipation of Drayton, whose *Polyolbion* muse thrived on riverine personification. The young Percy merges landscape and mythic grace, using the Severn to insert a heroic Mortimer into British history. During Hotspur's and

---

8 Lisa Hopkins inserts these lines within her larger discussion of the ambiguous liminality of Welsh borders in the *Henriad* (*Shakespeare on the Edge*, 26–7). For the Severn as crucial to defining the borders of early modern Wales, see Sullivan, *The Drama of Landscape*.

Glendower's later tense encounter in Wales, the Welsh magus is himself cast under a local chorographic spell, also alluding to the Severn to remind the arrogant youth of the former's successful battles with the king: three times, claims Glendower, he repulsed Henry 'from the banks of Wye / And sandy-bottomed Severn' (3.1.62–3). As if to prove himself the superior verse chorographer, Glendower lyrically demonstrates to Hotspur that only a Welshman can properly invoke this key border river – only a Welshman who once 'framed to the harp / Many an English ditty' (3.1.120–1) can effectively merge (Welsh) chorography and (British) history.

As long as Shakespeare's nationalism is self-contained within the island's borders, local rivers sustain their patriotic voice, such that even the enemies of a unified island are seduced by the 'swan of *Avon*'s' river-tropes. But in *Henry V*, Shakespeare's 'flights upon the bankes of Thames,' to echo Jonson, lead to the river's estuary, where brackish tidal currents undermine rather than enhance the freshwater river poetry's nationalist mystique. By the time of *Henry V*'s first performance in 1599, the popularity of the English history play was on the decline, evident in the play's well-documented ambivalent portrayal of the former prodigal son and now King Harry, both a heroic ruler of an ideal state and a font of hypocritical pieties;[9] and in this play, not even the nationalist vitality of riverine topography can close the gap of Shakespeare's ironic distance from his royal protagonist. This ambivalent play demonstrates how readily *I Henry IV*'s resonant river topoi deteriorate into mere provinciality, how readily local rivers shrink from geographic participants in British history to a local insignificance that contracts rather than expands the epic scope the play struggles to sustain.

One of the play's most familiar passages is the Chorus's metatheatrical anxiety that a tiny theater is not sufficient for staging Henry's invasion of France: 'Can this cockpit hold / The vasty fields of France?'[10] Invoking an ascendant 'Muse of fire' (1.0.1), the Chorus announces its ambition to frame the play within antiquity – namely, its goal of

---

9 A foundational study of the play's contradictions is Norman Rabkin, *Shakespeare and the Problem of Meaning* (Chicago: University of Chicago Press, 1981).

10 On the Chorus's self-deprecation as a form of the humility topos, see Lawrence Danson, '*Henry V*: King, Chorus, and Critics,' *Shakespeare Quarterly* 34, no. 1 (1983): 27–43. A more recent study of the role of the Chorus is Douglas Bruster and Robert Weimann, *Prologue to Shakespeare's Theatre: Performance and Liminality in Early Modern Drama* (New York: Routledge, 2004).

assuring Agincourt's place within a distinguished line of epic battle-fields. But the audience is also confronted with the Chorus's concern that the stage upon which the play will unfold may become a claustro-phobic, 'unworthy scaffold' (1.0.10–11) inadequate to the task of cred-ibly bounding an epic expanse.

One could argue that the Chorus's more pressing challenge should have been not France's 'vasty fields,' but rather the English Channel as the approach to the battle sites: the occasion for the Chorus's spatial crisis is dictated as much by the narrowness of the English Channel itself as by the restricted 'cockpit'-stage. In *3 Henry VI*, Richard, Duke of York, calls attention to the strait's narrowness when he insists that not everyone can be a king: 'As if a channel could be called the sea' (2.2.141). Richard's topographical analogy implies that the English Channel, in particular, is not a salt-water expanse, but a rivulet, a rut, a gutter between two sets of imposing headlands. Thus, if we cast a deaf ear to the Chorus's protests, then *Henry V*'s stage emerges as a plausi-bly adequate space for suspending disbelief and imagining the English troops' sea-passage from Southampton to northern France's Harfleur. The waterway is, in fact, so choked with the currents roiling within its narrow confines that the English and French coastlines, as the Cho-rus itself admits, glare at one another as 'high upreared and abutting fronts' (1.0.18).[11] Harry's giddy battle cry at Southampton, 'Cheerly to the sea! . . . / No king of England if not king of France!' (2.2.192–3), squeezes the channel even further: the adverb 'cheerly' (or 'speedily') threatens to recast his troops' 'epic' sea-passage as little more than a brief romp.

By the prologue to the third act, the Chorus appears finally to have hit its epic stride, turning to classical myth to widen the English Chan-nel. Harry is portrayed as a Phoebus propelled by 'the lofty surge' as his fleet plows 'the furrowed sea' (3.0.12–13). But, as it happens, the same prologue opens with an odd (textual? editorial?) error when the Chorus invites the audience to 'Suppose that you have seen / The well-appointed King at Dover pier' (3.0.3–4). Unintentionally – if no less errantly – relocating the king's embarking point from Southampton to

---

11 Lisa Hopkins cogently observes that France and England appear less as 'two mighty monarchies' than as crowded houses glaring at one another from opposite sides of narrow London streets ('Neighbourhood in *Henry V*,' in *Shakespeare and Ireland: History, Politics, Culture*, ed. Mark Thornton Barnett and Ramona Wray [Palgrave, 1997], 9).

Dover (the Dover that never came into focus in *Lear*), the Chorus compromises its own efforts to present the stage as an epic expanse. From the Dover Straits, the distance to the French coastline is a mere twenty-one miles; and thus Harry's fleet traverses not the mythic Phoebus's 'lofty surge' but rather a bottlenecked strait, its currents squeezed between the English and French shorelines. If Harry's sea-passage from England to France does succeed in echoing antiquity, then it echoes not so much the early antiquity of, say, the Achaians' eminently epic journey across the Aegean to Ilium as it does later antiquity's topos of *ultima Britannia*.

The inadequacy of *Henry V*'s topographical attempts to forge links with antiquity is evident in the play's deployment of the island's local rivers. But as the remainder of this section argues, what the Welsh Fluellen's and the English Bates's local habits of thought – not unlike Bardolph's thievish impulses – have in common is that they 'travel' all too easily across the narrow strait. Despite the Chorus's efforts to station these soldiers on a far-flung epic battlefield, their ready recourse to the local rivers they know so well (the Wye and Thames, respectively) suggests that they have scarcely left home.

Fluellen, comically speaking not in his Welsh compatriot Glendower's heroic blank verse but rather in his inimitable broken dialect, attempts to forge an analogy between the Macedonia of the legendary worthy Alexander and King Harry's birthplace at Monmouth. Recent criticism has often revisited this passage.[12] What I wish to emphasize is how the Welsh captain, so often attempting to overlay his speeches with a patina of antiquity, begins an infelicitous exercise in chorography that he cannot hope to complete: 'There is a river in Macedon, and there is also moreover a river at Monmouth' (26–7), the latter his native Wye. Almost immediately, Fluellen's analogy implodes when his linkage of contemporary Cambro-Briton king and classical exemplar requires filling in the blank with a corresponding Macedonian river.

---

12 For attention to Fluellen's dialect as an ethnic and regional cipher, see David Quint, 'Alexander the Pig: Shakespeare on History and Poetry,' *Boundary* 2 10 (1982): 49–68; Michael Neill, 'Broken English and Broken Irish: Nation, Language, and the Optics of Power in Shakespeare's Histories,' *Shakespeare Quarterly* 45 (1994): 1–32; David J. Baker, *Between Nations: Shakespeare, Spenser, Marvell, and the Question of Britain* (Stanford, CA: Stanford University Press, 1997); and Philip Schwyzer, *Literature, Nationalism, and Memory in Early Modern England and Ireland* (Cambridge: Cambridge University Press, 2004).

Comically unable to recall any such far-flung river companion – or, more consequentially, unable to achieve the river topos's goal of allying classical past and local geography – he (mercifully) shuts the analogy down: 'there is salmons in both' (30). And thus, via Fluellen, does Jonson's 'sweet swan of *Avon*' toy with how readily river topography can deteriorate into parody. Fluellen's river analogy expands not, as the captain had envisioned, into the classical past, but rather is reduced to a kind of 'choro-babble' that geographically and culturally distances Harry's Monmouth from Alexander's antiquity. It utterly sabotages the lyric capacity of local rivers both to narrate a national mythology and to connect with antiquity's distant past.

For that matter, the shrunken expanse of Fluellen's river tropes had already been anticipated several scenes earlier by the English soldier Bates, who briefly deposits audiences across the Channel back to the Thames estuary. Shrewder than Fluellen, Bates casts no sentimental eye on local rivers – let alone their capacity to enter into dialogue with antiquity. Shivering in France's night air, he curses the king for exposing his soldiers to the elements: the king 'could wish himself in Thames up to the neck and so I would he were' (4.1.115–16). As mentioned in the previous chapter, Spenser's Britomart proudly depicts Troynovant's triumphant foot on the neck of the Thames. But in Bates's vision, the neck of the Thames has freed itself from Troynovant to plunge the king in cold waters up to *his* neck. Emerging from the play's social margins, Bates's hard-bitten surliness could be read as another example of how the play's subversiveness in fact enhances the king's charisma.[13] But what remains unchallenged is Bates's utter mockery of what Jonson would later praise as Shakespeare's 'flights upon the bankes of Thames.' The English soldier's unceremonious act of stripping riverine topography of its mythic resonance exposes the Thames as not a swan-graced 'writing' of the nation but rather frigid waters fit for punishing a tyrant – waters more closely resembling Lyly's risible Thames estuary.

It bears mentioning that the prose chorography of Camden's *Britannia* traveled from west (the Severn) to east (to the Thames) – chorography's definitive direction modeled on Flavio Biondo's 1454 *Italia illustrata* and its tracing of eighteen Italian provinces. To read Shakespeare's *1 Henry*

---

13 For this subversion/containment reading of the play, see Stephen Greenblatt, 'Invisible Bullets,' in *Shakespearean Negotiations: The Circulation of Social Energy in Renaissance England* (Berkeley and Los Angeles: University of California Press, 1988).

IV and *Henry V* in tandem with one another is to witness the dramatist also tracing a chorographic path from the Severn to the estuarial
Thames – as well as a path, it should be noted, from blank verse to
prose.

With impeccable chorographic decorum, *I Henry IV*'s Severn and
Wye transcend their status as local rivers, with Hotspur and Glendower
both using river tropes to expand the space of theater into the larger
'theater' of the battlefields where British history unfolded. But in *Henry
V*, we also hear the uncertainties and ironies of Shakespeare's chorographic voice, casting increasing doubt on the capacity of rivers to ally
English provinciality and classical decorum. The storied Thames is no
longer auratic, no longer culturally encoded: it is simply a local estuary
mapped within Bates's provincial memory of the opposite side of the
English Channel. Just as, in *Henry V*, we see glimpses of a fading heroism, so also do we see local rivers – Fluellen's Wye and Bates's Thames –
disappearing into a parodic prose ('There is salmons in both.') that
offers neither the evocative blank verse of chorographic poetry nor the
kind of investigative rigor that characterized antiquarian prose. By the
time Shakespeare's river topos reaches the coastline, the magical spell
of chorographic verse has been broken; the Thames has been reduced
to the merely provincial.

'What ish my nation?' asks the play's confused Irish Captain Macmorris (3.3.122). As much literary criticism informed by the new British
history has pointed out, Macmorris's question resonates in a play where
Irish, Scottish, Welsh, and English identities are often set in competition
with one another, constantly tested for their ability to transcend ethnic division and coalesce into English 'unity.'[14] Lively debate on this
vital aspect of the play will undoubtedly continue. The point I wish
to emphasize is not only the play's overt struggle to shape an emergent nation out of ethnic diversity, but also the play's shadowing by

---

14 David J. Baker, '"Wildehirissheman": Colonial Representation in Shakespeare's *Henry
    V*,' *ELR* 22 (1993): 31–67; Christopher Highley, '"The Cause be not good": *Henry V* and
    Essex's Irish Campaign,' in *Shakespeare, Spenser, and the Crisis in Ireland* (Cambridge:
    Cambridge University Press, 1997); Graham Holderness, '"What ish my nation?":
    Shakespeare and National Identities,' *Textual Practice* 1991: 74–93; Patricia Parker,
    'Uncertain Unions: Welsh Leeks in *Henry V*,' in David Baker and Willy Maley, eds.,
    British Identities and English Renaissance Literature (Cambridge University Press, 2002):
    81–100; and the earlier-cited essay by Neill.

the spectral geography of antiquity's *ultima Britannia*, where Hibernian, Scottish, and Cambro-Briton coastlines were all viewed as equidistant from the *axis mundi*.

4. Antiquarianism's Paradoxical Embrace of *Ultima Britannia*

Several of the topographical sites discussed thus far in this chapter are overlain with a Galfridian patina, reminding Shakespeare's audiences of Geoffrey's *Historia*, even as Tudor/Stuart antiquarianism's debunking of Geoffrey had steadily become the dominant voice of the nation's chorography and historiography. The story line of *Lear* has, of course, long since been traced directly back to the Leir family saga of Geoffrey's *Historia*. Hotspur's and Glendower's Severn and Wye remind us of the riverrine lyricism of Drayton's *Polyolbion* and the poem's explicit indebtedness to Geoffrey. Fluellen's mention of King Harry's birthplace at Monmouth echoes Geoffrey's birthplace. Listening to these Galfridian echoes, we should also be aware of some attendant ironies. These sites are both Galfridian and, as we have seen, provide glimpses of a provincial island in the margins of antiquity's *mappae mundi*; and, thus, these ironies become all the more apparent at the coastline. Geoffrey was determined to rescue Britain from the charge of provinciality by rejecting *ultima Britannia* in favor of a 'history' of elite Trojan settlements on the East Anglian coast that could once and for all displace Caesar's eyewitness account of a Briton terror-coast. But Tudor/Stuart antiquarianism readily accommodated Caesar's *ultima Britannia* into its scholarly purview, paradoxically rendering provincial coastlines far more sophisticated than Geoffrey's outmoded Briton coastline.

Chaucer's *The Franklin's Tale* (alluded to in the first chapter) is a Breton lay whose characteristic magic – its success in making the impossible possible – turns to visual illusion to make the rocks of the Pedmark coast disappear. So also could we say that Geoffrey attempts to 'tidy up' the messy and menacing rock-strewn coastline documented in Caesar's *Gallic Wars*. In Geoffrey's history, as in the much later *Lear*, now we see coastlines – and now we don't.

Geoffrey's history of Britain begins with an acknowledgment of the island's rock-bound coast. At the beginning of the *Historia*, Britain's destiny as a pristine *totius insulae*, embodying insular unity within its coastal boundaries, is foreshadowed by Diana's prophecy that Aeneas's great grandson Brutus will sail from the Mediterranean to discover a 'sea-girt' island (*undique clausa mari*).[15] Geoffrey then inserts the island's coastline within the topos of an act of violence as a nation's founding moment. When the exiled Trojans first make landfall, they encounter a primal coastline inhabited by autochthonous, seacliff-dwelling giants who must be defeated before the island can be settled. In a vivid episode (narrated by Camden, as we have seen earlier), Brutus's companion Corineus wrestles the giant Gogmagog, hurling him over a cliff whose jagged rocks tear him apart. Thus, the Cornish ('Corinean') coast has its origins in coastal violence: 'in the beginning,' as it were, Cornwall's jagged rocks shred the giant's body to *become* Cornwall. But Geoffrey stages this founding violence less topographically than mythically: the coastal defeat of the giants is the necessary first stage of Britain's evolution into a new, westerly fertile crescent. Britain becomes, in Geoffrey's terms, an *insularam optima*, an idyllic *amoena situ* with abundant resources (*copia piscosorum*), and an island destined, under Brutus, to achieve the status of a *totius insulae*, or insular unity and integrity within its coastal boundaries.

Though Geoffrey did not make use of the Breton lay's miraculous recourse to the supernatural, he did succeed in summoning all his pseudo-historical forces, making the jagged rocks of the Briton coastline 'disappear' from the scope of his national mythmaking.

Caesar's hostile East Anglian shoreline, of course, is precisely what Tudor/Stuart antiquarianism was intent on reinserting into the nation's history. Before we turn to Caesar's *ultima Britannia* and Tudor/Stuart antiquarianism's embrace of it, a brief summary of antiquarianism's continental ambitions is warranted.

Thoroughly documented is Tudor/Stuart antiquarianism's rejection of Geoffrey's elite Trojans-in-exile, embracing instead the eyewitness, historical truth of Caesar's woad-decorated Briton indigenes. At this early juncture, what cannot be emphasized enough was the rich paradox of early modern English antiquarianism's search for the island's provincial origins as not an unreflective philobarbarism but a sophisticated, cosmopolitan act of cultural recovery. Antiquarianism's

---

15 All references to Geoffrey are taken from *Geoffrey of Monmouth: Historia Regum Britanniae*, ed. Jacob Hammer (Cambridge, MA: The Medieval Academy of America, 1951). Authoritative studies of the prominence in Tudor historiography of the Geoffrey myths and of Brutus's pre-Roman dynasty are T.D. Kendrick, *British Antiquity* (London: Methuen, 1950), and Arthur B. Ferguson, *Utter Antiquity: Perceptions of Prehistory in Renaissance England* (Durham, NC: Duke University Press, 1993).

scholarly ambition was to assure early Britain's inclusion in the cultural prestige of the Roman empire, to gain admission into the classical historical fraternity of Caesar, Tacitus, Suetonius, and Strabo. The nation's antiquarianism was deeply rooted in humanist continental scholarship, itself fundamentally influenced by classical history and ironically coming of age in countries (France, Germany) that had once been overrun by the Roman empire. Tudor/Stuart antiquaries sought to compete with such acclaimed northern European historiographers and chorographers as Ortelius, Justus Lipsius, and Joducus Hondius, scholars who had long since embraced the historical truth of the primitivism of their nations' early inhabitants. Recent histories of Tudor/Stuart antiquarianism have authoritatively established that the intended readers of, for example, the 1586 first edition of William Camden's *Britannia* (interestingly entitled after the island's ancient Roman name) were northern European scholars.[16] Shakespeare's king Cymbeline, as will be discussed in later detail, may have hoped to see Romans and Britons 'waving friendly together.' But contemporaneous with the king's fictive vision was Stuart antiquarianism's ambition to bring its methodology in line with the rest of northern European humanism by frankly acknowledging Britain's formerly colonized status under Rome, and by embracing a historical truth that replaced Geoffrey's elite Trojan ancestry with an indigenous primitivism redeemed by its proximity to an auratic Roman cultural prestige. Thus, the more Stuart antiquaries exposed the

---

16 Graham Parry has noted that this first edition was enthusiastically received by Ortelius who, early in Camden's career, encouraged his topographical research (*The Trophies of Time: English Antiquarians of the Seventeenth Century* [Oxford and New York: Oxford University Press, 1995], 26). F. Smith Fussner has argued, in no uncertain terms, that the *Britannia*'s first edition 're-established England's reputation in the European world of learning' (*Tudor History and the Historians* [New York and London: Basic Books, Inc., 1970], 279). F.J. Levy has observed that Camden's original intention was a tour of Roman Britain wholly in the spirit of Flavio Biondo's 1454 *Italia illustrata* (*Tudor Historical Thought* [San Marino, CA: The Huntington Library, 1967], 148). John Selden, Camden's student and arguably Stuart England's most methodologically advanced antiquary, also had many northern European acquaintances, including Scaliger and Bodin, as well as the prominent French medievalists Pierre Pithou and Jean du Tillet (D.R. Woolf, *The Idea of History in Early Stuart England: Erudition, Ideology, and 'The Light of Truth' from the Accession of James I to the Civil War* [Toronto: University of Toronto Press, 1990], 172). For the roots of antiquarianism in antiquity, see Arnaldo Momigliano, 'Ancient History and the Antiquarian,' *Journal of the Warbur and Courtauld Institutes* (1955): 285–315.

provincial early Britons as militarily primitive, the more sophisticated their historiography became.

In particular, Caesar's eyewitness account of the early Briton coastline was among the many reasons why the continental historian Jean Bodin, highly respected by Stuart antiquaries, reserved special praise for what he viewed as Caesar's distinctive ability to overcome his bias as a conqueror and achieve the status of an objective historian.[17] Stuart antiquarianism's embrace of Caesar's tide-battered coastline thrived on a paradox residing at the core of its historical inquiry: the longer antiquarian scholarly energies lingered on Caesar's coastline, the more humanist sophistication the discipline achieved.

At local coastlines, the antiquarian prose of Camden's *Britannia* demonstrated a particular capacity to shuttle between (Galfridian) fable and the material reality of British Isles coastlines. At one point in his survey of the Cornish shoreline, Camden paused to relate the mythic story of what he described as Corineus's 'fabulous wrestling' with the giant Gogmagog on Cornwall's rocky coast.[18] From Camden's antiquarian perspective, relating Galfridian anecdote (or 'fable') enhanced rather than detracted from the integrity of his coastal survey: though he judged Geoffrey's story as historically unfounded, Camden treated the anecdote as *itself* a history of how 'history' was written in earlier Britain. Camden's antiquarian prose both entertained his readers with a pseudo-mythic coastline and, via the chorographic detail of his prose, took them to the material reality of the Cornish coast itself. Camden's revisiting of Geoffrey's Cornish coastal fable amounted to a space-clearing for his eventual mapping of the real topography of the Devonshire and Cornish coasts, such as the Stert promontory where 'so soone as the shore hath drawn it selfe land-ward, the river Dert braketh out' (201). Camden's Cornish shorelines could both linger on the playgrounds of Galfridian myth and move to the rigorously topographical project of mapping fragmented local coastlines.

In his 1610 *Britannia*, Camden remarked that Caesar 'scarce made entry' into Britain (38). The renowned antiquarian's observation is a

---

17 Jean Bodin, *Method for the Easy Comprehension of History*, trans. Beatrice Reynolds (New York: Octagon, 1966), 51.

18 *Britain, or a Chorographicall Description of the Most Flourishing Kingdomes, England, Scotland, and Ireland*, trans. Philemon Holland (London: George Bishop & John Norton, 1610), 200.

reminder that Caesar, sailing from Calais and making landfall at what is now Kent, never penetrated very far inland. Caesar's Britain was always a coastal Britain – or, when viewed through Mediterranean eyes, an island *without* a recognizable coast. He eventually crossed the Thames near Brentford, managing to make military landfall (unlike his distant Mediterranean predecessor Pythias who, as Strabo reported, managed to keep the coastline in view only 'where accessible'); but he never put much distance between his soldiers and the Briton *apeiron*.

The point of emphasis here is the extent to which Caesar was impeded less by the island's Briton indigenes than by its coastlines, evident in his focus on the frequent North Atlantic storms and unnatural tides that toyed with his Mediterranean triremes. Even when his vessels were finally able to approach the coast, they were met by Briton charioteers plunging headlong into the surf and forcing them back into the deeper water that proved the invaders' even more formidable enemy. Caesar reported the difficulty his double-corseted soldiers experienced in having to fight not just the Britons but also the surf's unfamiliar tidal irregularities.[19] On the fourth day of his arrival, Caesar reported that his fleet was hampered by a coastal storm's moon-activated tides that left his galleys thoroughly water-logged.

A year later, in 54 BCE, he returned to Kent, this time with over eight hundred ships, many of which were destroyed when, once again, the fleet was outmaneuvered less by Briton military strategy than by raging coastal storms. The ever-tactical Caesar complained that the Thames could be forded on foot at only one point – and, even there, with great difficulty. (It may have occurred to Caesar how much more successful his invasion would have been had he encountered an estuary like Rome's *peirar*, the Tiber, where a small island disperses the river's current, making it easy to ford at Rome.) This time Caesar, evidently gauging the tides more accurately, did manage to ford the river: his soldiers, wading in water almost over their heads and avoiding the fixed stakes the Britons had planted on the opposite banks, succeeded in crossing the river and scattering the Britons into the woods. In sum, what emerges in the commentaries was Caesar's conviction that a defeat of the undisciplined Britons was a virtual certainty once he had completed an

---

19 Caesar's Mediterranean awe of North Atlantic tides is renewed in Pliny's *Historia Naturalis*, where the author refers to Pythias of Massilias report that north of Britain, the tides rose over one-hundred twenty feet (II.xcix.216–17).

against-all-odds defeat of the Thames estuary – the unpredictable tides and coastal storms that proved his far more tactical adversary.

Geoffrey, often writing what amounted to less a chronicle history than a Briton epic, promoted his Britons to the status of epic protagonists (most notably exemplified by the figure of 'Nennius' who fought in brave hand-to-hand combat with Caesar). To inflate Briton bravery, Geoffrey, relying on his concept of a *totius insulae*, all but eliminated the Thames tidewater judged so formidable by Caesar. Relevant here is a glance at Geoffrey's likely source materials and his inheritance of their (non)representation of the coastline's topography.

One of Geoffrey's sources was Bede's *Historia Ecclesiastica* (1.2), whose primary source, in turn, was the Christian apologist Orosius's early fifth-century *Historiarum adversus paganos*. We need not get bogged down with the manuscript errancies inherited by Geoffrey's Briton history, but one particular error exposed by Homer Nearing does help us understand how Caesar's coastline all but disappeared from Geoffrey. Nearing has pointed out that the manuscript version of Caesar's commentaries consulted earlier by Orosius had become confusingly intermingled with Suetonius's *Twelve Caesars*, an account that occasionally criticized Caesar's willingness to believe his troops' second-hand reports.[20] Orosius's reliance on this contaminated manuscript had particular consequences for representing the Briton coastline. In his condensed version of Caesar's second invasion, Orosius never actually stated that Caesar himself forded the Thames, leaving readers to speculate as to whether or not Caesar might have returned to his galleys and sailed up-river. Thus, one outcome of Orosius's engagement with this contaminated manuscript was not Caesar's preoccupation with the Thames estuary but rather something approximating a generically epic battle during which Briton valor was as much Caesar's adversary as tide and weather.

Bede transmitted Orosius's uncertain account, also making no clear allusion to Caesar's fording the Thames. Drawing on Bede (via Orosius via a compromised Suetonius), Geoffrey evidently justified his claim that when Caesar's ships sailed up the Thames to Trinovantum, they were shredded by the stakes the Britons had planted, leading to the

---

20 Homer Nearing, 'The Legend of Julius Caesar's British Conquest,' *PMLA* 64, no. 4 (1949) 893–4.

deaths of thousands of Romans. According to Geoffrey, what spelled disaster for Caesar was not the anonymous vagaries of tide and weather but the tactics of heroic Britons, never allowing Caesar to reach, in Geoffrey's words, 'dry land' and forcing him to retreat to Flanders.

A fast-forward to Spenser is appropriate at this point. The poet of *The Faerie Queene* was never reluctant to cast Geoffrey's *Historia* in an ambivalent light (as touched on in my previous chapter). But in the second book's *Briton moniments*, he could not resist a nostalgic opportunity to celebrate Elizabeth's 'greatest Isle' by revisiting Geoffrey's heroic coastal waters. Defeated by Cassibalane's troops, 'with blood they [the Romans] all the shore did staine, / And the gray *Ocean* into purple dy' (2.10.48). The 'purpling' of waters with the blood of slaughtered warriors is one of *The Faerie Queene*'s recurrent images, illustrated, for example, in Book 4's 'Diuine Scamander, purpled yet with blood / Of Greekes and Troians, which thence did die' (4.11.20). Despite Spenser's overall skepticism toward Geoffrey, his coastal, 'purpled' waters, a sure sign that he had settled into an epic high style, nostalgically acknowledged the aims of Galfridian pseudo-history.

But by the time of the first performance of *Cymbeline* (the subject of this chapter's next two sections), Stuart antiquarianism's well-known debunking of Geoffrey had so authoritatively succeeded in restoring the material reality of Caesar's coastline to British history that Spenser's 1590 'purpled,' Galfridian ocean, despite its self-conscious nostalgia, could only be read as outmoded. Camden's oft-quoted expression of 'much wonder why the *Britains* should so fondly adhere to their *Brutus*' (27) was both an implicit critique of what Frances Yates has termed the Jacobean stage's revival of an Elizabethan 'aura of chivalric Arthurian purity,' and a reinstating of the Briton coastline as Caesar's most formidable adversary.[21] Antiquarianism thrived on the paradox that the closer it embraced local shorelines as antiquity's *ultima Britannia*, the more sophisticated its historiography became. But Shakespeare's *Cymbeline*, despite its indebtedness to antiquarianism, becomes so entrapped within this paradox that its dramatic verse never succeeds in approaching the East Anglian shoreline it purports to celebrate.

---

21 Frances Yates, *Shakespeare's Last Plays: A New Approach* (London: Routledge and Kegan Paul, 1975), 17.

5. *Cymbeline's* Irreconcilable Shorelines

The critical reception of *Cymbeline* has come a long way since Samuel
Johnson's notorious protest against the play's 'confusion of the names
and manners of different times.'[22] More recently, readers and audiences have been invited to perceive the play not as a 'confusion' but
rather as a richly eclectic combination of myth, emblem, iconography,
and masque spectacle, virtuosic evidence that a mature Shakespeare
had reached the creative heights of his dramatic career. For example, to
embrace rather than resist the play's eclecticism is to appreciate how,
genealogically speaking, *Cymbeline's* celebration of James permits the
monarch to have it all. It is well known that James cultivated an imperial 'Roman' style at court, while also admiring the Trojan exile, Brutus,
the eponymous founder of Britain's pre-Roman dynasty and the king's
ancestor.[23] To embrace *Cymbeline's* eclecticism is to appreciate how the
play, where the lives of such Galfridian characters as Cymbeline, Imogen, Arviragus, and Guiderius intersect with such Augustan figures as
Lucius, was the ideal medium for catering to James's dual admiration
of Brutus and Augustus.

Representations of the Briton coastline figure prominently in *Cymbeline's* deep structural dialectic between *Romanitas* and *Troianitas*. Some
fifty years ago, Emrys Jones, among the first critics to take *Cymbeline's*
eclecticism seriously, called attention to the importance of the play's

---

22 *Johnson on Shakespeare: The Yale Edition of the Works of Samuel Johnson*, Vol. 8, 908.
23 For an account of James's 'Roman' style, see Jonathan Goldberg, *James I and the Poli-
tics of Literature: Jonson, Shakespeare, Donne, and their Contemporaries* (Stanford, CA:
Stanford University Press, 1989), 33–50. For James's goal of a *pax Britannia*, see Leeds
Barroll, 'Shakespeare and Roman History,' *Modern Language Review* 53 (1958): 327–43.
For a detailed reading of *Cymbeline* as firmly situated within Stuart court politics, see
Leah Marcus, *Puzzling Shakespeare: Local Reading and Its Discontents* (Berkeley and Los
Angeles: University of California Press, 1989), 106–59. Influenced by the new British
history's attention to British ethnicities, Mary Floyd-Wilson has recently investigated
the play's undercurrents of Anglo-Scottish tensions (*English Ethnicity and Race in
Early Modern Drama* [Cambridge: Cambridge University Press, 2006]). For the play's
Trojan resonances and indebtedness to the *Aeneid*, see Patricia Parker, 'Romance and
Empire: Anachronistic *Cymbeline*,' in *Unfolded Tales: Essays on Renaissance Romance*,
eds. George M. Logan and Gordon Teskey (Ithaca: Cornell University Press, 1989),
200; and Heather James, *Shakespeare's Troy: Drama, Politics, and the Translation of Empire* (Cambridge: Cambridge University Press, 1997).

local island geography. Noting that *Cymbeline* mentions only two British place-names, Lud's town and the Welsh port of Milford Haven, Jones posed the obvious question of why the Roman general and ambassador Lucius, returning to Rome from Cymbeline's court, travels via Milford Haven. He rightly answered (thereby countering Johnsonian accusations of spatial 'confusion') that *Cymbeline*'s geography 'is not a literal but a symbolic one,' a relocation motivated by – perhaps crucial for – the project of linking James with his ancestor Henry VII, and celebrating his rightful place within Tudor-British myth.[24] Extrapolating from Jones, one could argue that Lucius's out-of-the-way detour to Milford Haven amounted to Shakespeare's intentional going out of *his* way to use Tudor-Stuart nationalism to affirm James's Britain as marking the final obsolescence of Roman antiquity's *mappae mundi*.

As mentioned at the previous chapter's outset, James encouraged Parliament to view the British Isles as 'one island, compassed with one Sea.' But in *Cymbeline*, James's 'one Sea' encompasses two irreconcilable coastlines; and the viability of *Cymbeline*'s bold dialectic between Galfridian and Roman history is never more sorely tested than on the Thames estuary. The play strives to shorten the cultural distance between the colonized Briton margin and the Roman metropole, an ambition particularly evident in the play's final act where the king Cymbeline expresses his hope that Britons and Romans will 'wave friendly together' (5.3). But, as I will argue, the play never fully recovers from the destabilized patriotic blank verse of Cymbeline's queen: the more she touts Briton courage in combating the Romans, the more her Kentish coastline recedes into a provincial *ultima Britannia*.

Recent *Cymbeline* criticism has convincingly identified the play as a fraught site of Stuart Britain's engagement with and resistance to antiquarianism's increasingly authoritative demystification of Geoffrey's Brutus myth.[25] Expanding on this critical trend, I argue that *Cymbeline*'s engagement with antiquarianism becomes particularly conflicted at the

---

24 Emrys Jones, 'Stuart *Cymbeline*,' *Essays in Criticism* 11 (1962): 95.
25 See, for example, John E. Curran Jr, 'Royalty Unlearned and Honor Untaught: British Savages and Historiographical Change in *Cymbeline*,' *Comparative Drama* 31, no. 2 (1997): 277–303, and Jodi Mikalachki, *The Legacy of Boadicea: Gender and Nation in Early Modern England* (New York and London: Routledge, 1998). An authoritative history of the declining credibility of Galfridian history in early modern England is T.D. Kendrick, *British Antiquity* (London: Methuen, 1950).

Thames estuary (at some distance from Cymbeline's more inland Lud's town), with eventual consequences for how we might reassess some of the different generic aims of early modern English dramatic verse and antiquarian prose as they approach the water's edge. No investigation of antiquarianism as one of the play's key cultural and historical backdrops is complete without considering, as earlier discussed, how antiquarian prose successfully incorporated the material reality of British Isles coastlines, particularly the churning Thames estuary, into its scholarly purview. And, by extension, no investigation of early modern English verse approaches to east-facing shorelines is complete without thoroughly examining *Cymbeline*'s failure to reconcile Galfridian mythopoesis and Caesarean history within the constraints of its blank verse.

With this context in place, we can now turn to *Cymbeline*'s three Julius Caesars, only one of whom emerges as a real, historical Caesar. Lucius, reminding Cymbeline of the tribute the Britons owe to Augustus Caesar, hearkens back to 'Julius Caesar (whose remembrance yet / Lives in men's eyes, and will to ears and tongues / Be theme and hearing ever)' (3.1.2–4). Here, the Roman general's diplomacy (somewhat anachronistically) invokes Julius Caesar as a Renaissance humanist exemplar. Moments later, Cymbeline's zealously nationalist queen counters with a debased Julius Caesar: 'A kind of conquest / Caesar made here, but made not here his brag / Of "Came" and "saw" and "overcame."' As I will later expand on, the queen's eagerness to engage with the material reality of the coastline is fueled by her overcharged compulsion to view the Briton coastline through the lens of Geoffrey's *Historia* and its refusal to acknowledge just how many traces Caesar left behind on the Kentish coast for all to rediscover.

The play's status-seeking protagonist Posthumus alludes to the play's third Caesar. In anachronistic Rome, he discards his Galfridian identity in order to fashion his new role as a cosmopolitan Roman seeking to shed his Briton past.[26] When he first arrives at Philario's residence, Posthumus's worst nightmare about his outsider status is confirmed

---

26 Posthumus has long eluded critics' attempts to pin a national identity on him. David Bergeron has argued for Posthumus as the most Roman of the British characters ('*Cymbeline*: Shakespeare's Last Roman Play,' *Shakespeare Quarterly* 31 [1980]: 36); Knight has described him as a 'composite' of the British and the Roman (*Crown of Life*, 142); and Robert Miola has argued that, by the play's end, Posthumus's 'shows a British capacity for humility and spiritual growth' ('*Cymbeline*: Shakespeare's Validation of Rome,' in Annabel Patterson, ed., *Roman Images: Selected Papers from the*

when his host unceremoniously announces to his other guests, 'Here comes the Briton' (1.4.28). When Philario broaches the subject of impending Roman-Briton conflict, Posthumus banters with his host that the current Britons 'Are men more ordered than when Julius Caesar / Smiled at their lack of skill but found their courage / Worthy his frowning at' (2.4.21–3).

Lucius's Caesar, as we have seen, is less a real person than a mnemonic 'theme,' a humanist worthy displaced from history to cultural memory. The queen's repulsed Julius Caesar inhabits a historical gray area inherited from Geoffrey. Only Posthumus's Caesar is a historical Caesar, the first inhabitant of the Mediterranean to make something identifiable *as* landfall on Britain's hostile coastline. Indeed, Posthumus's Caesar was the Caesar increasingly relied upon by Tudor/Stuart antiquarianism as the author of the first recorded history of early Britain: his remark to Philario seems less a nationalist boast about the readiness of Cymbeline's troops than a preoccupation with *The Gallic Wars'* deference to the overmatched Britons' hapless courage, haunting Posthumus as Caesar's patronizing *noblessse oblige*.[27] Put another way, haunting Posthumus is history's explicitly coastal Caesar, who judged the Briton coastline as a far more formidable foe than the primitive Britons – not to mention the elite Trojans-in-exile so celebrated by both Geoffrey and, later in the play, Cymbeline's queen.

The Posthumus of the Roman metropole is not present to hear two topographical speeches by Cloten and his mother, Cymbeline's queen. Had Posthumus heard these doggedly nationalist speeches, one can

---

English Institute, 1982 [Baltimore: The Johns Hopkins University Press, 1984], 54–6). For a recent account of Posthumus as Shakespeare's paradigmatic *Inglese Italiano*, see Peter A. Parollin, 'Anachronistic Italy: Cultural Alliances and National Identity in *Cymbeline,' Shakespeare Studies* 30 (2002): 188–215.

27 Among other things, Posthumus's comment is an anxious response to Stuart antiquarian transmissions of Caesar's, Tacitus's, and Strabo's accounts of primitive, loin-clothed early Britons, as found in, for example, Camden's *Britannia*, Edward Ayscue's 1607 *Historie Contayning the Warres, Treaties, Marriages, and other Ocurrences between England and Scotland*, and John Speed's 1611 *Theatre of Great Britaine*. Three studies have usefully linked *Cymbeline* to Speed's frontispiece to his *Theatre*, particularly its engraving of the fierce 'Britaine' that dominates the front center: Peggy Muñoz Simonds, *Myth, Emblem, and Magic in Shakespeare's 'Cymbeline': An Iconographic Reconstruction* (Newark: University of Delaware Press, 1992), 159–61; Brian Gibbons, *Shakespeare and Multiplicity* (Cambridge: Cambridge University Press, 1993), 20; and Valerie Wayne, '*Cymbeline's* Severed Heads and the Stuff of Romance,' presentation for the 2005 SAA workshop 'Shakespeare and Romance.'

imagine him scrapping his project of promoting a 'new' Briton sophistication abroad as doomed. Both speeches, even as they celebrate a Galfridian heritage, ironically reinforce Britain's marginal status in Rome's *mappae mundi*.

Antiquity's world maps are of no cultural significance to Cloten, who boasts to the equally patriotic queen, 'Britain's a world / By itself' (3.3.13–14). On his hypermasculine world map, Britain is heroically isolated, anticipating liberation from Roman dominance and proudly adrift in what Greco-Roman geography mapped as North Sea isolation. But as J.P. Brockbank has noted, Cloten's description directly echoes Virgil's description of Britain in his first eclogue: *Et penitus toto diuisos orbe Britannias*, Britain as a region wholly sundered from the world.[28] The shadow of the topos of *ultima Britannia* is further lengthened in the queen's speech that follows.

Perhaps because of the aforementioned nature of its jumbled plot, *Cymbeline* has rarely been viewed as eminently quotable; and thus, much criticism has tended to cluster around the queen's patriotic speech as the play's most accessible entry into thematic discussion. The queen seizes the audience's attention by touting the Britons who fought against Julius Caesar; and, with isolationist fervor, she praises the island as

> ribb'd and pal'd in
> With rocks unscalable and roaring waters,
> With sands that will not bear your enemies' boats,
> But suck them up to th' topmast. A kind of conquest
> Caesar made here, but made not here his brag
> Of 'Came, and saw, and overcame:' with shame
> (The first that ever touch'd him) he was carried
> From off our coast, twice-beaten; and his shipping
> (Poor ignorant baubles) on our terrible seas,
> Like egg-shells mov'd upon their surges, crack'd
> As easily 'gainst our rocks.

>   (3.3.20–30)

Over the years, the queen's speech has become a *locus classicus* for investigating the complex nationalist currents running through the play. Some sixty years ago, G. Wilson Knight grouped the queen's speech

---

28 'History and Histrionics in *Cymbeline*,' *Shakespeare Survey* 11 (1958): 48.

with such notable examples of Shakespeare's 'island patriotism' as John of Gaunt's speech.[29] More recently, Jodi Mikalachki's important gender reading of this passage has complicated Knight's reading, arguing that the queen presents the worst face of British nationalism, a 'paradox of savage female patriotism' disrupting the kinship and male-bonding between the Briton king Cymbeline and the Roman ambassador Lucius.[30] However transparently or subversively one chooses to read the queen's patriotism, what lingers in this play's most quotable speech is the intractable material reality of the rock-bound Briton coast as, arguably, one of Shakespeare's most unsettled prosodic sites.

As noted earlier in this chapter, Gaunt's praise of England as 'This precious stone set in the silver sea' is a highly conflicted speech. But as, arguably, Shakespeare's most quoted speech, it is also Shakespearean blank verse at its proudest and most eloquent, anchored by an emphatic 'This' ('This precious stone,' 'This blessed plot,' etc.) repeated, with heightened rhetorical effect, eight times. The prosodic balance of Gaunt's blank verse allows Gaunt (somewhat) to trope away from the coastline. But the queen's 'savage female patriotism,' as if seeking competitive edge over Gaunt, becomes a kind of demonic coaster, keeping her audience in dangerously close contact with the material reality of the Kentish coastline – its 'unscalable rocks and roaring waters,' its vessel-cracking 'surges.' In place of Gaunt's perfectly carved maritime 'precious stone,' we glimpse the 'eggshell' – fragments of what remains of Caesar's tide-ripped galleys floating amidst jagged rocks. Unlike the lilting cadences of Gaunt's iambic pentameter ('This happy breed of men, this little world'), the queen's speech is as ragged and storm-tossed as Caesar's vessels – including pentameters that, at times, extend an extra half-syllable, as in line 28, so submerged in its own 'sea' of images that it swells into a hexameter. The 'shipping' that is the grammatical subject of line 29 does not link up with its verb until two

---

29 *The Crown of Life: Interpretation in Shakespeare's Final Plays* (London: Methuen, 1958), 30. For an overview of Holinshed's influence on the play, including the queen's speech, see Joan Warchol Rossi, '*Cymbeline*'s Debt to Holinshed: The Richness of III.1,' in *Shakespeare's Romances Reconsidered*, Carol McGinnis Kay and Henry E. Jacobs, eds. (Lincoln: University of Nebraska Press, 1978), 104–12.

30 *The Legacy of Boadicea*, 98. Mikalachki observes that even Cymbeline, by the play's end, repudiates the queen's patriotism – what, for him, amounts to 'her disruption of the masculine network of kinship, promises, and honor that binds Cymbeline to Rome' (98).

lines later – at which time the verb 'crack'd' severs line 29 from line 30, 'cracking' the blank verse like Caesar's 'egg-shell' galleys 'mov'd upon their surges.'

Unlike the rhythmic discipline of Gaunt's patriotic blank verse, the queen's speech is prosodically ragged, her idealizing of Briton nation-hood 'crack'd as easily' against Kent's coastal rocks as the Roman galleys she derides. Despite the fact that Caesar's fleet was badly damaged by the Kentish coast's tides, he still defeated the Britons. But the coastal poetics of the queen's Briton allegiances results in her enigmatic insistence that barely 'A kind of conquest / Caesar made here, but not here – his brag / Of "Came, saw, and overcame"' ('here, but not here' as another Shakespearean moment when now we see the coastline – and now we don't).[31] The queen denies that Caesar was victorious at the coastline; but she puts herself under no pressure to map where the Britons were defeated. Her Briton coast is 'here, but not here' – 'here' on the material reality of the coastline, but 'not here' in the truth of early Briton history. Offering neither Gaunt's idealized, emblematic coast, nor a coast grounded in historical fact, the queen's blank verse shows the strain of lingering too long on antiquity's *apeiron*.

The queen's blank verse both heroically embraces Galfridian (pseudo) history and suicidally hurls itself onto the material reality of the coastline. Her speech retreats into Galfridian myth, exposing the dissonance of the passage's historical content, as well as its verse form. On the one hand, as the queen would have audiences believe, her 'shame[d]' Caesar never disembarked at the coast, let alone forded the Thames, but rather was ingloriously 'carried / From off our coast.' On the other hand, her description is drained of much of its defamatory gall when we read Caesar's own frankly detailed accounts of how his galleys were the victims of the tides; and her catalogue of the dangers of the Kentish coast ends up ironically allied with *The Gallic Wars'* own emphasis on the Romans' encounter with the coastline as their more formidable combatant.[32]

---

31 The queen seemingly misquotes the lines from a Macbeth soliloquy that positions him 'here, / But not here, upon the bank and shoal of time' (1.7.5–6).

32 In the final analysis, the queen's portrait of a debased Caesar might have been more coherent had she spoken not in the voice of Galfridian patriotism but rather in the cynical voice of Lucan's anti-epic *Pharsalia*. Written in support of a lost Roman republic, this epic presents, in II.527, a Caesar who, 'terrified, showed his back to the Britons whom he had sought out' (*'Pharsalia': Lucan*, intro., trans. Jane Wilson Joyce [Ithaca: Cornell University Press, 1993]).

By the play's end, the queen has died, and the echoes of her 'savage female patriotism' have been silenced by her husband's goal of 'Let[ting] / A Roman and a British ensign wave / Friendly together at Lud's town.' But she does not exit *Cymbeline* until her speech's conflicted Roman and Briton historiography has further unbalanced the play's already precarious juggling of James's presumed Trojan, Arthurian, and ancient Briton ancestries. Weaving indiscriminately in and out of Geoffrey's celebration of Briton valor and Caesar's amphibious struggles with an anonymous coastline, her speech offers no guidepost for how to read *Cymbeline* as a nationalist play. The more her verse lingers not on Geoffrey's 'purpled' waters but rather on Britain's 'rocks unscalable' for its evocative power, the more audiences view her coastline through Caesar's eyes. Hailing the island as 'ribb'd and pal'd in [with] our terrible seas,' the queen's speech demonstrates that any allusion to the Kentish Coast necessarily falls prey to an entrapping tautology: her touting of Britain's impregnable insularity is itself dependent on Caesar's eyewitness account of the island as the tide-assaulted *ultima Britannia*.

6. Of 'swan's nests,' River Poetry, and Antiquarian Prose, 1545–1610

This section continues my discussion of *Cymbeline*'s conflicted East Anglian shorelines, eventually reading them in tandem with antiquarianism's frank acknowledgment of the historical validity of *ultima Britannia*. But first, I begin with a prelude to swans, again touching base with Jonson's 1623 ode to Shakespeare, praising his esteemed predecessor as the 'sweet swan of *Avon*! What a sight it were / To see thee in our waters yet appeare, and make those flights upon the bankes of Thames, / That so did take *Eliza*, and our *James*' (71–4).

Swans were the sacred bird of Apollo and poetic creativity; and the swans that graced the Thames were avian symbols of the kind of nationalist mythopoetics the queen's coastal verse fails to script.[33] But their 'swan song' also made them symbols of mortality, another inheritance from classical poetry. In a preface to the reader that introduces his 1590 *Tale of Two Swannes*, the poet William Vallans writes that swans 'before their death do sing, as Virgil, Ovid, Horace, Martial with all the Poets

---

33 Further contributing to the topos of the Fortunate Isles was the legend that Apollo and the Muses had deserted the ancient world and arrived in England.

do constantly affirme.'[34] The 'swan of *Avon*' was all too familiar with antiquity's swans as a trope for mortality. In *The Rape of Lucrece*, the heroine, revealing to her husband the violation she has endured, knows her life is nearing its end: 'And now the pale swan in her wat'ry nest / Begins the sad dirge of her certain ending' (1611–12). Here, the narrator alludes to the dying swan's compulsive return to its nest to sing its final 'swan song.' In *3 Henry VI*, Richard, Duke of York, ponders the inevitability of death: 'I have seen a swan / With bootless labor swim against the tide, / And spend her strength with overmatched waves' (1.4.30–3). Shakespeare's tropes reveal not only the swan as the image of an inspired poetics but also the 'swan's nest' as a symbol of mortality – particularly if the swan, as in Richard's image, became stranded by the estuarial tide, too exhausted to reach its inland death-nest.

No discussion of *Cymbeline* is complete without at least attempting to interpret one of the play's more enigmatic passages, Imogen's metaphoric map of her native island: 'I'th' world's volume / Our Britain seems as of it but not in't, / In a great pool a swan's nest' (3.4.13–40). Nor is any critique of the queen's failed coastal poetics complete without inserting its contradictions with the context of Imogen's enigma.

The play's editors have customarily provided useful commentary on Imogen's metaphor of Britain as a 'volume,' such as the *Norton* edition's depiction of her island as a loose-leaf page that, although included within, is not yet bound into the 'volume' of world history.[35] But editors have never successfully glossed her second, not readily reconcilable metaphor of the island as 'In a great pool a swan's nest.'[36] Her metaphors of Britain as both a 'volume' and a 'swan's nest,' their strange admixture of nationalist pride and remoteness on a colonial periphery, of poetic inspiration and dirge-like 'swan song,' elude glib summary. But I would like to suggest Tudor/Stuart antiquarianism as

---

34 William Vallans, *The Tale of Two Swannes* (Oxford: Printed at the Theater, 1769).

35 See also Willy Maley's discussion of this image as reflecting Britain as an 'invention . . . with which Shakespeare's culture is only just coming to terms' ('Postcolonial Shakespeare: British Identity Formation and *Cymbeline*,' in *Shakespeare's Late Plays: New Readings*, eds. Jennifer Richards and James Knowles [Edinburgh: Edinburgh University Press, 1999], 150).

36 Years ago, J.M. Nosworthy's authoritative edition of the play may have come closest when he asked: 'Is it not possible that 'swan's nest' incorporates Shakespeare's vision of Britain as a nest of singing birds, as poets?' (*Cymbeline*, ed. Nosworthy [London and Cambridge, MA: Methuen and Harvard University Press, 1964], 101).

at least tentatively bridging the odd synapse between these two metaphors, thus maintaining its importance as the play's historiographic
backdrop. Relevant here was antiquarianism's intriguing ability to, as
it were, act globally and think locally. Antiquarianism shuttled between
continental historiographic ambition and (as will be discussed in this
section) provincial contentment, demonstrating its generic capacity to
embrace both an ambitious prose agenda of inserting ancient Britain
within the growing 'volume' of world history, and an at-times equally
ambitious verse project of merging the tropes of classical poetry with
the quaintness of local topography. Antiquarianism's dual generic affinities for historical prose and river poetry – and its immaculate distinction between the genres – established the protocols for how to
'write' the material reality of the East Anglian coastline, protocols the
queen's speech fails to observe.

Imogen's first metaphor suggests that in the 'volume' of world history, the king Cymbeline's insular, undocumented Britain is perhaps
not yet sufficiently evolved to welcome Jove's westward-soaring eagle
at court, still inhabiting the shadowy margins of an older Roman geography. And thus, it hints at the urgency of ongoing antiquarian scholarly searches for the forgotten pages of Briton history and their promise
of eventual inclusion within the growing 'world's volume' of histories
of northern European indigeneity. Imogen's allusion to a 'swan's nest,'
as mentioned earlier, is not as clear, however; and eventually I would
like to speculate on its relevance as a critique of the queen's speech. In
the meantime, however, I will turn to antiquarian poetry – namely how
and why it succeeded at the Kentish coast where *Cymbeline*'s queen
fails, deftly avoiding her entrapping tautology. By conceding antiquity's perception of Britannia as an island *without* a coast – without a
peirar – antiquarian poetry composed a historically consistent national
mythopoetics under the sign of the swan. Shuttling between prose and
poetry, Tudor/Stuart antiquarianism co-existed happily with what the
queen's blank verse disavows – antiquity's quarantining of British Isles
coastlines from the domain of verse itself.

Imogen's swan trope metonymically recalls the swan-graced Thames
of Tudor/Stuart antiquarianism's verse cousin, chorographic river poetry (for example, Spenser's hailing of the Thames's 'Swannes of goodly
hue' in *Prothalamion*, 37). This chorographic poetry is situated not on
Caesar's tide-battered coastline but rather, more often than not, on a
gentler, inland Thames – inland from the shadow of *ultima Britannia*
and from the estuarial currents at times fatal to chorographic poetry's

beloved swans. The antiquarian verse of John Leland and Camden, spanning a sixty-five year period between 1545 and 1610 (a year before *Cymbeline*'s first performance), provides prooftexts for this claim. Although these two figures are most often associated with antiquarian prose, the historian F.J. Levy (cited earlier) has pointed out that Leland, throughout his career, thought of himself not as a prose writer but a poet (129),[37] and Ben Jonson, in a marginal note to his 1604 *Part of the Coronation Entertainment*, referred to the antiquary Camden as also 'a learned Poet of our time.'[38] Moreover, in their poetic roles, both Leland and Camden took seriously the challenge of bringing verse to the Kentish coast without violating classical decorum.

Before turning to this poetry, I wish to investigate how Leland's and Camden's antiquarian prose lenses viewed the material reality of what could only loosely be termed the island's coast-*line*. In general, the most recognizable feature of antiquarianism's topographical discourse was its meticulous listing and detailing of England's shires, villages, woods, footpaths – loci always rewarding antiquarian curiosity. England's battered coastline, however, presented a number of natural obstacles to antiquarian habits of exhaustive local scrutiny. To be sure, Leland's antiquarian prose unabashedly celebrated the ruggedness of English coastlines, sharing, in his *Itinerary*, his regard for them with his monarch Henry VIII:

> I was totally enflammid with a love to see thoroughly al those Partes of this your opulente and ample Reaulme, that I had redde of yn the aforesaid Writers: yn so muche that al my other Occupations intermitted I have so traveled yn yowr Dominions booth by the Se Costes and the middle Partes, sparing nother Labor nor Costes, by the space of these vi. yeres paste, that there is almost nother Cape, nor Bay, Haven, Creke or Peere, River or Confluence of Rivers, Breches, Waschis, Lakes, Meres, Fenny Waters . . . but I have seen them; and notid yn so doing a hole Worlde of Things very memorable.[39]

---

37 Levy does not elaborate further. Leland's credentials as a humanist poet are evident in his 1542 threnody on Sir Thomas Wyatt, *Naeniae in mortem Thomae Viati*, comparing his former Cambridge colleague to Dante and Petrarch.
38 *Ben Jonson*, eds. C.H. Herford and Percy and Evelyn Simpson (Oxford, 1925–52), 7: 92.
39 *The New Year's Gift*, in *The Itinerary of John Leland*, 9 vols., ed. T. Hearne, 3rd edition (Oxford, 1770), I:xxii.

In his antiquarian wanderings (some of which may have resulted from the king's fear of French invasion) Leland claimed to have traced almost every indentation, every cape, marsh, tidal creek, and mud flat that broke up Henry's coastline. Only a passionately 'enflammid,' hydrophilic Leland could have even imagined the seemingly infinite project of tracing on foot every topographic feature of Europe's longest coastline, a project impossible to have realized during a lifetime.[40] (One hopes it is not simply uncharitable to remind readers here that Leland eventually went mad – unable, like Spenser's Eumnestes, to sort through the mounds of material he had accumulated over the years.) William Lambarde, England's first county chorographer, might have been more realistic about the challenges of exploring and cataloguing local coastlines. In his 1576 *Perambulation of Kent*, he confessed a wish to have spent more time on local watersheds, 'Ebbes, Floudes & Tides of the Sea, Riuers, Flattes, Barres . . . ,' but, in the end, spending more time inland.[41]

As discussed in my introductory chapter, Greek mariners' hugging of the coastline was made possible by the Mediterranean *peirar*. The mode of early modern antiquarian travel was, of course, not sailing but rather ambulation – an investigative traversal that seldom rendered a hugging of British coastlines practical. Derived from the Latin *perambulare*, the term 'perambulation' means to walk through. But on England's coastlines, the more accurate term for antiquarian traversals might well have been not *per–* but rather '*circum-*ambulation.' In other words, coastal antiquarianism entailed not a perambulatory hugging but rather a circumambulatory skirting that as often as not led away from the coastline (in the general direction of what Leland termed the island's 'middle Partes'): the coastline induced antiquaries to walk *around*, before they could ever claim they had walked *through*, the island's indented borders.

Camden, orienting his antiquarian studies from west to east, described the counties 'on one hand, to the Severn sea and the Thames on

---

40 Decades later, in 1587, William Harrison claimed to have tracked all the island's rivers, ranging from the urban ebbs and flows of the Thames around the London Bridge to the obscurest rills 'which falleth into the Rother from Bendyshe Hall' (*William Harrison: The Description of England*, ed. George Edelen [Ithaca: Cornell University Press, 1968], 404).

41 *Perambulation of Kent* (London: Printed for Matthew Walbancke and Dan Pakeman, 1656).

the other' (1.379). That is, he frequently traveled not from tide-battered cove to cove but rather from river to river (as well as from county to county) as the most accommodating way of describing England's varied terrain. Surveying Devonshire, Camden followed its south-facing coasts only long enough to strike inland at the estuaries that provided him more sequestered opportunities for antiquarian reflection. And in his section on Cornwall, Camden attempted to trace a coastal trajectory:

> From Plims mouth, where the South shore of this region beginneth, the country runneth along with a large and great front as farre as to *Stert*, a cape or promontorie (for, so the word in the English Saxon tongue signifieth) but so soone as the shore hath drawne it selfe back land-ward, the river *Dert* braketh out, which arising from the inward part of the country runneth downe apace, through certain leane and high grounds, called thereupon *Dertmoore* . . . (201)

Camden's antiquarian attention to the Saxon word for 'cape' lies all but buried beneath the welter of promontories, rivers, and effluvial plains competing for the privilege of the label of shoreline. From Plymouth, a sea-cliff extends to the Stert promontory – only to have its inward-veering shoreline collide with the Dart River. The broken Cornish coast (though literally dubbed 'Land's End') is an indeterminate commingling of cliff, moor, river shallow, tidal wash, and estuary that antiquity never acknowledged *as* a coast. In this indefinite zone between land and sea, we can view Camden's efforts to document coastal topography as mirroring early modern English coasters' struggles to chart the shoreline's watery hazards from the other side of the liminality where sea became land.

Between the two investigative purviews of antiquarianism and coasting lay antiquity's *apeiron*, wholly exposed at the swirling Thames estuary between Kent and East Anglia. Given its relative proximity to the island's most populous city, the estuary was, naturally, one of antiquarianism's most thoroughly documented coastal sites; and its emptying into the English Channel was described at length in William Harrison's 1587 *Description of England*, published as a preface to Holinshed's *Chronicle* (1577 and 1586):

> For the more that this river is put by of her right course, the more the water must of necessity swell with the white waters which run down from the land, because the passage cannot be so swift and ready in the winding as in the straight course. These landfloods also do greatly strain the fineness

of the stream, inso much that after a great landflood you shall take had-
docks with your hands beneath the bridge . . . whose eyes are so blinded
with the thickness of that element that they cannot see where to become
and make shift to save themselves . . . [42]

No Latinate 'finny droves' were observable in these abnormal currents. Harrison's chorographic zeal effectively outed the terminus of
the statelier inland Thames as a churning *apeiron*, at times so sediment-
choked that its own haddock were blinded and disoriented. Harrison's
description of the estuary's stunned haddock demonstrated why antiquarian prose was the literary medium best suited to capture the estuary's idiosyncrasies.

Thus Leland's, Harrison's, and Camden's prose reflected antiquarian certainty that the mud flats and tidal beds collecting the waters of
the Thames basin were most effectively approached not poetically but
rather by an *ad hoc* prose more adaptable to the estuary's anecdotal
quirks. As we will see, Leland and Camden did at times bring their
poetry to the English Channel; but their poetry never ceased viewing
the coastline through the mediating lens of classical models, including
the topos of *ultima Britannia*.

This context allows us to reconnect with Imogen's 'swan's nest,' turning from antiquarian prose to its cousin chorographic poetry, synec-
dochalized by her swan trope. A favorite chorográphic focus was, of
course, the rich history unfolding along the banks of the swan-graced
Thames, returning us to Leland, who not only wrote antiquarian prose
but also invented the chorographic river poem as a genre unique to
England (a poetic invention perhaps best indicating why Leland preferred to view himself as a poet). Interestingly, on those occasions when
Leland was inspired to write topographic poetry, he most often lingered
not on the island's capes, bays, and estuaries, but rather on the island's
more protected inland rivers, where an inherently English genre of chorographic poetry could be born and nurtured.

As touched on in my previous chapter, the genre was a studied response to the early modern English humanist challenge of integrating

---

42 *The Description of England*, 421. Some three centuries earlier, the port charted by
England's first tide-table, found among some manuscripts written at St Albans, was,
not surprisingly, the Thames estuary, where river and sea collide to form what the
tide-table termed, with unceremonious accuracy, a 'Flod at London Bridge' (quoted
in Taylor, 135).

classical poetic subtexts within local riverine purviews. The earliest example of the English river poem, anticipating by some fifty years Spenser's cantos of the marriage of the Thames and Medway, was Leland's 1545 neo-Latin *Cygnea Cantio*. In this poem a flock of companion swans, gracefully floating down the Thames as it wound its stately way through the countryside, illuminated the local charms of the river bank's antiquities and suggested local English rivers as descendants of the classical muses.[43] Not just trivially (or locally) quaint, the *Cygnea Cantio* defined the river poem as the point at which literary influences and riverine confluences triumphantly merged: classical antiquity's influence deposited its rich resources at the confluence of the Tame and the Isis, and its riverine narrations of English national mythology. In such a scheme, Leland's poem confirmed that the swan-graced Thames was as inherently adaptable to classical models as it was inherently English.

Thus, Imogen's metaphor of Britain as a 'swan's nest' becomes more coherent when inserted within the context of the chorographic river poem, where swans sustained their appeal as symbols of national myth-making. Tudor England's ongoing experiments with swans was evident in Vallans' aforementioned 1590 *A Tale of Two Swannes*, whose lengthy subtitle, *Wherin is comprehended the original and increase of the riuer lee commonly called Ware-riuer*, hints at how much he savored versifying the island's network of rivers. Vallans was not destined to become a household name in the literary history of early modern England. But he was instrumental in promoting the river poem as a genre of poetry circulating at court, and he urged not only Spenser but also Leland's antiquarian successor Camden to publish their experiments with the river genre: in his preface, Vallans aimed to 'animate, or encourage those worthie Poets [Spenser and Camden], who haue written *Epithalamion Thamesis*, to publish the same.'[44]

In addition to what was eventually published as *The Faerie Queene*'s marriage of the Thames and Medway, Vallans alluded to Camden's Anglo-Latin poetic tribute to the Thames, *De Connubio Tamae et Isis*, a

---

43 For one of the earliest scholarly discussions of this poem, see Charles G. Osgood's essay 'Spenser's English Rivers,' *Transactions of the Connecticut Academy of Arts and Sciences* 23 (1920): 102.

44 The first scholar to identify Vallans' 'worthie Poets' as Spenser and Camden was Leicester Bradner, *Musae Anglicanae: A History of Anglo-Latin Poetry, 1500–1925* (London: Oxford University Press, 1940), 40–1.

series of eleven verse fragments scattered throughout various editions of his *Britannia* from 1586 to 1610.[45] For the virtuosity of these fragments, we need look no further than Leicester Bradner's praise of the poet's graceful hexameters: 'There is a remarkably sculptural effect in the figure of Isis pouring the streams of the nascent river out of her urn, reminiscent of the great Roman fountains.'[46] Flowing past the towns that dotted its banks – Oxford, Reading, Windsor, Richmond, Kew – Camden's Latinate Thames effortlessly merged sound and sense, classical poetics and local English place. In a felicitous account of the wedding ceremony of the Tame and Isis, Camden even attempted a brief 'translation' of antiquity's *peirar* into English verse: his sea-nymph Britona plucked a harp and sang of Nereus' first glimpse of Britain's 'victorious Sea / [which] Through cloven rocks did passe.'[47] Britona's gently domesticated, 'cloven' sea-cliffs were not wave-thrashed but rather caressed by the tides' silken 'pass[ing].' And thus, Camden's Thames flowed not into chorographic specificity but rather into a benignly paternal ocean, seemingly on brief loan from antiquity:

> And in one connected stream,
> With hearts united now, Isis and Tame
> Arose exulting in united name;
> And onwards moving in harmonious boast
> Join Father Ocean in the Eastern Coast.

> (2.10)

But not even *De Connubio*'s earlier deft triumph (replete with dryads, water nymphs, and satyrs inherited from Virgil, Ovid, and Statius)

---

45 For the authoritative dating of these fragments, as well as evidence that these fragments were as carefully revised as Camden's prose, see Jack B. Oruch, 'Spenser, Camden, and the Poetic Marriages of Rivers,' *Studies in Philology* 64, no. 4 (1967): 606–24.

46 Bradner, 41. Bradner has usefully traced the complex editorial path of Camden's river-poem. The 1586 edition includes twenty-nine lines on the conjoining of the two rivers at Oxfordshire; the 1590 edition adds nine lines on the head of tide-water at Surrey; and twenty-nine lines on the source of the Isis at Gloucestershire, and new lines on the junction of the two rivers; and the 1600, 1607, and 1610 editions include still more lines (40–1).

47 Fragment VI, 56–7, trans. Holland, in 'Poems by William Camden, With Notes and Translations from the Latin,' ed. George Burke Johnston, *Studies in Philology* 72 (1975): 95.

was inclined to linger on the Thames that progressed from Greenwich and Deptford to the sea.[48] Camden's prose *Britannia* was evidence of his awareness that his eminently poetic Thames was, at its terminus, on the verge of forfeiting its Latinate identity, on the estuarial verge of dissolving within the incomplete embrace between the North Atlantic and antiquity's Mediterranean *peirar*, his graceful Latin hexameters on the verge of disintegrating into something no longer recognizable *as* poetry. Scattered throughout, embedded within *Britannia*'s prose, the verse fragments of *De Connubio* were swallowed as wholly by Camden's antiquarian prose as the inland Thames' stately flow is swallowed by estuarial salt water.[49]

A defining principle of humanist continental chorography was the movement from west to east; and in the case of the early modern English river poem dedicated to the Thames, this eastward direction expedited a generic shift from hexameters to a more durable prose better equipped to record such regional – and nonclassical – quirks as Harrison's sediment-blinded haddock. Even as Camden's inland Thames, like Leland's, kept competitive pace with classical models, so also did he defer, at the estuary, to the cultural authority of antiquity's *ultima Britannia*. Thus did his Thames's 'harmonious boast' cede place to the intractable realities of *The Gallic Wars*' shoreline, marking the point at which Camden the chorographic poet passed through a looking-glass to become Camden the antiquarian prose historian: he no longer viewed the Thames through the inland eyes of the genre of the river poem, but rather through the coastal eyes of Caesar's prose commentaries.

Before observing the significance of Leland's and Camden's river poetry as commentary on the troubled shoreline poetics of *Cymbeline*'s queen, let us briefly return to the *Cygnea Cantio*, whose chorographic vision at one point pauses to view the coast through the eyes of a Kentish Caesar. In his prose *Itinerary*, Leland discussed the probability that Caesar had first landed (to a certain extent, at least) at Dover and, in the

---

48 Oruch notes Camden's discovery, between 1600 and 1604, that the Elbe River (running through what is now Czechoslovakia and Germany) and the Low Countries' Schelde River suffered a similar tidal turbulence as they emptied into the North Sea (610).

49 Relevant here is Oruch's observation that Camden never combined the *De Connubio*'s fragments into a whole poem that could be published separately (611).

next year, some eight miles northeast at Deal, on sandy, tide-washed flats:

> Deale, half a myle fro the shore of the se, a fisscher village iii. myles or more above Sandwice, is apon a flat shore and very open to the se, wher is a fosse or a great bank artificial betwixt the towne and se, and beginneth aboute Deale, and rennith a great way up toward S. Margaret's Clyfe, yn so much that sum suppose that this is the place where Caesar landed *in aperto litore*. Surely the fosse was made to kepe owte ennemyes there, or to defend the rage of the se; or I think rather the castings up beche or pible. (III.50.55)

In this passage, Leland's Kentish Caesar was not Geoffrey's Caesar, so assailed by the Britons that he never reached dry land. Rather, he was the Caesar celebrated by continental and English antiquaries alike as not just a general but an architect, a builder of camps, 'fosses,' coastal bulwarks, barricades, fortresses, walls – the traces of engineering feats that would eventually demarcate the borders of towns, the foundational traces of future *civitas*. This coastal engineer is the Caesar praised in Leland's *Cygnea Cantio*:

> Renowned Dele doth vaunt itself,
>   with Turrets newly rais'd:
> For monuments of Caesars host,
>   A place in storie prais'd.

This stanza is Lambarde's English translation of the *Cygnea Cantio*, included in his *Perambulation of Kent*. (Though Lambarde himself composed no Anglo-Latin chorographic poetry, his *Perambulation*'s translation of Leland reinforced the alliance between antiquarian prose and poetry, and perhaps even provided Camden with the impulse to enfold poetry within his own antiquarian prose.) In Leland's stanza, we hardly encounter the poetics of genius. But the stanza does offer insight into Leland's self-perception as a poet even more than a writer of prose – and, more specifically, the centrality of Kentish coastlines to this self-perception. Unlike the dramatic verse of *Cymbeline*'s queen, exposing her Galfridian blank verse to the hazards of Caesarean coastlines, Leland contains Kent's 'raging se' within his prose *Itinerary*. His poetry, rather than self-destructing amidst rocky coasts or tidal washes, celebrates the castle at Deal that owns a Roman 'monument.' At the coast,

Leland's verse continues the *Cygnea Cantio*'s overall project of merging local landscape and classical decorum, while also keeping in his sights the historical truth of Caesar's *ultima Britannia*.

In their various ways, Leland and Camden reflected antiquarian history's facility to shift gears from prose to poetry (and back), recruiting Caesar's triumph on a provincial coastline for the larger cause of an authentically humanist British history. But the *apeiron* of *Cymbeline*'s queen – 'ribb'd and paled in / With rocks unscalable and roaring waters,' plagued by sucking sandbanks that swallow enemy galleys 'to the topmast,' assaulted by the tides that 'cracked' Caesar's galleys 'Like eggshells' – belongs to no genre: neither the prose of an antiquarian historiography nor a coastal verse, like Leland's and Camden's, observing classical decorum, the queen's headlong plunge into the material reality of coastal Kent ends up justifying antiquity's quarantining of the region's shores from the domain of poetry. Depicting a Caesar ingloriously 'carried / Off our coast' by the tides of a spurious Galfridianism, the queen scours her own verse on the shoreline's 'rocks unscalable,' where her meters are as 'crack'd' as Caesar's galleys.

I make no claim to have solved the mystery with which this section began – i.e., Imogen's metaphor of Britain as a 'swan's nest.' But the queen's topographical verse – namely the conspicuous absence of the river swan as a conventional symbol of an inspired local mythopoetics – can return us full circle to the 'swan's nest' as an emblem of mortality. Leland's *Cygnea Cantio* was, in fact, composed as a 'swan song,' sung by a swan that, anticipating its death, sends its swan-companions back to Oxford and prepares for Heaven. But the verse of *Cymbeline*'s queen, stranded in waters graced by no Apollonian sacred birds, struggles – much like Richard's swan paddling with 'bootless labor' – to swim against the tide of Stuart antiquarianism; and her coastal poetics is left without so much as a dying swan to sing the 'swan song' of her failed revival of Geoffrey's *totius insulae* for British history.

7. Losing Perspective on the Ever-Receding Rocky Coast

The dual aims of antiquarian chorographic verse and prose warrant a brief, concluding glance at Drayton's *Polyolbion*, whose doomed project of preserving a robust Galfridian history that could survive an increasingly consolidated antiquarian historiography can serve as a useful coda to *Cymbeline*. The 1612 edition of Drayton's poem was published at roughly the same time as *Cymbeline*'s first performance; and it also exposes some of the cognitive dissonances of engaging with Geoffrey on a rock-bound coastline. Drayton sought to bring Galfridian history and early modern English chorography into viable proximity with one another, but, in the process, his poem ran afoul of antiquarianism's protocols for how to avoid unwitting entrapment within the shadow of antiquity's *ultima Britannia*.

Over a century ago, Oliver Elton's study of Drayton, intriguingly – if somewhat awkwardly – observed: 'Into Drayton, English as he was, had sunk the Renaissance feeling of the wreck and destruction accomplished by Time upon beauty, and power, and noble visible monuments, and the glory of the great . . . '[50] Elton does not elaborate on his epithet for Drayton ('English as he was'), but it does glance back at the poet's familiarity with shipwreck-strewn local shores, and his predisposition to view them as apt emblems of the 'wreck and destruction' of historical time. Like the queen's blank verse, *Polyolbion*'s hexameter couplets seek to preserve intact the 'ship' of Galfridian history. But, like the queen's blank verse, Drayton's poetry, faithful to Geoffrey, also at crucial moments splits apart on the rocks of the Briton coast and its relationship to the historical past.[51]

Several storied rivers in the 1612 *Polyolbion* lament Tudor/Stuart antiquarianism's privileging of the historical integrity of Caesar's *Gallic Wars* over Geoffrey's *Historia*. The river Wye, at one point, 'bitterlie exclaime[s]' against the growing historical trend that has robbed the river of its once grand, Galfridian resonances (6.305–9).[52] The river Dee, both a gentle inland river and an angry estuary when its churning waters empty into the Irish Sea, is even more confrontational: Britain was not such a barbarous nation as '*Caesars* envious pen would all the world perswade' (10.298). The Dee unleashes a verse accusation of Caesar's prose account of the Romans' amphibious assault on the tide-battered Thames estuary as having been written by an 'envious pen' wrongfully slandering Geoffrey's elite, paradisal Trojans-in-exile as primitive indigenes residing in *ultima Britannia*. Not only does the river Dee implicitly defend its companion estuary on the English Channel, but it also insists on designating the material reality of British Isles coastlines as

---

50 Oliver Elton, *Michael Drayton: A Critical Study* (London: A. Constable, 1905), 110.

51 For recent discussions of *Polyolbion*'s troubled historical voice, see Claire McEachern, *The Poetics of English Nationhood, 1590–1612* (Cambridge: Cambridge University Press, 1996); and John E. Curran Jr, 'The History Never Was Written: Bards, Druids, and the Problem of Antiquarianism in *Polyolbion*,' *Renaissance Quarterly* 51 (1998): 498–525.

52 All references to *Polyolbion* are from *The Works of Michael Drayton*, ed. J. William Hebel (Oxford: Shakespeare Head Press, 1931–41).

the stage for continuing the historical debate (or what Drayton hoped still had the magnitude of a debate) over the island's origins. Exposing the folly of attempts, such as Caesar's, to retrieve the distant historical past, the river demands to know: 'As what so great a Work, by Time that is not wrack't?' The Dee implies that the historical truth of Caesar's commentaries, lost in a murky, distant past, has been 'wrack't' on Time's metaphorical coastal rocks as surely as the general's triremes foundered on the real rocks of the Kentish coast.

Not unlike *Cymbeline*'s queen, *Polyolbion*'s Galfridian Dee urges readers to regard Caesar's historical truth as mere fiction. But what the river cannot bracket from the debate is the reality of local coastlines, ironically the driving force behind the Dee's argumentative space-clearing as it seeks to cast doubt on Caesar's documentation of a hostile coast. The Dee would insist that we know Caesar's commentaries (and, by extension, his account of the Kentish shoreline) are not wholly reliable because of historical inquiry's tendency to founder on the rocks of Time. That the metaphor of 'wracking' comes all too instinctively to the Dee (particularly in its incarnation as a churning estuary) can give us pause, for the river allows, through the back door, the truth that even the most committed Galfridian could not ignore for long – i.e., the East Anglian coastline not as the welcoming shores of Geoffrey's Trojan *locus amoenus* but rather the tide-assaulted coast of Roman antiquity's *ultima Britannia*.

Compounding the confusion, the river Dee ends up ironically doubling back on the historical discourse of Camden, Drayton's friend but also one of Geoffrey's most influential detractors. Years earlier, in his 1586 *Britannia*, Camden himself had viewed the difficult antiquarian task of recovering the obscure historical origins of pre-Roman Britain through the lens of a similar coastal metaphor: 'who is so skillful as in this dark ocean of antiquity to struggle with time without splitting on the rocks?' (I, liv). Camden's implicit target was Geoffrey's effort to build a Trojan ancestral 'house' on a hostile, rock-strewn coast. Sooner or later, Camden predicted, even the stoutest vessel of antiquarian historical inquiry will founder on a rock-ribbed coast, the graveyard of Britain's fragmented and largely undocumented early history. But for Camden, fear of the historical unknown was no reason not to continue drifting amidst these rocks in persistent attempts to shed light on history's gaps. All of which is to argue that Camden's coastal metaphor lends perspective on how thoroughly antiquarian prose (unlike the queen's blank verse and *Polyolbion*'s couplets) was reconciled to – worked in concert with – antiquity's perception of Briton shores as the catastrophic breakdown of the sacred barrier between land and sea. Predating *Polyolbion* by a quarter of a century, Camden exposes the Dee's defense of Geoffrey as belated, too late to recruit the shipwreck metaphor to promote Geoffrey's pristine *totius insulae* over the 'wracking' menaces of Caesar's coastline.

Elsewhere in *Polyolbion*, the river Dee deploys a second coastal metaphor as it continues expanding on the difficulties of historical recovery: 'in things past so long (for all the world) we are / Like to a man embarqu't, and travelling the Deepe' (308–23). In the effort to lay claim to a coastal metaphor that can once and for all preserve the integrity of Galfridian history, the Dee now imagines the ship of the historian not as headed toward the coast (not toward the threat of being 'wrack't'), but as carried away from the coast. Dee's historical past is no longer a looming promontory threatening the vessel of history but rather a barely perceptible vanishing point on the horizon.

The conflicting perspectives of the Dee's coastal metaphors are further evidence that *Polyolbion*'s alliance of poetry and Galfridian history may have been doomed from the start. As is well known, Drayton invited the prestigious Stuart antiquarian John Selden, Camden's student, to annotate *Polyolbion*'s first eighteen books, hoping the prose annotations would give his poem's Galfridian fables and legends more historical heft. But Selden's notes, as Drayton might have predicted, both engaged with and sustained a scholarly distance from the fables *Polyolbion* sought to preserve in the amber of its couplets.[53] The charmingly personified Wye and Dee rivers illustrate Drayton's indebtedness to antiquarianism's own cartographic eagerness to recruit legend and fable in the service of mapping local landscapes. But when antiquarianism reached the water's edge, Galfridian and Caesarean histories quickly parted company: antiquarianism's prose project was not a dallying in legend but rather a sailing amidst the material reality of the coastline until it had pieced together the fragments of Briton history. The willingness of antiquarian prose to stay the course and brace itself for an inevitable splitting on the rocks of *ultima Britannia* exposed Drayton's couplets as perhaps too delicate to negotiate Caesar's coast.

---

53 Anne Lake Prescott has referred to Selden's annotations as 'a study in urbane ambivalence' ('Drayton's Muse and Selden's "Story": The Interfacing of Poetry and History in *Poly-Olbion*,' *Studies in Philology* 87 [1990]: 128–35).

In the final analysis, readers witness *Polyolbion*'s river Dee still attempting to decide whether it should face the history of the Briton coastline,
or turn away – whether it should attempt to face (down) the 'wracking'
Caesarean coastline and risk destruction, or turn its gaze away from the
coastline and concede defeat to an antiquarian prose far more adept at
addressing the material reality of local coastlines.

   Polyolbion's conflicted perspective of the shoreline can serve as the
backdrop of a brief, final return to *Cymbeline*'s rock-bound coast, particularly as viewed from the perspective of Posthumus. I am thinking of
the aforementioned status-seeking Posthumus who, at key moments in
the play, seeks to shed his marginal Briton identity in favor of a Roman
(or early modern Italian) identity – the Posthumus who is 'undelvable to the root' not only by members of Cymbeline's court but also
by decades of Shakespeare scholarship. When, in anachronistic early
modern Rome, we last saw the play's protagonist, he was spending
less time mourning his separation from Imogen than attempting to rewrite Caesar's patronizing of the primitive Britons (depicting, as we
have seen, the current Britons as 'men more ordered than when Julius
Caesar / Smiled at their lack of skill but found their courage / Worthy
his frowning'). Indeed, Posthumus further unsettles the play's troubled
dialectic between remembering and forgetting. If the queen, in one of
her Galfridian outbursts, urges her husband the king to 'Remember,
my liege / the kings your ancestors' (3.1.18), Imogen, as early as the
opening act, worries that her wayward husband 'Has forgot Britain'
(1.6.113) – Galfridian heritage and all. At one point in the play, Posthumus seemingly forces Shakespeare's audiences to 'remember' Britain's
otherwise obsolete marginality in the spectral geography of the Roman
empire. Though the protagonist of a play invested in James's idea of
'Britain' and 'Britainness,' Posthumus's name, entirely Shakespeare's
invention, suggests an obscure state of being 'born after.' Though born
when Britain was a Roman tributary, one could argue that Posthumus
has also seemingly been born 'after' the topos of *ultima Britannia* had
long become embedded in the Roman geographic imagination. 'Undelvable to the root,' as the First Gentleman describes him, Posthumus
is ostensibly Galfridian but, at key moments, also a parody of Brutus as
he heads eastward in the wrong direction, away from Lud's town and
his 'Imogen.' And thus does Posthumus seek not just asylum from the
angry Cymbeline but also a full-fledged cultural assimilation within
the Roman metropole.

Not insignificantly, before departing for Rome, Posthumus leads audiences to the Briton coastline – not, unlike the queen, to focus on the Kentish rocks as emblems of Briton nationalism, but rather to gaze into the distance as his ship disappears out of sight of the queen's turbulent shores. Put another way, we watch as he seemingly converts his banishment from the island into what amounts to an abandonment of the Briton shoreline where the zealously patriotic queen will eventually founder. That the play's protagonist (though himself of Galfridian descent) seemingly cannot escape the queen's dissonant coast soon enough may be evident when Pisanio informs Imogen that Posthumus 'would not suffer me / To bring him to the haven . . . ' (1.1.172–3). Here, Pisanio assures Imogen that her husband wished to be alone with the grief of spousal separation. But Posthumus, always 'undelvable to the root,' might also be viewed as tipping off a readiness to put distance between him and the queen's shoreline. As Pisanio narrates,

> for so long
> As he could make me with this eye or ear
> Distinguish him from others, he did keep
> The deck, with glove, or hat, or handkerchief
> Still waving, as the fits and stirs of's mind
> Could best express how slow his soul sailed on.
> How swift his ship . . .
>
> (1.3.8–14)

On the one hand, Pisanio's narration lyrically rehearses a frequent romance motif, the lovers' poignantly extended farewell. On the other hand, his effort to assure Imogen that her grieving husband was reluctant to leave his wife (and his native Britain) behind also ends up, however inadvertently, emphasizing the relentlessly widening distance between the coastline and Posthumus's 'swift'-sailing vessel, which disappears on the horizon's vanishing point. In such a scheme, Posthumus is neither a committed Galfridian (like the queen) nor a stalwart antiquarian willing to stay the course and risk 'splitting' on the shoals of time in the service of a reliable historiography. It will soon be the case that the glove, hat, and handkerchief he uses to wave farewell to Imogen-via-Pisanio will also serve as the well-appointing fashion accessories aiding in his cultivation of a 'new' Briton sophistication not at home but abroad. Both Pisanio and the Briton coastline can only watch from a distance as the ship of the once Galfridian Posthumus points its stern to the queen's shores and their tautological entrapment in Caesar's *Gallic Wars*. The ship eventually crosses a time-warped, anachronistic threshold into its passenger's new life as an early modern, humanist Roman well-schooled in antiquity's topos of *ultima Britannia*. Posthumus's departure is, in effect, a mirror reversal of the route of Caesar's invasion, sailing away from antiquity's *apeiron*, away from the queen's sea-cliffs and their chalky defiance of the continental Europe the play's protagonist so admires. Imogen is left to measure 'the diminution / Of space' (1.4.18–19) that, from her perspective, has reduced her exiled husband to a speck on the horizon. But from the perspective of Posthumus, later suspected by his wife of having 'forgot Britain,' a receding, evanescent Briton coast is an escape valve from the queen's suffocating Galfridianism, from the queen's galley-smashing Briton coastline, and all that it exposes of a provincial Britain as Rome's *ultima Britannia*.

In the play's fourth act, a Briton lord announces to Cymbeline that 'The Roman legions, all from Gallia drawn, / Are landed on your coast' (2.25–6). The Romans, in other words, have landed not on the queen's fraught Kentish coast but rather, in the play's strategic geography, at the king's and Henry Tudor's Milford Haven, where Briton mythohistory has a better chance of recruiting local coastlines in the service of British history.

Chapter Four

Exiled Shorelines: Early Milton and the Rejection of the *Mare Ovidianum*

1. 'Love your Naso's name . . .'

There are several productive pathways into revisiting the ambitious poet to whom Milton biography has customarily referred as the early or 'young' Milton – including the religious (his thoughts of entering the priesthood), the political (his political aims as pamphleteer), and the literary historical (his ambitions as a laureate poet).[1] This, my most biographical chapter, explores the literary historical path. It can go without saying that the early Milton mapped out his literary career in sharply different historical and cultural circumstances than Spenser and Shakespeare. But a significant literary historical linkage of the young Milton with his two esteemed predecessors is enabled by Leicester Bradner's still-useful identification of the young Milton as 'the last of the Elizabethans.'[2] I argue further that the young Milton may also have been the last of the great humanist-trained early modern English writers to labor in the shadow of the otherwise obsolete topos of *ultima Britannia*.

If Spenser often self-indulgently cultivated the pose of exile (particularly as Colin Clout piping on the banks of the Mulla or in the spirit-filled woods of Acidale), the young Milton rejected the exilic pose as a significant obstacle in his laureate career path. Prior to and during his tour of Italy, Milton was seemingly impervious to the kind of cultural melancholia that at times visited any humanist-trained early modern

---

1 For a perspective on religious and political career reflections in Milton's early poetry, see David Norbrook, *Poetry and Politics in the English Renaissance*, rev. ed. (New York: Oxford University Press, 2002), 227–46.
2 *Musae Anglicanae*, 116.

English poet aware of composing on antiquity's margin. If the young poet, on the verge of traveling to Italy and gazing on the Mediterranean for the first time, indeed brooded on the ironies of shaping a poetic career on what was antiquity's edges of the world, he left no obvious trace. Following the heady successes of his Italian tour, Milton, in his 1642 *Reason of Church Government*, pointedly anticipated writing a vernacular English epic while 'content with these British islands as my world.'[3]

Bradner's pathway to the young Milton was Ovid: 'in Milton's early Latin verse, we find the last and most important appearance of the all-pervasive Ovidian influence in Renaissance Latin poetry' (111). Ovid's poetry often prompted early modern thoughts about how – or how not – to shape a literary career,[4] and Milton proved no exception. One of the more durable *leitmotifs* in Milton scholarship has been tracking the poet's carefully planned soaring from the 'middle flights' of poetic apprenticeship to the eventual loftier heights of vernacular epic. Early in his poetic career, Milton committed himself to the *rota Virgilii* and a concomitant rejection of Ovid.[5] Intimately related to his epic ambition (or so he would have readers believe) was his aforementioned 'content with these British islands as my world'; and as part of affirming his 'content' on antiquity's margin, the young Milton distanced himself not only from the 'young' Ovid of amatory elegiacs, as is well known, but also from the 'older' Ovid of exile. But he also revealed difficulties in disentangling himself from the exiled Ovid. Thus, to investigate in detail Milton's literary responses – as well as his strategic non-

---

3 All references to Milton's prose are taken from *The Complete Works of John Milton*, gen. ed. Don M. Wolfe (New Haven: Yale University Press, 1953–82). The definitive early studies of Milton's Italian tour are Masson, *The Life of John Milton*; James Holly Hanford, 'Milton's Italy,' *Annuales Medievale* 5 (1954): 49–61; and John Arthos, *Milton and the Italian Cities* (New York: Barnes and Noble, 1968).

4 For Ovid's influence on Marlowe's mapping of his literary career, see Patrick Cheney, *Marlowe's Counterfeit Profession: Ovid, Spenser, Counter-Nationhood* (Toronto: University of Toronto Press, 1997).

5 Bradner, *Musae anglicanae*; E.K. Rand, 'Milton in Rustication,' *Studies in Philology* 19 (1922): 109–35; Davis P. Harding, *Milton and the Renaissance Ovid* (Urbana, IL: University of Illinois Press, 1946); Louis Martz, *Poet of Exile: A Study of Milton's Poetry* (New Haven: Yale University Press, 1966); R.W. Condee, *Structure in Milton's Poetry* (University Park, PA: Penn State University Press, 1974). For a definitive study of Milton and the *Metamorphoses*, see Richard J. DuRocher, *Milton and Ovid* (Ithaca, NY: Cornell University Press, 1985).

responses – to Ovid's literary response to exile on the remote shores of the Black Sea is to reconfigure, or view in a different light, some of the well-established details of the young Milton's career trajectory as it unfolded in the shadow of antiquity's *ultima Britannia*. In the *Tristia* 3.14, Ovid seemingly confessed, 'Misfortunes have broken my talent, whose source was even aforetime unproductive and whose stream was meager' (*ingenium fregere meum mala, cuius et ante / fons infecundus parvaque vena fuit*, 33–4).[6] But to accept Ovid's claim at face value (as Milton, despite his remarkable sensitivity to Ovidian self-parody, tended to do) was to overlook the extent to which, on the shores of the Black Sea, Ovid's exile poetry set the standard for how to dictate to the muses on an *apeiron* of the Roman empire's remote periphery.

This chapter's itinerary will begin with the absent presence of the exiled Ovid in Milton's *Epitaphium Damonis* and how differently the elegy would have read had its poet not overlooked Ovid's significant linkage of alien estuaries and poetic genre. The chapter will then travel back in time to glance at some of the elegies Ovid wrote while exiled on the shores of the Black Sea, a necessary backdrop for returning to the young Milton and some of the poems written prior to his Italian tour. I will read the Latin *Elegia Prima*, *Elegia Quarta*, *Elegia Sexta*, and the English *Lycidas* with the aim of teasing out how Milton pointedly rejected the pose of Ovidian exile as an obstacle to his well-documented plans for writing a great English vernacular epic. The chapter then turns to selected poems written during Milton's successful Italian tour, namely *Ad Salsillum* and *Mansus*, where he self-consciously presented himself as a poet who, unlike Ovid, flourished on the remote shorelines of ancient Rome's *mappae mundi*. The chapter concludes with Milton's stay in Geneva, the site of a complex engagement with one of Horace's epistles (1.11) and its critique of remote shorelines. Returning full circle to Milton's rejection of the exiled Ovid, I argue that audible in his salute to Horace, just prior to his return to the shores of *ultima Britannia*, is the voice of the rejected Ovid never recognized by the young Milton as a master at linking alien estuaries and poetic genre. Phrased broadly, the chapter, seeking to add to biographical portraits of the young Milton, offers a perspective on continuing pressures on early modern English

---

6 All references to the *Tristia* and the *Epistulae ex Ponto* are taken from *Ovid in Six Volumes*, ed., trans. Arthur Leslie Wheeler, vol. 6, *Tristia, Ex Ponto* (Cambridge, MA: Harvard University Press, 1988).

writers, well into the seventeenth century, to shape a poetic career on an island antiquity had once banned from poetry itself.

A topos running throughout Ovid's exile poetry is his fear that he has been abandoned and forgotten by friends and patrons back in Rome. In one of the *Tristia*'s most emotional appeals, Ovid begs an anonymous friend to 'love your Naso's name – the only part of him not yet in exile: all else the Scythian Pontus possesses' (*Nasonsique tui, quod adhuc non exulat unum, / nomen ama: Scythicus cetera Pontus habet*, 3.4.45–6). Jo-Marie Claassen gets to the core of what Ovid urges here, noting just how important the name 'Naso' is in Ovid's poetics of exile: the poet persistently invites his friends to distinguish Ovid, the famous Roman poet, from Naso, the suffering protagonist of his exile poetry.[7] An undercurrent in this chapter is the possibility that there is something eerily incantatory about Ovid's exhortation to 'love your Naso's name' – almost as if the otherwise-abject exile powerfully predicts that nothing good can befall a poet who seeks to cultivate a poetic voice on the periphery of the Roman empire without first passing through and at least acknowledging the *Tristia* as a model for how to dictate to the muses on alien shores. What should not be underestimated at this point is what much recent Ovid scholarship has demonstrated (to be discussed later in detail) – i.e., the extent to which Ovid, though a self-confessed *flebilis exul*, had every intention of securing his place within the Greco-Roman literary tradition; and he was well aware that the poems he wrote in Tomis would likely become a new genre of exile poetry – well aware, that is, of the enriching paradox that his poetry was never as virtuosic as it was on inhospitable Pontic shores.

The later Milton composed his great epic during the Restoration, a span of years during which the republican poet himself could loosely be termed a poet in exile, writing about biblical history's prototypical exiles Adam and Eve.[8] And yet, in those moments of writing *Paradise Lost* when he was predisposed to remember Ovid, it was the opulent *Metamorphoses*, not the lonely poems Ovid wrote during his exile, to which Milton turned.[9] In this context, we can be reminded of Brooks Otis's analysis of the *Metamorphoses*' compelling compilation of my-

---

7 See the second chapter of *Displaced Persons: Literature of Exile from Cicero to Boethius* (Madison, WI: University of Wisconsin Press, 1999).

8 Milton explores the theme of Israelite exile in his translations of the Psalms.

9 Martz has argued that during the years he composed *Paradise Lost*, Milton viewed the *Metamorphoses* as 'one of his best loved books' (*Poet of Exile*, 204).

thology as a type of heroic poem demonstrating exemplary epic unity.[10]
Otis's claim has long occasioned debate; but we can stop well short
of calling the *Metamorphoses* an epic and still appreciate the extent to
which Milton, immersed at last in writing the epic he had planned for
so long, undoubtedly responded to the *Metamorphoses'* resonant conclusion where Ovid proclaims that if the prophecies of poets hold true, he
will live forever in fame (*perque omnia saecula fama, / siquid habent veri
vatum praesagia, vivam*, 15.878–9).[11] At this later stage in his career, Milton was clearly unresponsive to Ovid's fears, expressed years later in
the *Tristia*, that he would die unmourned by his friends back in Rome.
'So I shall die on unknown shores far distant' (*Tam procul ignotis igitur
moriemur in oris*, 2.1.7).

In his 1643 *Apology for Smectymnuus*, Milton somewhat patronizingly
glanced back at his youthful imitations (both Latin and English) of the
classical elegists Ovid, Propertius, and Tibullus, 'Whom both for the
pleasing sound of their numerous writing, which in imitation I found
most easie, and most agreeable to natures part in me, and for their
matter . . . I was so allur'd to read that no recreation came to me better
welcome' (*CPW*, I: 889). Milton glanced back at his days as an apprentice with a naturally gifted affinity for these poets' 'numerous' writing
(their alternating hexameters and pentameters), mastering the rules of
elegiac prosody so precisely that he found them 'easie' to imitate. These
imitative elegies were what he had alluded to a year earlier in *Reason* as
his youthful 'trifles,' circulated among his Italian colleagues as 'proof
of his wit and learning,' proof that he was indeed prepared to begin
ascending the loftier heights of epic. Thus, Milton made clear that his
early experiments with classical elegiac meter were a training ground
that his epic ambitions had left behind.

The passage in *Reason* is an inclusive allusion to Ovid, Propertius,
and Tibullus. But when Milton boasts that he found their elegiac
meters 'most easie' to write, it was to Ovid that he turned, echoing
Ovid's autobiographical reminiscences in the *Tristia* 4 that 'poetry in
meter came unbidden to me' (*Sponte sua Carmen numeros ueniebat ad
aptos*, 25). Thus, as much of this chapter will unfold, did Milton reveal

---

10 *Ovid as an Epic Poet* (Cambridge: Cambridge University Press, 1966).
11 All references to the *Metamorphoses* are taken from the *Metamorphoses*, trans. Frank
   Justus Miller, 2 vols., 3rd ed., rev. G.P. Goold, The Loeb Classical Library (Cambridge, MA: Harvard University Press, 1977).

the difficulty of fully disentangling himself from the Tomitan Ovid he rejected as a poetic model; and thus did the Tomitan Ovid of remote Black Sea shorelines succeed in haunting the young Milton from the grave.

2. Poetry, Place, and the *Mare Ovidianum*

Milton's rejection of Ovidian elegiac meter is profoundly linked to place – specifically, what he termed in *Reason* his newly discovered 'content with these British islands as my world,' indicating that as he begins planning to write vernacular epic, he is entirely 'at home' on the *unheimlich* shores of antiquity's *ultima Britannia*. In this context, we can contrast Milton's carefree, thoroughly Ovidian 'trifle' *Elegia Quinta* (1629–30) with his high Virgilian pastoral elegy *Epitaphium Damonis* (1639–40), written in hexameters in memory of his closest friend Charles Diodati upon the poet's return from his Italian tour.[12] *Elegia Quinta* was the young Milton's contribution to the classical and Neo-Latin genre celebrating the return of spring and the renewal of poetic inspiration. His renewed creativity transported him to the venerable shadows and grottoes of antiquity (*Perque umbras, perque antra feror*, 19) – to the green lawns where the hunter Aeolides waited for the sun; to the flowery fields where satyrs darted; to the copses where the Maenalian Pan roamed; to the benign seas where fleets of dolphins accompanied sailors. As pointed out in the *Variorum Commentary*, the poem alluded frequently to Ovid, perhaps most notably to such episodes in the *Metamorphoses* as Daphne's transformation into a laurel, and Aurora's theft of Cephalus from his wife Procris.[13] So faithfully was the English spring viewed through Ovidian eyes that, some forty years ago, David Daiches identified a central problem of Milton's Latin verse,

---

12 Key studies of Milton's and Diodati's friendship include Donald C. Dorian, *The English Diodatis* (New Brunswick, NJ: Rutgers University Press, 1950); John Shawcross, 'Milton and Diodati: An Esssay in Psychodynamic Meaning,' *Milton Studies* 7 (1975): 127–63; and, most recently, Thomas H. Luxon, *Single Imperfection: Milton, Marriage and Friendship* (Pittsburgh, PA: Duquesne University Press, 2005), 78–85. For a reading of *Elegia Prima* as a chorograhic, 'river'-dialogue between Milton and Diodati, see Elizabeth Jane Bellamy and Rachel Trubowitz, 'A River Runs Through It' (paper given at the 2006 RSA, Cambridge, England).

13 *Commentary on the Poems of John Milton*, ed. John Shawcross and A. Bartlett Giamatti, Vol. I (New York: Columbia University Press, 1970), 74–111.

the poet's problem 'in establishing himself as a native English poet on almost too solid a classical foundation.'[14]

Among other things, Milton seemingly wrote *Epitaphium Damonis*, the last of his Latin poems and generally recognized as the culmination of his early poetry, to solve this problem – to establish himself 'as a native English poet' who, even when composing Latin verse, could transform English landscapes into numinous sites that his poetics could claim as its own. Milton, as the Virgilian shepherd Thyrsis, has lost the friend with whom he planned to share his vernacular epic ambitions. But in *Epitaphium Damonis*, the poet nevertheless attempts, in noticeable contrast to the Ovidian *Elegia Quinta*, to link poetry and a rediscovered appreciation of (local) place. After his turn to British epic, he anticipates being read by the river Ouse (flowing through Buckinghamshire – this is the river Great Ouse, distinct from other rivers with the name Ouse, where the poet long resided), and those who drink the waters of the Alne and Humber, or those who inhabit the forests near Cornwall's Tamar – and, of course, the Thames (175–8). The poet's allusion to the region near 'the Idumenian river' (*Idumansi . . . fluent*, 90) may be the most earnest indication that he is 'content' to write in what was once antiquity's *ultima Britannia*. This estuarial river was identified in Camden's 1607 *Britannia* as the Chelmer flowing into the Blackwater Bay near Essex and, as the famous antiquarian noted, identified in Ptolemy's *Geographia* as *Idumanias fluvius* (II, 45).[15]

As one of the many rivers where early modern English antiquarianism meets ancient Greco-Roman geography, Milton's otherwise obscure Idumenian river also becomes one of the elegy's definitive chorographic ciphers of his readiness to return to British shores to write an epic. Such is the measure of Milton's poetic genius that he is, at one and the same time, never so Virgilian and never so 'English' (i.e., ready to write a vernacular epic) as when he bids farewell to Virgilian pastoral on the shores of what Virgilian pastoral itself (*Eclogues* 1.6) had once identified as *ultima Britannia*. *Epitaphiums Damonis* is the last of Milton's Latin poems – and, arguably, an authoritative final sign that the topos of *ultima Britannnia* had become not just geographically obsolete, but had also lost its power to quarantine early modern English estuaries from the domain of poetry.

---

14 'Some Aspects of Milton's Pastoral Imagery,' *More Literary Essays* (Edinburgh and London, 1968), 100.

15 *Variorum Commentary*, Vol. I, 308.

In Milton's richly allusive farewell to pastoral, not every classical poet was destined to make an appearance. But one poet whose relative absence is worth noting is Ovid.[16] Specifically, I argue for the significance of the fact that entirely absent from *Epitaphium Damonis* are any references to the poetry Ovid wrote in exile on the shores of the Black Sea – an oddity in light of the exile poetry's status as, among other things, an extended meditation on the link between poetry and (loss of) place. To unpack this observation, we should remember that *Epitaphium Damonis* is an attempt to work through two sources of grief – the loss of a close friend and the loss of Diodati and/as Italy, and all that country meant for Milton's development as a poet.[17] One of the elegy's more melancholic lines reveals that Milton's loss of Italy as western literary history's conventional site of a numinous poetics is just as apparent as his reconnection with local English sites: Thyrsis had to bid poignant farewell to his Florentine friend Buonmattei's murmuring Arno (*Arni murmura*, 129–30), as well as to the beautiful Bay of Naples and to Tasso's patron Manso, 'glory of the Chalcidean shore' (*Mansus, Chaleidicae non ultima gloria ripae*, 182).

Throughout literary history, great epic poets have conventionally been associated with bodies of water: Virgil had his Mincius; Tasso had his Sebeto emptying into Manso's Bay of Naples; even Spenser, beyond the Dublin pale, had the 'Mulla mine whose waues I whilom taught to weep.' But the local chorography of *Epitaphium Damonis* prompts a consideration of the extent to which Milton had to convince himself that he could be 'content' with the Ouse, and not Diodati (nor his Italian colleagues writing in sight of the murmuring Arno), as the audience for his epic. At this point, let us turn to Ovid's *Tristia* and its own

---

16 Harding observed that by the time *Epitaphium Damonis* was published, 'concrete evidence of Ovid's influence is almost completely lacking' (56).

17 Culling through Dorian's study of Milton's friendship with Diodati yields ample evidence of the many opportunities Milton had to associate his friend's Anglo-Italian family heritage with *cinquecento* epic. Charles's father, Theodore Diodati, who had immigrated to England from Italy in 1598, served as tutor to the young son of Sir John Harington of Exton, whose first cousin, Sir John Harington of Kelston, was the first English translator of Ariosto's *Orlando furioso* (1591). When the Anglo-Italian John Florio, in the dedicatory epistle to his 1603 English translation of Montaigne's *Essais*, lavishly praised Theodore for his help with the translation, he invoked Tasso: alluding to the seventh book of the *Gerusalemme liberata*, Florio described Diodati as his '*bonus genius*, and sent [to] me as the good Angel to *Raimond* in *Tasso*' (quoted in Dorian, 40).

laying claim to a body of water – not Rome's storied Tiber, but the alien shores of the Black Sea, where the exile, too, had suffered a double loss of friends and of Italy.

Earlier in his career, in the *Fasti*, Ovid conventionally praised Rome as the circuit of the world (*Romanae spacium est urbis et orbis idem*).[18] But such was the irony of the urbane poet's fate that, in 8 A.D., he was exiled by an offended Augustus to the rock-bound regions of the Black Sea near Tomis (*in extremis ignoti partibut quare; Tristia,* 3.3.3). Upon Ovid's reaching Tomis, he claimed that the extreme climate and the tedium of exile had conspired to take their toll on his poetry; and the exile openly declared that his poetic successes were now far behind him. Ovid's exile poetry was, among other things, a detailed chronicle of the demise of a poet whose creativity, or *ingenium*, faded on alien shores far from Rome; and in Tomis, Ovid persistently calibrated the waning of his *ingenium* according to the Black Sea shores' distance from Rome. He devoted the *Tristia* 1.3 to a poignant narration of his last glimpses of Rome. In 3.2, he grieved for sites lost to him forever – Caesar's forum, ancient Numa's palace, the gate of Palatine: 'Rome steals into my thought, my home, and the places I long for' (*Roma domusque subit desideriumque locorum*, 21). In 5.9, he wondered if, exile that he was, his Tomitan poetry would ever be read by his friends back in Rome (*Exul in amissa si tamen Vrbe legor*, 61). And thus, Ovid no longer composed amatory elegies near his beloved Tiber as it flowed into the Mediterranean, but rather elegies of exile on the *apeiron* of the Danube delta as it flowed into the lonely Pontic Sea (*inhospita litora Ponti; Tristia* 3.11.7) – flowed, that is, only on those occasions, as Ovid ruefully recorded, when its waters were not frozen solid by frigid winter winds.

In 5.4, the poetic persona was not Ovid himself but rather one of his exilic epistles, addressed to a friend back in Rome: 'From the Euxine shore have I come, a letter of Naso's' (*Litore ab Euxino Nasonis epistula veni*, 1). Unlike his epistles of exile, Ovid himself would never see Rome again. But Ovid's composing in the voice of one of his own epistles indicated the extent to which 'the Naso of the Euxine' perceived himself as inseparable from his poetics of exile. And although he had lost the Roman *axis mundi*, where he garnered poetic fame for the *Amores*, the *Heroides*, and the *Metamorphoses*, in Tomis, the Euxine's Naso gained a remote shoreline, the material substrate for a new poetics of exile.

---

18 Sir George James Frazer, ed., *Ovid's Fasti*, The Loeb Classical Library (Cambridge, MA: Harvard University Press, 1951), 106.

In her essay on what she terms the *Tristia*'s 'rhetoric of naming,' Ellen Oliensis has observed that Ovid's Pontic shoreline bounded 'a body of water that is certainly ripe for renaming (Mare Ovidianum?).'[19] Her provisional labeling of the Black Sea as the *Mare Ovidianum*, though suggested only in passing, nonetheless gets to the heart of the strange commingling of abjection and poetic ambition that characterized Ovid's shoreline exile; and throughout this chapter I elevate the term *Mare Ovidianum* to the status of a critical concept for discussing the exiled Ovid. In *Tristia* 5.2, the poet narrated: 'I have come to the formless shores of the Euxine waters – this land lies beneath the frigid pole' (*iussus ad Euxini deformia litora veni / aequoris – haec gelido terra sub axe iacet*, 65–66). Ovid's attention to *Euxini deformia litora* left no doubt that he perceived the Black Sea as an *apeiron* of the sort he might have once thought existed only in *ultima Britannia*. But even as the Pontic shoreline threatened to dismantle his poetry, so also did Ovid strive to gain writerly control over this deformed body of water, to incorporate this *apeiron* into his poetry, to claim it as a sea (or anti-sea) 'of his own' in order to define a poetics of exile. The *Mare Ovidianum* resides at the core of what could be read as the epic Ovid supposedly never wrote. And Milton, before writing *Epitaphium Damnis*, might have chosen to reflect further on the extent to which this unlikely body of water set the standard for how to sustain poetic creativity far from the Mediterranean *peirar*.

The obvious explanation for the absence of the *Tristia* in *Epitaphium Damonis* is, of course, what has been discussed earlier as Milton's rejection of the Ovidian elegiac meter that was once – but no more – the source of his youthful 'recreation.' Bradner specifically implicated the *Tristia* in this rejection, the increasingly epic imperative for Milton to spurn 'the softness of the *Amores* and *Tristia*' in order to pursue 'a new seriousness.'[20] For Milton, the elegiac *Tristia* would have been final proof of the received opinion that Ovid's career ended without producing an epic. Ovid composed the *Tristia* in his customary elegiac meter, the prosody that the hexameters of *Epitaphium Damonis* pointedly sought to surpass.

---

19 Ellen Oliensis, 'Return to Sender: The Rhetoric of *Nomina* in Ovid's *Tristia*,' *Ramus* 26 (1997): 183.

20 *Musae Anglicanae*, 116. Ovid himself had described his elegiac meter as 'soft' in the *Amores*, 1:22.

Amidst this discussion of Ovidian meter, we should advance no further without also pausing to consider the always difficult task of assessing Ovidian tone – the Ovidian topos of self-deprecation, so often
challenging readers to penetrate beneath the layers of wit to see if they
can locate a bedrock of seriousness.

Ovidian tone and meter intersected complexly when Ovid himself
once wittily confessed the likelihood that his courting of the *Musa iocasa*
would never allow him anything more than a 'soft' flirtation with epic.
In the famous opening lines of the *Amores*, the poet narrated that he
was prepared to write of 'arms and violent wars,' with meter suiting
matter (in dactylic hexameter). But when he attempted to write the second hexameter, the mischievous Cupid stole a foot, leaving him with
merely an elegiac couplet (*Arma graui numero uiolentaque bella parabam /
edere, material conueniente modis. / par erat inferior uersus: risisse Cupido /
dicitur atque unum surripuisse pedem*, 1–4).[21] No prosodic harm done, as
it turned out, for the poet preferred composing not in epic hexameters
but in the alternating hexameters and pentameters of the elegiac meter
that defined the lamenting and lamentable poet-lover. For the poet of
the *Amores*, form most effectively mirrored content – i.e., meter was
best suited to matter – not when he wrote of arms and wars, but when
his 'limping' verse reflected the 'matter' of his lamentable state. All of
which is to say, the shrewd Ovid knew that suffering was never more
inherently poetic than when his verse 'limped' in elegiac lament.

'Mournful is my state,' writes Ovid, 'mournful therefore is my song,
for the work is suited to its theme' (*flebilis ut noster status est, ita flebile
carmen, / materiae scripto conueniente suae*). Here, Ovid again strives to
match content, his mournful 'matter,' to form, the 'limping' meter of
elegy. But these lines appear not in the *Amores* but in the *Tristia* (5.1.5–6),
where Ovid, no longer the Roman poet but the Tomitan Ovid of exile,
suggests to the reader that his 'limping' verse may, indeed, be a version
of epic.

In the *Tristia*'s second epistle, Ovid claims to write verse even as he
embarks on the dangerous journey to Tomis on a storm-tossed Adriatic. He laments: 'Wretched me! What vast mountains of water heave
themselves aloft! Now, now, you think, they will touch the highest
stars. What mighty abysses settle beneath us as the flood yawns apart!

---

21 The reference to the *Amores* is taken from *Ovid's 'Amores': Book One*, ed., trans. John
    A. Barsby (Oxford: Clarendon Press, 1973).

Now, now, you think they will touch black Tartarus' (*me miserum,* *quanti montes volvuntur aquarum! / iam iam tacturos sidera summa putes. / Quantae diducto subsidunt aequore ualles! / iam iam tacturas Tartara nigra putes,* 1.2.19–22). From Ovid's perspective, elegy's 'limping' meter is, indeed, the most appropriate prosodic form for presenting the content of his suffering: his otherwise 'limping' meters mark perfect time to the stomach-churning ascents and plunging descents of his helpless vessel. In the *Tristia* 3.1, Ovid observes that if his poetry strikes readers as damaged, 'if the lame couplets halt in alternate verses, 'tis due to the metre's nature or to the length of the journey' (*vel pedis hoc ratio uel via longa facit,* 12). In this carefully crafted line, Ovid links elegy's limping verse with the voice of exilic suffering itself: his poetry limps because he has deliberately chosen elegy as the definitive meter of his exiled persona. More to the point, only the virtuosic poet – the preeminently suffering poet bereft of friends and home – can recruit the 'lame feet' of elegy in the service of composing what he insists, in the *ex Ponto,* could resemble the scope of epic: 'Should I attempt to a full record of them [my misfortunes] in verse, there will be a long Iliad of my fate' (*quae tibi si memori coner perscribere versu, / Ilias est fati longa futura mei,* 2.7.33–4). If in the *Amores,* he confessed, in some sense, that he fell one metric foot short of an epic, in the *Tristia,* the missing foot is, as it were, no 'impediment' to an exploration of epic suffering.

The *Tristia*'s epic posturing will be discussed in more detail in the next section. At this point, suffice to say that Milton's *Epitaphium Damonis* refused to entertain Ovid's debonair argument that his 'limping' meter had composed an epic. Put another way, the young Milton seemed disinclined to become an older Ovid, marking time in elegiac meter, an exiled poet Milton viewed as perpetually deferred from epic destiny. But what *Epitaphium Damonis* and its exploration of the link between poetry and place (specifically, the loss of numinous poetic sites) could not deny was that on the desolate shores of the Euxine, Ovid's poetics had converted loss of friends and Roman home into a shoreline of his own.

3. Tomitan Ovid: Writing a Pontic Epic on the *Apeiron*

One of this chapter's earlier claims was that even the Tomitan Ovid had every ambition to secure his place within the Greco-Roman literary tradition. In the context of this claim, worth rehearsing are samplings of his many descriptions of the Black Sea and how banishment on remote shores far from the Roman *mare nostrum* culminated in the *Mare*

Ovidianum as the definitive trope of his poetics of exile. Upon entering the Pontic, he prays for safe passage (*nunc quoque tuta, precor, vasti secet ostia Ponti, / quasque petit, Getici litoris intret aquas,* 1.10.15). He is benumbed by the Black Sea's frost (*ustus ab assiduo frigore Pontus habet,* 3.2.9); and he insists to potentially skeptical readers that 'I have seen the vast sea stiff with ice, a slippery shell holding the water motionless. And seeing is not enough; I have trodden the frozen sea' (*vidimus ingentem glacie consistere pontum,/ lubricaque inmotas testa premebat aquas. / nec vidisse sat est; durum calcavimus aequor, undaque non udo sub pede summa fuit,* 3.10.37–40). The unnaturally shaped Black Sea (*iussus ad Euxini deformia litora veni,* 5.2.65) seemingly defines the *apeiron* itself. Though Tomis is located at the mouth of the Danube, one encounters not the rhythmic flow of estuarial currents emptying into the sea, but rather waters eerily frozen into place (2.198). In the *ex Ponto*, Ovid reports that the once dark-blue waters of the eastern Danube, as it flows to the sea, are frost-congealed when 'the winter makes even the sea a highway for one foot' (*hic freta vel pediti pervia reddit hiems,* 4.10.27–9). No estuary could be more antithetical to the Tiber of his beloved Rome; on the Danube's delta, no exile could be further from his native land (*viterior nulli quam mihi terra data est; Tristia* 2.198).

One way Ovid cultivated his exilic pose was to interweave the threads of his shoreline trope within the Black Sea's conflicted etymology. At one point, the poet hopes he will not have to endure another birthday on 'the remotest part of the world, Pontus, falsely called Euxine' (*dum me terrarum pars paene novissima, Pontus / Euxinus falso nomine dictus, habet,* 3.13.27–8). As noted in the Loeb edition, one meaning of the name 'Euxine' is 'hospitable.' Thus does Ovid tease out the central irony of this ill-named body of water when he laments that 'the cold shores of the Pontus Euxinus keep me' (*frigida me cohibent Euxini litora Ponti,* 4.4.55), confirming that the *inhospita litora Ponti* are imprisonment itself. He responds, then, to the challenge of attempting to take verse possession of a body of water that has been named both a 'hospitable' Euxine and a hostile, ice-bridged Pontus. Philip Hardie puts this challenge in further perspective when he observes that the poet's Scythian Pontus 'is both the geographic name of Ovid's place of exile – and a Greek word for 'sea,'' so alien it resists 'proper' naming.[22] Seeking to

---

22 Philip Hardie, *Ovid's Poetics of Illusion* (Cambridge: Cambridge University Press, 2002), 295.

rename the Pontus, Ovid is instead immersed in the Pontic Sea's play on words, its 'inhospitable' waters' satiric play on the 'hospitable' Euxine name, and a cognate *pont*-ic sea punningly defined by its remote ice-bridges. Hence, the more Ovid seeks to merge the literally named Pontic and the absurdly named Euxine shores, the more his verse willingly indulges in linguistic contamination: 'I'm afraid amid my Latin, Sintic or Pontic words you'll find I use' (*timeo ne Sintia mixta Latinis inque meis scriptis Pontica verba legas*, 3.14.49–50).[23] On the remote shores of the Black Sea, his poetic *ingenium* is reduced to speaking 'Pontic,' the language of Pontus – and, hence, a topos in two senses of the word. 'Pontic' is both a regional dialect (the degraded Greek of a Roman colony), and the language of the *apeiron* as the topos of a no-place between land and sea.

In the *Tristia* 3.4, as mentioned earlier, Ovid begs an anonymous friend in Rome to 'love your Naso's name – the only part of him not yet in exile: all else the Scythian Pontus possesses.' All of which is to argue that although Pontus has no 'proper' name, Ovid has succeeded in inscribing *his* name within a play on naming itself: he urges his (un-named) friend to remember 'Naso' back in Rome, even after the body bearing his name perishes on a shore that itself has no 'proper' name. And thus, one of the *Tristia's* most resonant lines is the conclusion to 3.4.46: *All else the Scythian Pontus possesses,* Ovid writes in 'Pontic'; and as the *Mare Ovidianum* writes an epitaph for his exilic poetics, the poet sends back to Rome a self-confessed inelegant volume of poems, 'as becomes the book of an exile' (*incultus, qualem decet exulis esse,* 1.1.3).

But paradoxically, Ovid's abjection also constitutes a witty account of survival, a calculated commingling of the modesty topos (i.e., an invitation to readers to witness his waning poetic powers on frozen shores) with a shrewd awareness that he is shaping a new poetic genre on his *Mare Ovidianum*. The Tomitan Ovid's poetry is both *incultus*, inelegant, and a sophisticated exploration of the paradoxes and punning etymologies that constitute a new poetics of shoreline exile.

I now briefly ponder (without definitively answering) the question: was Ovid's effort to take writerly possession of this *Mare Ovidianum* tantamount to writing (with whatever degree of attendant irony) a Pontic epic? In an aforementioned line from *ex Ponto*, Ovid alerts his readers to expect a long Iliad of his misfortune. To be sure, this claim can be dismissed as nothing more than Ovid's empty recitation of the

---

23 Ovid alludes to some Getic verses he wrote in *ex Ponto*, 4.13.ff.

post-Homeric topos of an 'Iliad of suffering.'[24] But there can be no ig-
noring that he inventively plays with the topos, almost daring his readers to mock his epic pretensions.

Discerning readers of Ovid (including Milton – along with Marlowe,
perhaps early modern England's ablest reader of Ovidian wit) could
scarcely be blamed for guarding against a possible Ovidian trap. A formidable obstacle to assessing the tone of Ovid's claim that, on Pontic
shores, he experienced suffering of Iliadic proportions is his aforementioned career-long courting of the *Musa iocosa* that has notoriously
eluded attempts to separate the man from the poetic persona. Since the
1980s, an influential trend in Ovid criticism, taking issue with a long
scholarly tradition that mined Ovid's Pontic elegies for concrete biographical information, has paid far greater attention to the perceived
ambiguity of Ovid's exilic voice.[25] Gareth Williams, for example, reveals the Tomitan poet as a 'dissimulating,' self-deprecating Ovid, who
often cultivates an exilic pose (2). In such a scheme, Ovid's exile poetry
is not simply a transparent series of pleas for sympathy (not only from
his friends but also from his emperor Augustus), but just as often self-
conscious experiments in a shoreline epic unfolding not in Ulysses's
Aegean but on Pontic shores.

In the final poem of the *ex Ponto*, Ovid complains that it is uncharitable for readers to point out shortcomings in his poetics of exile, for
he himself has long since surrendered to the label of 'a Getic poet,' a
poet among barbarians (*nec te mirari si sint uitiosa decebit / carmina, quae
faciam paene poeta Getes*, 4.17–18). This is just one of many moments in
the exile poetry where the Ovidian modesty topos deploys the tactic of
the preemptive strike – a well-timed art of self-deprecation (describing
his poetry as *incultus*, for example) before his readers can find fault. But

---

24 For Plutarch's use of the topos, see Matthew McGowan, *Ovid in Exile: Power and
Poetic Redress in the 'Tristia' and 'Epistulae ex Ponto'* (Leiden and Boston: Brill, 2009),
173n16.

25 One of the most respected examples of the earlier era of Ovid scholarship is L.P.
Wilkinson, *Ovid Recalled* (Cambridge: Cambridge University Press, 1955). Notable
examples of the more recent trend include Betty Rose Nagle, *The Poetics of Exile:
Program and Polemic in the 'Tristia' and 'Epistulae ex Ponto' of Ovid*, Collection Latomus,
170 (Brussels, 1980); E.J. Kenney, 'Ovid,' in *The Cambridge History of Classical Literature*, eds. W.V. Clausen and E.J. Kenney, Vol. 2 (Cambridge, 1982): 420–57; Gareth
D. Williams, *Banished Voices: Readings in Ovid's Exile Poetry* (Cambridge: Cambridge
University Press, 1994); Claassen, *Displaced Persons*, 1999; Hardie, *Ovid's Poetics of Illusion*, 2002; and McGowan, *Ovid in Exile*, 2009.

within this pattern of self-deprecation, there is no overlooking a lingering Roman sophistication that underwrites the Pontic exile's lament. And at this stage, we can connect with some recent scholarship that reads Ovid's exilic poetry as challenging the long-accepted view that the famous poet of amatory elegy never wrote an epic. E.J. Kenney and Sidney Hinds have argued that Latin elegy in general 'can be defined negatively as "not-epic" . . . epic is constantly immanent within elegy as the term against which it defines itself.'[26] Turning to Ovid in particular, Stephen Harrison has recently argued that if the *Tristia*, especially the first book, 'is concerned to differentiate itself from love elegy, it is also concerned to assimilate to epic.'[27] Did Ovid accept that elegy was the genre that had to be abandoned in order to write an epic? This is not to suggest that Ovid formally wrote an epic (and he certainly wrote nothing that the Renaissance would recognize as an epic); but he did sustain poetic ambition on the shores of the Black Sea where, in *ex Ponto*, he makes the aforementioned prediction that his lasting poetic legacy will be 'an Iliad of misfortune.'

In the *Tristia* 1.1, Ovid instructs his reader to 'Pray bring the Maeonian and cast just as many dangers about him; all his genius will fall away in the presence of such great ills' (*da mihi Maeoniden et tot circumice casus, / ingenium tantis excidet omne malis*, 47–8). In 1.3, the poet, gazing upon his Tomitan isolation, writes: 'If one may use in a lowly case a lofty example, such was the appearance of Troy in the hour of her capture' (*si licet exemplis in paruo grandibus uti, / haec facies Troiae, cum caperetur, erat*, 25–6). In 1.5, he persistently competes with Ulysses: 'He wandered over but a narrow space in many years between the homes of Dulichium and Ilium; I, after traversing seas whole constellations apart, have been banished by Caesar's anger to the bay of the Getae' (*ille brevi spatio multis errauit in annis / inter Dulichias Iliacasque domos: / nos freta sideribus totis distantia mensos / detulit in Geticos Caesaris ira sinus*, 58–62). Whereas Ulysses was often accompanied by a band of loyal comrades, Ovid reminds his readers that in his exile he has been abandoned by friends (*me profugum comites deseruere mei*, 64). In Ovid's estimation, Ulysses's temporary exile from Ithaca was not really so earth-shattering. Ovid, after all, was exiled from Rome, whose seven

---

26 'Elegiac poetry, Latin,' in *The Oxford Classical Dictionary*, 3rd ed. (Oxford: Oxford University Press, 1998).

27 'Ovid and Genre: Evolutions of an Elegist,' in *The Cambridge Companion to Ovid*, ed. Philip Hardie (Cambridge: Cambridge University Press, 2002), 90.

hills gaze on the world, on the gods – on sovereignty itself (*sed quae de septum totum circumspicit orbem / Montibus, imperii Roma deumque locus*, 69–70). The same gods finally permitted Ulysses to return to Ithaca, but for Ovid there is no end in sight to exile. He insists to his readers that he has suffered so much misfortune on sea and land that Ulysses was lucky in comparison (*tot mala sum fugiens tellure, tot aequore passas / te quoque ut auditis posse dolore putem. / crede mihi, si sit nobis collates Vlixes*, 3.11.59–61). In 1.5.57, he urges: 'Ye learned poets, write of my evils instead of the Neritian' (*pro duce Neritio mala nostra, poetae, / scribite: Neritio nam mala plura tuli*, 57–9).[28]

Perhaps what is finally at stake here is not whether Ovid wrote an epic, but rather the virtuosity with which he places the burden of proof on even his most skeptical readers to argue that he did *not* write an epic.

Throughout his exile poetry Ovid persistently links his suffering (*mala*) and the toll it took on his creativity (*ingenium*), as in his aforementioned lament that misfortune has broken his talent (3.14). But Ovid's complex mutual interplay between *mala* and *ingenium* produced something more than mere pathos: it became his epic subject – in the process calling into question his own claims that the decline of his poetic career directly correlated with his distance from Rome. To be sure, Homer wrote a stirring epic about separation from home. But on the shores of the Black Sea, one should not completely dismiss Ovid's aim to become his *own* epic protagonist, inserting the *Mare Ovidianum* within the fabric of the literary history of epic. The *Mare Ovidianum*, far from dismantling his poetry, gave the poet his own 'Pontic' epic vernacular voice. And thus did Ovid succeed in writing a version of epic on the *apeiron* of the Black Sea. I now turn to the young Milton who rejected the Ovid of exile.

4. Rejecting the Pose of Ovidian Exile

Though dated, James Holly Hanford's account of the young Milton's ambition still makes for compelling reading. Hanford emphasizes the

---

28 Wilkinson has observed that 'we find ourselves congratulating him on each new point he wins in this odd contest of rivalry' (319). Hardie has also pointed out an Ovidian parallel with Aeneas. In the *Tristia* 1.2, the poet narrates the violent storm that almost drowned him during the first stage of his journey from Rome to Tomis. Whereas a storm-tossed Aeneas eventually made it to Rome, the storm-tossed Ovid never saw Rome again (285).

poet's 'studied decorum, the result of a strong personal reserve and of the strict tradition under which Milton had so carefully schooled himself.'[29] After discussing three of the young Milton's Latin elegies, written prior to his Italian tour, I will focus on the years immediately following his return from Italy – in particular, the 'studied decorum' with which the poet expelled the *Mare Ovidianum* from his career trajectory.

Milton's rejection of Ovid as he soared to epic heights is, of course, a significant moment in the English poet's literary biography. Although the Roman poet's potent mix of naive abjection and sophisticated, learned wit had once enticed the precocious Milton of St. Paul's and Cambridge, the excesses of Ovidian wit, as Milton scholarship has amply demonstated, diminished in appeal for the apprentice poet. But this diminished appeal exposed Milton as an inconsistent reader of the *Tristia*. On the one hand, Milton did not take seriously the truth value of the not-Virgil Ovid's claim to have written an epic, least of all on Pontic shores. But on the other hand, Milton seemed particularly prone to take seriously Ovid's topos of a failed poetics – the Tomitan poet's exile as hostile to poetry. That is, Milton seems to have read the *Tristia*'s complex commingling of *mala* and *ingenium* at face value as a serious cautionary tale for declaring one's creative vulnerability on remote shores, an unwelcome message for a poet 'content' to reclaim *ultima Britannia* 'as my world.'

Milton was, of course, intimately acquainted with the poetry Ovid wrote during his Tomitan exile; and at this point we are well-reminded that the exilic final stage in Ovid's poetic career was, in fact, the *first* stage of Milton's poetic career. Years ago, Harding traced a clear-cut trajectory for the young Milton's engagements with Ovid, from his education at St. Paul's to Cambridge to the years following his tour of Italy.[30] Harding noted that the curriculum at St. Paul's began pupils' study of Ovid with the *Tristia*, later advancing to the *Heroides* and the *Metamorphoses*. The *Tristia* served as a kind of training ground for learning the rules of Latin prosody, a first step before eventually turning to Ovid's more sustained narrative poetry. For Milton, shedding not only

---

29 James Holly Hanford, 'The Youth of Milton: An Interpretation of His Early Literary Developments,' in *Studies of Shakespeare, Milton and Donne* (by members of the English Department of the University of Michigan) (New York: MacMillan, 1925), 9.

30 Harding, *Milton and the Renaissance Ovid*. For Ovid's influence on the early modern English curriculum in general, see Baldwin, II.

the erotic poetry of the earlier Ovid, but also the exilic poetics of the Roman poet's final career phase was a necessary first step in his carefully choreographed epic ambitions. Though he resided in antiquity's *ultima Britannia*, there was, from the ambitious young poet's perspective, no reason to feel inadequate about composing on the edges of the Roman world. After all, the poetry Ovid wrote on *his* periphery of the Roman empire was reducible to a mere first stage in Milton's imitation of Latin poetry – and his eventual turn to vernacular epic.

For Milton, a rejection of Ovid was tantamount to forgetting to 'love your Naso's name,' particularly evident in three of his Latin elegies, two written to Diodati and one written to Thomas Young, a former tutor. These elegies indulge in the somewhat risky business of expressing a false sympathy for an Ovid who knew best how to convert self-mockery of his *mala carmina* on the remote shores of the Roman empire into a poetics of the *Mare Ovidianum*.

Martz once described *Elegia Prima* as 'that playful and thoroughly Ovidian elegy composed by the arrogantly clever and quite unrepentant sophomore' during his rustication by Cambridge' (37). The elegy does not disguise the poet's irreverence toward the Cambridge officials responsible for his rustication. But at least partially informing Martz's description of the poem's tone is what editorial commentary has long noted, i.e., Milton's assuming an Ovidian pose to record the delights of London during his rustication – most notably, his glimpsing, just beyond the city limits, of London's young virgins (50–3), an obvious imitation of Ovid's description of the virgins of Rome in *Ars Amatoria* 3.168.[31] In returning to *Elegia Prima*, I wish to explore the extent to which Milton was just as inclined to forget the exiled 'Naso's name' as he was to ventriloquize Ovidian eroticism.

Throughout the elegy, Milton plays fast and loose with the pose of Ovidian exile, seemingly testing Diodati on when the poet adopts an

---

31 Milton's gazing at the virgins is best read tropically rather than autobiographically. Stella Revard has cogently noted that Milton's verb *videas*, meaning 'you may see [the virgins],' is noncommittal, opposed to the more definite *video*, or 'I see' (*Milton and the Tangles of Neaera's Hair: The Making of the 1645 'Poems'* [Columbia, MO: University of Missouri Press, 1997], 15). For Milton's self-presentation as an Ovid in exile in this poem, see Hanford, 'The Youth of Milton,' 109, and Walter MacKellar, *The Latin Poems of John Milton* (New Haven: Yale University Press, 1930), 22. For the elegy's implicit parallels between Milton's London and Ovid's Rome, see Condee, *Structure in Milton's Poetry*, 22.

exilic pose and when he holds it in disdain. Engaging in breezy, competitive banter with his addressee, Milton notes that Diodati's letter has reached him from a distant land (*terras remotas*, 5); and he uses chorographic tropes to displace Diodati onto shores that resemble antiquity's *apeiron*: 'At last, dear friend, your letter has come to me and its news-laden pages have brought me your words – brought them from the western bank of the Dee beside Chester, where with precipitate current it seeks the Irish Sea' (*Tandem, care, tuae mihi pervenere tabellae, / Pertulit et voces nuntia charta tuas, / Pertulit occidua devae Cestrensis ab ora / Vergivium prono qua petit amne salum*, 1–4).[32] Within this bantering framework, Milton represents Diodati as a kind of Ovidian exile, with the poet himself playing the role of one of Ovid's Roman friends, reading the poet's exilic elegies at a safe distance from Pontic shores. (It may be no mere coincidence that Ovid and Diodati – for the moment – both reside on the 'western' shores of, respectively, the Danube and Dee estuaries.)

The young Milton's Rome, following his rustication by Cambridge, is, of course, 'the city which the Thames washes with its tidal waters' (*Me tenet urbs reflua quam Thamesis alluit unda*, 9). The poet's local tidal waves do not scour (like the Dee of his addressee) but rather gently lave their shores, even suggesting that Milton has regained a kind of Mediterranean *peirar* denied the Tomitan exile forced to bid farewell to the benign shores of the Mediterranean and reside in the frozen Danube. Milton continues portraying himself as, paradoxically, an exile alternately free from or, unlike the Tomitan Ovid, thriving in exile. The poet revels in his new-found urban freedom and leisure during his rustication from Cambridge: 'The bare fields, so niggardly of pleasant shade, have no charm for me. How wretchedly suited that place is to the worship of Phoebus' (*Nuda nec arva placent, umbrusque negantia molles / Quam male Phoebicolis convenit ille locus*, 13–14). He claims that if his pleasant interlude in London is indeed exile, then he welcomes banishment; and he speculates: 'Ah! Would that the bard who was a pitiful exile in the land of Tomis had never had to bear anything worse! Then he would have yielded nothing to Ionian Homer and you, O Maro, would have been conquered and stripped of your prime honors' (*Ille Tomitano flebilis exul agro; / Non tunc Ionio quicquam cessisset Homero / Neve foret victo laus tibi prima, Maro*, 22–4). In this brash rewriting of the *Tristia*, the London-

---

32 Milton's chorographic greeting could also be read as a coded tribute to Diodati as a fellow poet who, two years earlier, had a poem included in a volume of verses dedicated to the memory of Camden, *Camdeni Insignia*.

dwelling Milton converts exile into freedom and regains the 'Rome' forever lost to the Tomitan Ovid. Thus, the lines are less a poignant tribute to Ovid than a window through which to view Milton's future intention to 'overgo' the exiled poet who never wrote an epic. Paying tribute to Homer's native home of Ionia and customarily addressing Virgil by his family name of 'Maro,' Milton refers to Naso only as the *flebilis exul*.

Milton's allusion is a prime example of irreverent play with the exiled Ovid. The allusion addresses neither Ovid the Roman poet, nor Naso, the Tomitan exile: he casts a deaf ear to Ovid's exhortation and, forgetting his 'Naso's name,' eulogizes the poignant Naso as an exile without a name. And thus had the curriculum at St. Paul's tutored the precocious poet well in how to counterpose Ovid's favored epithet of abjection with his own poetic ambitions to become not a Naso writing on remote shores but a Homer or a Maro.

Rand explicitly identified the poet of the 1629 *Elegia Sexta* as 'a young Ovid' (111). But perhaps more to the point is how the young Milton-as-Ovid again strategically defines his poetic voice in opposition to the 'older' Ovid of exile. The elegy can readily be included among those early poems that document the young Milton's poetic ambitions; again written to Diodati, the elegy also articulates his ambition over and against the trope of Ovidian exile. Early in the elegy, the poet robustly celebrates the drunken feasts of Bacchus as a source of poetic inspiration, but it concludes with the poet mentioning that he has finished composing *The Nativity Ode*. In response to Diodati's complaint that he himself has been abandoned by the muse, Milton encourages his friend to take advantage of the merriment of the Christmas holidays to continue composing. Bear in mind, he writes, that Ovid 'sent bad verses from the Corallian fields because there were no banquets in that land and the vine had not been planted' (*Naso Corallaeis mala carmina misit ab agris; / Non illic epulae, non sata vitas erit*, 19–20). Exiled in desolate Tomis, bereft of vinous inspiration, even Ovid could send no more competent verse back to Rome than *mala carmina*.

As in *Elegia Prima*, Milton's sustains a competitive and highly allusive banter with Diodati at the expense of the exiled Ovid, from whom he is determined to keep an urbane distance. But there may be no exit from the allusive density of Ovidian wit – no exit from the *Mare Ovidianum* and its thwarting of any attempt to reduce Ovidian exile to a mere cautionary tale of the perils of writing verse in isolation.

The difficulty of locating an exit from the labyrinth of Ovidian wit is no better illustrated than in Milton's *Elegia Quarta* (1627), written to the

Scots Presbyterian Thomas Young, his former tutor at St. Paul's and a
pastor residing amidst religious turmoil in Hamburg. The elegy is written with affection and concern for Young's safety; but it also reveals a
young poet underestimating the complexities of the 'old' Ovid's poetics
of exile.

It was under Young's tutelage that Milton had first learned to lis-
ten to the *Tristia*'s voice of exile; and thus, in the elegy's opening lines,
Milton expresses his concern for Young, who is 'alone on that strange
soil,' banished to war-torn 'Teutonic' lands (*Vivis et ignoto solus inopsque
solo*, 84). The poet worries that 'in regions bordering upon you wars are
ready to burst out' (*In tibi finitimus bella tumere locis*, 72); and the surrounding fields are blood-soaked and carcass-strewn. Thus does Milton, safely tucked away on English shores (*Mittit ab Angliaco littore fida
manus*, 52), portray Young as a version of the Tomitan exile to whom his
tutor had introduced him.

Milton explicitly alludes to the *Tristia* when he urges his letter to
soar swiftly to its addressee: 'Obtain for yourself, if you can, the swift
team by which the Colchian was borne away in her flight from the face
of her husband, or that by which the boy, Triptolemus, reached the
bounds of Scythia, when he was sent, a welcome messenger, from the
Eleusinian city' (*At tu, si poteris, celeries tibi sume iugales, / Vecta quibus
Colchis fugit ab ore viri; / Aut queis Triptolemus Scythicas devenit in oras, /
Gratus Eleusina missus ab urbe puer*, 9–12). As Milton's editors have noted,
the young poet's allusion echoes as many as three of Ovid's works -
the *Heroides* (6, 129–38), narrating Medea's flight in a dragon-drawn
chariot after murdering Jason's children; the *Metamorphoses* (5, 643–50),
narrating Triptolemus's flight to Scythia to introduce agriculture to the
remote region; and the *Tristia* 3.8. Of the three sources, Milton most
likely alluded to the *Tristia*, where Ovid pointedly juxtaposes these two
mythic figures. But Milton's otherwise thoughtfully chosen allusion to
the *Tristia* proves unable to contain the complexity of Ovid's coupling
of Triptolemus and Medea. Teasing out the full context of Ovid's invoking of these mythic figures reveals how the 'swift teams' of Milton's
Triptolemus and Medea run with the bit, transforming the young poet
into a Phaeton no longer in control of his allusion.

To pursue this argument, we should detour first through the *Tristia*
3.10, not insignificantly judged by Ovid scholarship as the exiled poet's
most vivid account of the extreme winters that ravaged his poetry –
or so he claimed. He is under constant threat not only from freezing
coastal winds but also from marauding tribes (hence the allusiveness of

Milton's portrayal of the endangered Young) – the Sauromatae, the Bessi, the Getae – barbarous names 'unworthy of my talent' (*quam non ingenio nomina digna meo!*, 6). But when he narrates how these savage hordes routinely cross the iced-over Danube to invade Tomis and lay waste to the countryside, Ovid's presumably declining *ingenium* deftly tests the alertness of his readers, who are expected to recognize his echoes of the well-known 'Scythian digression' in Virgil's *Georgics* 3.349–83.[33] In this passage, Virgil, playing on Scythian remoteness as a founding axiom for Roman poetry, praises his beloved Italy as the cradle of agriculture, opposing his native country to an abhorrent Scythia, where both the extreme climate and roving barbarians discourage the cultivation of crops. The purpose of Virgil's digression is not to present his readers with an actual geographical Scythia (for example, he never mentions by name the Black Sea that was destined to become the particular locus of Ovid's exile); rather, he invokes a generically remote region – most likely mediated by Herodotus's own mediated Scythia – in order to set up a telling contrast to the benign climate of his beloved homeland.

Unlike the generic topoi that characterize Virgil's discursive Scythia, the exiled Ovid offers memorable details of a *real* Scythia: large patches of snow that do not melt for two years; icicles that form on beards; frozen wine that can be consumed only when broken into chips (13–24). His Scythia, no longer relegated to Virgilian digression, is now the central focus of Ovidian poetic labor. And even as Ovid must now concede that he is himself a Scythian (an inhabitant of the *Georgics'* not-Italy), so also do his eyewitness reports pointedly rewrite Virgil's Scythian digression: if nothing else, Ovid's exile means that he, not Virgil, is the more reliable authority on Scythia. Though expressing concern that the recitation of the names of the Scythian barbarians who cross the icy Danube may strike readers back in Rome as inherently unpoetic, Ovid suggests that he has at least earned some measure of ethnographic authority – however dubious the honor may be judged by Roman sensibilities. Even if readers will not accept his claim that he was the protagonist of his own Pontic epic, they must nonetheless accept that his poetry of exile succeeded in charting a real Scythia for Roman *mappae mundi*.

---

33 For Ovid's echoes of Virgil's Scythian digression, see L.P. Wilkerson, *The Georgics of Virgil: A Critical Survey* (Cambridge, 1970), 98; S. Besslich, 'Ovid's Winter in Tomis,' *Gymnasium* 79 (1972): 177–91; Harry B. Evans, 'Winter and Warfare in Ovid's Tomis,' *Classical Journal* 70, no. 3 (1975): 1–9.

All of which is to point out that even on the Black Sea's frozen shores, Ovid's presumably fading *ingenium* thrives, transforming self-deprecation into a hyper-literary competitiveness not only with his Augustan rival Virgil but also with his own earlier Roman persona. Later in 3.10, Ovid wryly contends that had Leander lived near the frozen shores of a wintry Black Sea, the ill-fated lover would never have drowned (37–40). In a display of poetic virtuosity, Ovid both critiques his own earlier account of Leander in *Heroides* 18, while also wittily implying that the ethnographic authority resulting from his exile in Virgil's not-Italy has exposed the potential meaningless of mythic legend itself. Decades ago, the classicist Hermann Fränkel made an observation that, in this context, deserves excavation: in *Tristia* 3.8, he writes, mythic legend 'lost its point in the absurd country in which the poet was banished.'[34]

The extent to which exile, if nothing else, had inspired Ovid's muse of debonair self-reference is also evident two poems earlier in *Tristia* 3.8, where the poet alludes to the two mythological figures of Triptolemus and Medea (now, late in his career, essentially Ovidian *exempla*) to express his longing to return to Rome: 'Now would I crave to stand in the car of Triptolemus who flung the untried seed on ground that had known it not; now would I bridle the dragons that Medea had when she fled thy citadel Corinth' (*Nunc ego Triptolemi cuperem consistere curru / misit in ignotam qui rude semen humum; / nunc ego Medeae uellem frenare dracones / quos habuit fugiens arce, Corinthe, tua*). Triptolemus, charged by Ceres to spread agriculture throughout the world, journeyed from Athens to Europe to Asia and, finally, to Scythia; and it was in Tomis where Medea murdered her brother Absyrtus. But Ovid's preoccupation is not with Triptolemus's and Medea's mythic identities (as, respectively, seed-bearer and perpetrator of fratricide) but with their Scythian associations. Ovid wishes he could guide Triptolemus's chariot or the Colchian Medea's yoked dragons back to Rome – perhaps yet another plea for sympathy from the *flebilis exul* from whom Milton was so intent on distancing himself. But the poet of the *Tristia* also wryly signals that his poetics of exile has now forever allied the mythic prestige of Triptolemus and Medea with the frozen remoteness of his Scythian 'home' on the *Mare Ovidianum*.

Earlier in his poetic career, in happier times, Ovid himself had narrated the stories of both figures. But in an elaborate exercise in

---

34 *Ovid: A Poet Between Two Worlds* (Berkeley and Los Angeles: University of California Press, 1945), 125–6.

self-reference, the poet once again opposes the Roman and Tomitan Ovids. In effect, he overrides and rewrites the earlier works that had rewarded him with poetic fame (the same works that, we are well-reminded, supplanted the *Tristia* in the curricular hierarchy of Milton's St. Paul's): he drains Triptolemus and Medea – herself a fugitive – of their mythic aura and relocates them from dreamy myth to the nightmares of Scythian geography. The Tomitan Ovid confirms for his readers that the Roman Ovid's recounting of the stories of Medea and Triptolemus had insensitively neglected these figures' explicit ties to Scythia. No one was more aware than Ovid that Virgil had never mentioned the Black Sea by name. And thus does Ovid drive home the point that only by enduring the trials of exile on the shores of the Black Sea can a poet learn that these *exempla* must be repositioned geographically within a real Scythia, where mythopoesis cedes place to the *Mare Ovidianum*. The Tomitan Ovid exposes the Roman Ovid as having gotten it all wrong: Leander could not possibly have drowned on the Black Sea's frozen waters; and Scythia's barren steppes are clear evidence that Triptolemus never visited there. Exposing the lies of myth becomes the 'truth' of the *Mare Ovidianum*.

With incantatory resonance, Milton hopes his letter will reach his former tutor as swiftly as the Colchian Medea fled Corinth, or as swiftly as Triptolemus arrived in Scythia to sow seed. But no allusion to Ovid's Triptolemus and Medea can be complete without first passing through the *Tristia*'s deployment of these figures to undermine myth itself. The young Milton consistently distances himself not just from the Ovid of abject exile but also from the Tomitan Ovid of poetic virtuosity, who learned to transport the *ars poetica* from Rome to a bleak region that Virgil had quarantined from poetry itself.

I now reconnect with Milton and his strategic rejection of the pose of Ovidian exile in the years immediately following the English poet's Italian tour.

In the process of collecting his early poems for publication in the 1645 *Poems of Mr. John Milton, Both English and Latin*, Milton appended to *Elegia Septima*, generally recognized as his most erotic poem, a palinode. This oft-cited palinode took the form of the ambitious poet's renunciation of his imitations of the excesses of the Ovid of the *Ars Amatoria*: 'These are the monuments to my wantonness that with a perverse spirit and a trifling purpose I once erected' (*Haec ego mente olim laeva, studioque supino, / Nequitiae posui vana trophaea meae*). The palinode continues in the same Ovidian meter as *Elegia Septima*, the meter that he once 'found most easie, and most agreeable to natures part in me.' But as John K. Hale has observed, the palinode 'corresponds in length and tone with the *following* elegiacs, which are more epigrammatic (more after Martial than Ovid).'[35] And thus, as Hale adds, does Milton ' "graft" epigram upon the erotic' (40). The point I wish to emphasize here is that the carefully crafted palinode is yet another illustration of what Hanford termed the young poet's 'studied decorum.' The palinode signals that although he may not quite yet be prepared to give up Latin elegiac meter, he is ready to renounce one of its most notable practitioners, Ovid. Working with Hale's horticultural metaphor of 'grafting,' the remainder of this section also argues that encoded within Milton's palinode is a hastened 'withering' not only of the Ovidian pose of amatory excess but also the Ovidian poetry of exile.

Martz has memorably alluded to the apprentice-poet Milton as 'the rising poet.' There are many pathways for discussing the choices 'the rising poet' made as he pursued his ambitions to write an epic, not the least of which was his rejection of the Ovid who wrote no epic – and the English poet's related turn to Virgil. On the title page of his *Poems*, Milton pointedly quoted from Virgil's seventh eclogue, where Thyrsis (Milton's poetic persona in *Epitaphium Damonis*), though losing his singing contest with Corydon, makes clear his desire for future poetic fame: *Baccare frontem / Cingite, ne vati noceat mala lingua futuro*. Martz, examining Milton's choice of Thyrsis's self-presentation as a bard of destiny, has usefully filled in the context of the *Poems'* motto: *Pastores, hedera crescentem ornate poetam, / Arcades* ('Bring ivy-leaves to decorate your rising poet, shepherds of Arcady').[36] It is not simply idle to observe that Milton did not choose for his title page, say, Ovid's urging those who possess his portrait: 'remove from my locks the ivy, the chaplet of Bacchus. Such fortunate symbols are suited to the happy poets' (*deme meis hederas, Bacchica serta, comis, / ista decent laetos felicia signa poetas, Tristia* 7.1–3). One can imagine the exiled Ovid's claim that he is too unhappy to remember his earlier portrait as close to unnerving for the Milton of 1645, so resolutely focused on his future as an epic poet that even Ovidian wit had lost much of its charm. Hence, the *Poems'* title page features not the Tomitan Ovid of waning *ingenium* but rather 'the rising poet' Thyrsis, Virgil's emblem of career ambition.

---

35 John K. Hale, 'Milton's Self-Presentation in *Poems . . . 1645*,' *Milton Quarterly* 25, no. 2 (1991): 40; italics in original.
36 Martz, 36.

No one was more aware than Milton that renunciations of juvenilia were a time-honored poetic convention. But the 'studied decorum' of Milton's palinode offers an additional biographical window through which to view his rejection of Ovidian excess. We can speculate that Milton, in the process of compiling his *Poems*, may have reflected not only upon his imitations of the young Ovid but also upon his occasional allusions to the older Ovid of exile. Perhaps Milton concluded (with no small measure of Ovidian wryness) that the Roman poet, too, would have benefited from writing a retraction of his *Ars Amatoria* and the putative passage so offensive to Augustus that it prompted the Roman poet's exile to Tomis. Perhaps, had Ovid retracted some of his earlier poetry, he might have avoided the shores of the Pontic Sea and, like Virgil, progressed to epic.

Though, as we have seen, we can somewhat productively speak of a Milton-in-exile during his writing of *Paradise Lost*, Milton discouraged analogies with the exiled Ovid; and in addition to his poetic commitment to the *rota Virgilii*, what undoubtedly played a role in this discouragement was his deeply felt politics. Had Milton, with his growing republican sentiments, ever paused to historicize Ovid's exilic poetry within his own poetics in exile, the post-Cambridge Milton might have found objectionable the extent to which Ovid deferred to monarchical power, praising the ostensibly republican authority of Augustus as, in fact, imperial (*res est publica Caesar*; *Tristia*, 4.4.15).[37] It is hard to conceive of Milton looking favorably on the exiled Ovid's depiction of Augustus's power as, in Philip Hardie's words, 'consolation and potential source of salvation.'[38] Perhaps from Milton's political perspective, it was justifiable that Ovid's exile poetry, its passivity in the face of imperial power, signaled not only the end of the Roman's poetic career, but also the end of a poetic career that failed to culminate in epic, the test of poetic greatness.

Finally at the threshold of realizing his epic ambition, what a mature Milton may have judged most repellent about Ovid's exile poetry was the relentless abjection of the Roman poet's exilic persona, the latter's frequent reminding his readers of his 'fearful state' (*flebilis status*), and his persistent self-depictions as *flebilis exul* and *miser* – the latter epithet, as Milton well knew, a topos of Roman elegy but also, in the context of

---

37 For a study of Augustus as both head of a republic and an imperial monarch (*princeps*), see A. Wallace-Hadrill, '*Civilis princeps*: Between Citizen and King,' *JRS* 72 (1982): 32–48.

38 Hardie, *Ovid's Poetics of Illusion*, 9.

the *Tristia*, an overemphasis on exilic helplessness.[39] The sheer repetitiveness of Ovid's exilic pose was no doubt a major reason why the curriculum at St. Paul's perceived the *Tristia* as so pedagogically valuable
for beginning students of Latin. But these Ovidian epithets of suffering,
once valuable tools of Latin language acquisition, evidently wore thin
as the maturing poet pursued epic's 'vast design.'

5. 'At last he twitch't his mantle': *Lycidas* and Milton's 'Writing' of Local Coastlines

Ovid temporarily drops out of the discussion in order that we might
reexamine Milton's happy state of mind just prior to his Italian tour,
a time when he was utterly unpreoccupied with the topos of Ovidian
exile. Acutely aware that he was shaping his poetic career on antiquity's *ultima Britannia*, a younger Milton made sure his early poems
reflected a sophisticated sense of being 'at home' with an *unheimlich*
topos. The patently Protestant *In Quintum Novembris* opens with a geographical salute to the 'devout' King James from the remote north (*pius
extrema veniens Iacobus ab areto*, 1). The arch-fiend Satan instigates the
pope by reviling a rebellious and savage nation born under the northern sky (*Hyperboreo gens barbara nata sub axe*, 95). The pope, rallying
his consistory, also hurls invectives at the odious English, living in
isolation, cut off from the continent (*prudens natura negavit / Indignam
penitus nostro coniungere mundo*, 158–9). But these insults directed at
a barbarous England end up reinforcing the poet's youthfully robust
national pride in an island nation remote from a decadent Catholic
Italy. The young Milton seemingly never worried that the raw winds
of *ultima Britannia* would dampen his creativity. Rather, to echo Prince
Hal, he was self-assured that his poetry, 'like bright metal on a sullen
ground, / . . . glitt'ring o'er my fault' (206–7), would shine all the more
brightly for being penned by a 'northern' hand.[40]

In turning to *Lycidas*, the last of the English poems collected in the
1645 *Poems*, I hope to place in sharper relief the ways in which Milton,

---

39 A helpful classicist context for appreciating the pedagogical value of the *Tristia* is
   McGowan's observation that in his exile poetry, Ovid's repetitiveness 'becomes itself
   an oft-repeated theme' (6).
40 This same 'northern' self-confidence is evident in the invocation to Book 9 of *Paradise Lost*. The poet, aiming for 'higher Argument' (34), hopes that England's 'cold /
   Climate' will not 'damp my intended wing' (44–5). Milton's allusion to Aristotelian
   climate theory is less insecure than boastful.

on the verge of departing for his Italian tour, succeeded in endowing English shorelines with, to echo Rosalie Colie, 'the numen of poetic significance.' And I wish to tease out the remarkable and ironic ease with which Milton's English verse, written just prior to his departure for Italy, refused to founder on the shoals of *ultima Britannia*.

In his introductory note to *Lycidas* for his volume of poems, Milton wrote that his Cambridge colleague Edward King 'drown'd in his Passage from *Chester* on the *Irish* Seas.'[41] The spare, pragmatic accuracy of Milton's prose map belies the scope of his underlying poetic ambition. Along with the elegy's many oft-noted triumphs – its rich texture of pastoral, political, theological, and national threads – we glimpse the poet's ambition to settle two scores on the eve of his tour to Italy: to introduce authoritatively an inspired poetry to the shorelines of the British Isles – and, by extension, to counter *cinquecento* Italy's poetic perception of British coasts that, in the aforementioned words of Guarini, 'were with no measures grac'd.' (See this book's first chapter.) In this elegy, we witness the apotheosis of the drowned shepherd-swain as the Irish Sea's 'genius of the shoreline' (183). So too do we witness Milton becoming a kind of presiding genius of an English shoreline poetics that he anticipated sharing with his Italian interlocutors during his upcoming tour of Italy.[42]

To place the 'genius' of Milton's shoreline poetics in fuller perspective, we can begin with a brief glance at some of the other poems that appeared with *Lycidas*. The shipwreck that drowned King off the Anglesey coast was evidence that well into the seventeenth century, the coastlines of the British Isles often lived up to the reputation of antiquity's *ultima Britannia*. Moreover, with the notable exception of *Lycidas*, the poems published in the 1638 commemorative volume *Justa Edouardo King naufrago* more than justified antiquity's *ultima Britannia*. In his poem, John Cleveland, one of the volume's better-known contributors, bluntly summarized the main obstacle to commemorating *King naufrago*: 'the sea's too rough for verse.'[43]

---

41 *Poems of Mr. John Milton*, 1645, facs. ed. (Menston, York: Scolar, 1973), 57.
42 For a reading of the 'Genius of the shore' as evidence of Milton's patent nationalism, particularly his anti-Irish sentiments, see Lawrence Lipking, 'The Genius of the Shore: Lycidas, Adamastor, and the Poetics of Nationalism,' *PMLA* (1995): 205–21.
43 All quotations from the contributions to *Justa Edouardo King*, except *Lycidas*, are taken from *Justa Edouardo King: Reproduced from the Original Edition, 1638, with an Introduction*, intro. Ernest C. Mossner (New York: Columbia University Press [for the Facsimile Text Society], 1939).

160

King drowned somewhere between North Wales and Ireland; and the uncertainty as to where, precisely, the shipwreck occurred was a direct result of the maritime region's inadequately charted dangers.[44] The title *Justa Edouardo King* is followed by a motto from Petronius's *Satyricon*: *si recte calculum ponas, ubique naufragium est* ('If you rightly cast the reckoning, there is shipwreck everywhere'). Petronius's adage has less to do with shipwrecks as such than with an overarching fatalism about human tragedy. Notwithstanding, Petronius's shipwreck metaphor (originating in antiquity, no less) was particularly apt for the notoriously treacherous North Welsh coast, where shipwrecks were frequent. Although a tide-table for the Thames estuary had been compiled some four centuries earlier, it was not until 1644 that a detailed atlas of the North Welsh coast appeared; and even that long-awaited atlas was inaccurate, incapable of pinpointing the region's offshore rocks and sandbanks that were hidden by tides swirling in competing directions.[45] Of all the coastlines of the British Isles, Anglesey was perhaps Guarini's most 'ungrac'd' coast.

Of *Justa Edouardo King*'s anonymous prefatory Latin paragraph that summarized the circumstances of King's accident, David Masson offered the following translation: King's ship was reported as 'having struck on a rock not far from the British shore and been ruptured by the shock.' As Masson hastened to assure his readers, his translation is 'not more clumsy than the original' (651). And indeed, with the exception of Milton's famous contribution, the volume showed little evidence of having been visited by the Muse – little evidence, that is, that its poetry had been any more skilled than King's ship in avoiding foundering on the brute reality of Anglesey's 'rock-shock.' One 'W. Hall' forgettably described the drowned King as 'thus embalm'd in brinie casket lid.' Isaac Olivier leveled the less-than-felicitous accusation that 'The Ocean't self's a stain.' The aforementioned Cleveland penned his anguish thus: 'But can his spacious virtue find a grave / Within th' impostum'd buble of a wave?' An 'R. Brown' could not get past tidewater-as-tears: 'Weep forth your tears, then; pour out all your tide: / All waters are pernicious since King died.' In the poem printed just

---

44 For a recent attempt to locate the shipwreck, see J. Karl Franson, 'The Fatal Voyage of Edward King, Milton's Lycidas,' *Milton Studies* 25 (1990): 67–88. For an overview of the region's coastal dangers, see Ivor W. Jones, *Shipwrecks of North Wales* (Newton Abbot, Devonshire: David, 1973).
45 For details of this atlas, see Waters, *The Art of Navigation*, 11–14.

before *Lycidas*, 'T. Norton,' lapsing into the topos of the Fortunate Isles, drew an uncompelling coastal map: 'haste thee to the northern shore; / I' th' Irish sea one jewel lies.' But smug mockery of these contributions misses the point. (Any number of the contributors, after all, frankly admitted they were not poets.)[46] To quote selected lines from these mediocre poems is to place in sharper relief the extent of Milton's poetic genius – namely, *Lycidas*'s attempt to disprove Cleveland's maxim that the Anglesey coast is 'too rough for verse.'

Milton's oft-discussed choice of the name 'Lycidas' for King is not without significance for assessing the poet's awareness of the perils not only of sailing on the Anglesey coast, but also of attempting to versify it. Milton's 'Lycidas' might have been motivated by Sannazaro's piscatory eclogue 'Phyllis.' As discussed in the second chapter, the fisher-swain Lycidas revisits his dead beloved's coastal grave where he envelops readers in his erotic coastal *pietas*. But we are well-reminded here that King's body was never found, a body not draped in mournful seaweed but rather most likely dashed on jagged coastal rocks. Milton knew his elegy would have to construct its own shoreline monument – not on the blue shores of the Mediterranean basin's Bay of Naples but in *ultima Britannia*. Perhaps it was at this point that Milton chose to adopt not Sannazaro's but Virgil's 'Lycidas,' the protagonist of the ninth eclogue. Among other things, Virgil's poem was an interrogation of poetry's ability to shape events meaningfully – and, by extension, a challenge to Milton to convert senseless happenstance, coastal death-by-drowning on *ultima Britannia*, into a transcendent emblem of tragic dignity.

No poet likely foresaw with greater clarity than Milton the awkward inappropriateness of the overused topos of the Fortunate Isles for mourning a body left to 'welter to the parching wind' (130); the topos was too abstract to 'build the lofty rhyme' in rhythmic tandem with a body hurled against the base of a wind-raked 'beaked Promontory' in Anglesey (11, 94). And thus does a moment in *Lycidas* draw inspiration not from the highly stylized topos that required British poetry to abstract away from the coastline, but rather from a visit to the coastline itself, to the mysterious coastal haunts of 'your old *Bards*, the famous *Druids*' (47). These ancient bards inspire the poet of *Lycidas* to rediscover, amidst the harsh topography of Anglesey, sacred sites of

---

46 The contributions of the most prominent poets in the collection, Cleveland and Joseph Beaumont, are discussed by Ruth Wallerstein, *Studies in Seventeenth Century Poetics* (Madison: University of Wisconsin Press, 1950), 97–103.

poetic inspiration (where immanent spirits might yet keep company with Lycidas) on 'the shaggy top of *Mona* high,' or 'where *Deva* spreads her wizard stream' (54–5). Mona is 'shaggy' with the sacred ceremonial groves of the Druids; and the divine Dee is a 'wizard' celebrated by the Druids for its shape-shifting capacity to metamorphose from a gentle inland flow to the turbulent tidal waters of the Dee channel. Long before the Romans gave these sites the place-names of 'Mona' and 'Deva' (and long before the names were inherited by such early modern antiquarian and cartographic luminaries as Ortelius, Mercator, and Camden, not to mention the poet Drayton), these shorelines were the sites of an inspired Druidic poetry. Somewhere amidst these turbulent waters King was tragically drowned; but at the same time, Milton assures Lycidas's mourners that he died near a sacred coastal site where the island's poetry originated.[47]

Milton's turn to the Druids could have been an occasion to expose antiquity's unpoetic *ultima Britannia* as a bad faith historical gesture. But the ambitions of *Lycidas*'s classically trained apprentice-poet would not allow him to linger on local bardic shorelines, content to borrow inspiration from the Druids. To track his coastal poetics' classical ambitions, let us turn to the passage that culminates in one of the poem's most-quoted lines:

> Ay me! Whilst thee the shores and sounding Seas
> Wash far away, where'er thy bones are hurled,
> Whether beyond the stormy *Hebrides*,
> Where thou perhaps under the whelming tide
> Visit'st the bottom of the monstrous world;
> Or whether thou, to our moist vows denied,
> Sleep'st by the fable of *Bellerus* old,
> Where the great vision of the guarded Mount
> Looks toward *Namancos* and *Bayona*'s hold:
> Look homeward, Angel now, and melt with ruth:
> And, O ye *Dolphins*, waft the hapless youth.
>
> (156–64)[48]

---

47 Years later, of course, Milton would reject the historical value of the fables of the bards in his prose *History of Great Britain*.

48 My discussion of this passage will not enter into the thorny thickets of debate about syntactic ambiguities potentially allowing either Lycidas or Michael to be identified as the angel 'looking homeward.' For an argument that Lycidas is the angel, see

The passage maps what could be termed as nothing less than a long European coast, moving from the Hebrides and Bellerus (or 'Bellarium,' the Latin designation for Cornwall's Land's End) to southwest Galicia's 'Bayona' (south of Cape Finisterre) and 'Namancos,' gazed upon by the angel Michael from his vantage point on St. Michael's Mount.[49] But in the passage that culminates in the famous imperative to 'Look homeward, Angel,' antiquity's Mediterranean also beckons the poet to remember the dictates of classical prosody. At this point, I defer to the prosodic ear of Clay Hunt, whose commentary on these lines from his monograph on *Lycidas* is perhaps the most detailed analysis of the poem's pastoral meter:

> These lines are remarkable for their sustained prosodic coherence and impulsion, which drive the verse, check it, build tension by rhetorical suspensions, and finally release the accumulated force of the verse-paragraph in the two concluding lines, letting it fall, at last, to the firm but lilting cadence of the closing line. The lines are striking also for their steady, even flow, achieved by the use of long vowels, which give the verse a movement and metric more quantitative than accentual, and for their resonant verbal sonorities. Verse music of this kind had scarcely been heard in English before Milton . . . and to my ear it suggests less the prosodic patterns of English decasyllabic verse than the power, weight, and sonority of the hexameters not just of Virgil but more particularly of Homer.[50]

As the poet's grief and anguish modulate into serenity and acceptance of tragedy, so also do his Galician, Welsh, and Cornish shores echo the cadences of ancient Mediterranean poetics. Following the impulsive violence that 'hurled' Lycidas's bones beyond the Hebrides or, perhaps, 'under the whelming tide,' the passage concludes with dolphins gently 'wafting' Lycidas. In the final analysis, *Lycidas*'s local coastal map is

---

G.W. Pigman III, *Grief and English Renaissance Elegy* (Cambridge: Cambridge University Press, 1985), 117. For a more recent revisiting of this debate, see Joad Raymond, 'Look Homeward Angel: Guardian Angels and Nationhood in Seventeenth-Century England,' in *Early Modern Nationalism and Milton's England*, eds. David Loewenstein and Paul Stevens (Toronto: University of Toronto Press, 2008), 139–72.

49 Allan H. Gilbert suggests that Milton's 'Namancos' may have been taken from Mercator's map of Galicia in his 1628 atlas (*A Geographical Dictionary of Milton* [New York: Russell & Russell, 1919], 202).

50 Clay Hunt, *'Lycidas' and the Italian Critics* (New Haven: Yale University Press, 1975), 141.

not a monument to the bardic past of Welsh and Cornish shores but rather a monument to Milton's disciplined use of classical quantitative metrics to harness raw maritime energy for early modern English poetry.

As editors of *Lycidas* have frequently noted, when, early in his elegy, Milton poses the lyric question, 'Who would not sing for *Lycidas*?' he self-consciously echoes Virgil's 'Who would refuse to sing for Gallus?' (*Eclogue* 10.3); and in so doing he announces a manifestly Virgilian agenda for his pastoral elegy. That Milton had judged himself successful in bringing Virgilian pastoral convention to bear on British Isles shorelines is evident in the poem's confident conclusion, where, as the sun sets, 'At last he [the poet himself] rose, and twitch't his Mantle blue: / Tomorrow to fresh Woods and Pastures new' (192–3). Shortly after writing his pastoral, Milton would depart for Italy, in the hopes of wandering the Arno Valley and conducting internal dialogues with his epic mentor Tasso, author of the *Gerusalemme liberata* but also author of the pastoral romance, the *Aminta*, echoed frequently throughout *Lycidas*.[51] Perhaps he also imagined an internal dialogue with Tasso's almost-as-esteemed countryman Guarini, who authored the renowned pastoral romance *Il pastor fido*. That is to say, as the apprentice-poet penned his elegy's last two lines – as, in effect, his poetic persona turns away from local shorelines – he could have been reminded of Samuel Daniel's dedicatory sonnet to his English translation of *Il pastor fido*, conveying Guarini's judgment that British coastlines were 'with no measures grac'd,' itself anticipating Cleveland's axiom that local shores were 'too rough for verse.' The *Lycidas* poet's 'twitch't' mantle signals that Milton had achieved satisfying closure on two poetic fronts. Not only had he succeeded in singing for Lycidas to the tune of Virgil's classical prosody, but he had also sung for Lycidas in a pastoral voice so virtuosic that no longer would English poetry have to labor in the shadow of *cinquecento* Italian pastoral disdain for English shorelines.

Lycidas left no doubt that the poet from *ultima Britannia* had completed a key rite of passage for glimpsing the Mediterranean for the first time. But the next section investigates the conflicted undercurrents of *Mansus*, the poem Milton wrote to Tasso's patron, and a poem written as he glimpsed the Mediterranean for the final time before returning to *ultima Britannia*.

---

51 For *Lycidas*'s echoes of the *Aminta*, see F.T. Prince, *The Italian Elements of Milton's Verse* (New York: Oxford University Press, 1954).

6. The *Londini Milto, Mansus,*
and the Thames

As pointed out in the previous section, the young Milton yet to travel
to Italy enjoyed playing the role of a precocious poet improbably hailing from *ultima Britannia*. Nor during the Italian tour so crucial to his
poetic development was the poet any less reluctant to foreground his
'northernness' for his Italian colleagues, who themselves enjoyed the
rhetorical game of praising the visiting *Giovanni Miltone Inglese* of the
Thames. Among the 'Written Encomiums' included in Milton's 1645
Poems is a quatrain by the Roman poet Giovanni Salzilli:

> Conquered is Homer's Meles; Virgil's Mincio wears willows;
> Tasso's Sebeto now ceases to babble so free;
> Thames, as the victor, carries highest of any her billows.
> In that Milton's muse equals the one to the three.[52]

One can both agree with Masson's assessment that the quatrain's flattering lines are 'so gross that honest prose is ashamed of them' (805),
and still pause to consider how Milton responded to Salzilli's chorographic praise. Linking riverine place and one's place within the pan-
theon of great epic poets, Salzilli predicts that the muse of Milton's
estuarial Thames will eventually sweep the promising poet beyond the
'middle flights' of verse (such as the Latin elegiacs of Salzilli's own quatrain) to the loftier heights of epic heroic poetry, where he will surpass
even Homeric and Virgilian epic.

Milton's 1638 poem *Ad Salsillum*, written during his first visit to
Rome, responds in kind to the admiring quatrain's chorographic discourse. In line 9, Milton identifies himself as the *Londini Milto* (mirroring Salzilli's status as 'The Roman poet' of the poem's subtitle, *Poetam
Romanum*), hailing from a distant land where the lungs of winds blow
with uncontrollable force (*pessimus ubi ventorum, / Insanienti impotensque
pulmonis, / Pernix anhela sub Iove exercet flabra*, 11–13). Proving that the
Londini Milto knows how to pay homage to a Mediterranean *peirar*, the
poet concludes by wishing the ailing Salzilli good health so that his
poetry can once again tame the swelling Tiber itself (*Tumidusque et ipse*

---

52 English translation quoted in Masson, 805. Virgil praises the verdant banks of the
    Mincio in his *Eclogues*, 7.12–13, and *Georgics*, 3.14–15.

Tibris, 36).[53] In sum, if we read the lavish praise of Salzilli's quatrain in tandem with Milton's *Ad Salsillum*, then we witness the English poet graciously accepting the Thames as a *peirar* 'of his own.'

But the literary figure whom the touring Milton had most sought out to impress, Tasso's former patron Manso, was not so willing to play the game of praising *Londini Milto*. Before Milton left Naples and eventually returned to England, Manso presented the English poet with a farewell Latin distich:

> *Mens, forma, decor, facies, mos, si pietas sic*
> *Non Anglus, verum hercle, Angelus ipse fores.*[54]

The distich can be roughly translated: if your piety matched your many other talents, then you would be no Angle but an Angel. Manso obviously echoed the words of Gregory the Great that the foreigners he had seen in the forum who hailed from what was once *ultima Britannia* were so pleasing in aspect that he was tempted to call them not *Angli* but *Angeli*. But Manso's distich also echoed Gregory's conviction that the foreigners were nonetheless unenlightened pagans in need of conversion. And thus did Manso not-so-subtly take Milton to task for his Protestantism.

William Riley Parker has remarked in passing that Manso's distich was 'qualified admiration' (II, 827n34). Anthony Low, revisiting this 'qualified' distich in greater detail, wisely doubts that Milton took offense. The poet did, after all, include the lines in his 'Written Encomiums'

---

53 Milton's fondness for antiquity's Tiber appears as early as *In Quintum Novembris* where Satan glimpses 'the furtive kisses which you are giving to the sea, O Tiber' (*nec non / Te furtive, Tibris, Thetidi videet oscula dantem*, 51–2). His classical training had acquainted him well with the varying faces of antiquity's Tiber – sometimes calm, sometimes stormy. He would have been familiar with the tranquil Tiber residing at the core of one of the *Aeneid*'s great epic moments, when the reed-crowned river god Tiberinus appears at night to Aeneas, promising him calm waters for his passage up the river banks to Pallanteum. Milton was also familiar with the portentous Horatian Tiber of *Odes* 1.2.17, whose swollen flood waters protested the death of Julius Caesar, a river outraged on behalf of his wife Ilia, Caesar's relative. But whether calm or disturbed, Milton well knew that the Tiber defined the *peirar* itself: Horace's tumultuous Tiber stemmed not from congenitally angry tides but from the occasional anger of the gods, for whom the river and its estuary was one of their cherished playgrounds.

54 *The Works of John Milton*, ed. Frank A. Patterson et al. (New York: Columbia University Press, 1931–40), I:154.

to his 1645 *Poems*; and, as Low argues, 'he saw nothing to be ashamed of in being charged with Protestantism, and he liked a good joke.'[55] Nonetheless, Low concedes that *Mansus*, the 1639 poem that Milton wrote in gratitude to his host for the kindness shown his guest during his visit to Naples, itself shows signs of a guarded response to what Low terms the 'sting' of Manso's distich. And R.W. Condee has found it outright odd that *Mansus* makes no mention of the usual subject matter of panegyric, such as the addressee's high rank and military prowess.[56]

Though there is no evidence that Milton took offense at being labeled a Protestant, I would like to speculate on the possibility that he chafed at Manso's belaboring the point of his Englishness so close to his return to England. He surely noticed that Manso's brittle humor ran counter to the smooth rhetoric of praise to which the *Londini Milto* had become accustomed during his earlier visits to the Italian academies. The triumphs of *Lycidas*'s shoreline poetics threatened to become a distant memory; and a heavy sense of transition – made heavier by what amounted to Manso's hasty farewell distich – might have been one reason for the bittersweet tone of *Mansus*. Embedded within this Latin poem was Milton's realization that he was about to leave Italy as the definitive site of, to echo Rosalie Colie, the numen of poetic significance, the definitive intersection of poetry and place – and that he would, of necessity, soon have to content himself with the distant Thames as his *peirar*. He would have to come to terms, that is, not with the Thames of Salzilli's rhetorical flourish but with a marginal estuary scarcely locatable in literary history.

On the one hand, *Mansus* has deservedly become a *locus classicus* for charting Milton's ambitions to become a great epic poet – an English poet, to be sure, but also an English Tasso. In an oft-quoted line, Milton anticipates returning to England and writing an Arthurian epic where he promises, with a *brio* bordering on self-satire, to 'shatter the Saxon phalanxes under the British Mars!' (*frangam Saxonicas Britonum Marte phalanges!*, 84). But on the other hand, as the English poet stole his final glimpses of the Bay of Naples from Manso's villa (a numinous site gazed upon by Milton's revered Tasso), any confidence in his

---

55 '*Mansus*: In Its Context,' *Milton Studies* 19 (1984): 107.
56 '"Mansus" and the Panegyric Tradition,' *Structure in Milton's Poetry* (University Park, PA: Penn State University Press, 1974): 85–103.

epic future would almost certainly have been attenuated by a melancholic sense of what was all too quickly receding into the past – i.e., his
intimate contacts with the Mediterranean that, ever since his days at
St. Paul's, had nurtured his poetic creativity, and, in Italy, had enabled
the casual wit of his identity as *Londini Milto*. Even as Milton shared
with Tasso's former patron his own ambition to be a great epic poet,
so also, on the eve of his return to England, did *Mansus* entertain some
doubts that literary history would ever acknowledge an epic written on
the shores of the not-Mediterranean.

Perhaps by way of pointed response to what Parker has termed the
'qualified admiration' of Manso's distich, Milton celebrates not so much
the glories of the Italian *cinqucento* that his tour had rendered so vivid
and immediate (that is to say, he experiments not with the potential
voice of an 'English Tasso') but rather retreats to the Virgilian pastoral
mode that had shaped so much of his poetic identity on English shores
(most notably, *Lycidas*) long before he ever laid eyes on the real Mediterranean. The poem begins by mentioning Gallus, the first Roman elegist
lamented in Virgil's sixth eclogue, and a paradigm of poetic patronage
(who even Manso, perhaps, could only aspire to be?).

As in *Ad Salsillum*, Milton again presents himself, by now almost for-
mulaically, as an alien muse, 'a young pilgrim sent from Hyperborean
skies' (*Missus Hyperboreo iuvenis peregrines ab axc*, 26); and thus does the
poet, in a wittily ambiguous response to Manso's distich, suspend himself between the twin topoi of England as the Fortunate Isles and England as *ultima Britannia*. He then alludes to the Thames, the river Salzilli
had identified as the new 'victor' over Virgil's Mincius (celebrated in
Milton's own *Lycidas* as the 'Smooth-sliding *Mincius*,' 86) and Tasso's
Sebeto, flowing into the Bay of Naples.

But as Milton penned *Mansus* on the verge of taking up permanent
residence near the Thames, his estuarial poetics seems as tinged with
sadness as embroidered with playful wit: 'I believe that in the dim shadows of night I too have heard the swans singing on our river, where the
silver Thames with pure urns spreads her green locks wide in the swell
of the ocean' (*Nos etiam in nostro modulantes fllumine cygnos / Credimus
obscuras noctis sensisse per umbras, / Qua Thamesis late puris argenteus
urnis / Oceani glaucos perfundit gurgite crines*, 30–3). In this complex allusion, Milton officially reclaims the swelling Thames as an eminently
poetic river 'of his own.' But as noted in the *Variorum Commentary*,
the last phrase of line 30, *flumine cygnos*, is the last line in the *Georgics*
2.199 (273n30–4). Perhaps Milton attempts to remind *himself* as much as

Manso that he had once written inspired poetry in the silvery, nocturnal light of the Thames – and that he would soon be under pressure to do so again, this time as an epic poet. Milton gazes at his once-and-future estuary through the regressive eyes of Virgilian pastoral – perhaps the only way the *Londini Milto*, on the eve of his return to England, could transform antiquity's *apeiron* into English literary history's *peirar*.

On the one hand, Milton's reminiscences of swans singing on the Thames echo Virgil's and Horace's own lyrical tributes to the Tiber's swans. But the voice of the exiled Ovid is also audible in Milton's allusion. To be sure, the river swan was a trope of poetic inspiration, but also, as discussed in the previous chapter, a trope of mortality. An absent presence in Milton's swan trope is the exiled Ovid's lament in the *Tristia*: 'As the bird of Cayster is said to lie upon the banks and bemoan its own death with weakening note cast far away upon the Sarmatian shores, take heed that my funeral rites pass not off in silence' (*utque iacens ripa deflere Caystrius ales / dicitur ore suam deficiente necem, / sic ego, Sarmaticas longe proiectus in oras / efficio tacitum ne mihi funus eat*, 5.1.11–13).

When Milton once again sings, swan-like, on the Thames, he hopes he will sing as a Virgilian swan. But the swan trope of *Mansus* also hints that the English poet, upon recrossing the Channel, could end up singing an Ovidian swan-song on remote shores.

7. Milton, Horace, and Ovid in Geneva

This chapter returns full circle to Milton's rejection of the Tomitan Ovid discussed in the opening sections – namely, the Ovid so often dismissed by the young Milton, yet so crucial for teasing out what might have been the latter's frame of mind on the eve of his return to England. The exiled Ovid, as we saw earlier, seemingly predicted that nothing good could befall a poet who ignored his injunction to remember to 'love your Naso's name.' I pick up in Geneva, not long after Milton wrote *Mansus*, in order to explore how the poet may have continued struggling with the prospect of wrapping up his successful tour of Italy and returning to England. I will investigate how the Milton who departed from Italy forgot his 'Naso's name,' thereby convincing himself, as he stated some three years later in the *Reason*, of his 'content with these British islands as my world.' Winding down his Italian tour, Milton bade farewell to Benedetto Buonmattei's Florence, and made comparatively unmemorable journeys to Bologna, Ferrara, Venice, Milan – finally crossing the

Alps and returning to Geneva. In this city, Milton sought the company not of the Tomitan Ovid but of Horace – in so doing, forgetting 'his Naso's name' and/as Ovid's triumphant poetic conversion of a remote estuary into the *Mare Ovidianum*.

During his tour of Italy, Milton, as we have seen, enjoyed playing the role of the 'northerner' from *ultima Britannia*, circulating his poetry in the country where the topos originated. While residing in Florence in 1638, Milton wrote a Latin letter to Buonmattei, who was completing a treatise on Tuscan grammar, *Della langua Toscana*. In his his letter, Milton, always effusive about the elegance of the Tuscan dialect, urged Buonmattei to include an appendix on correct pronunciation, particularly for the benefit of those 'beyond the bound of the Alps.'[57] Here, Milton's allusion to the presumably ruder French, German, and English vernaculars casually concedes his 'northern' distance from Italy. In point of fact, Milton knew that his Italian colleagues had been so impressed with his command of Tuscan that his remark to Buonmattei would have been received as an inside joke.

But the pose of a *Londini Milto* likely at last wore thin. Near the end of his tour of Italy, Milton received news of the unexpected death of Diodati, eventually (belatedly?) mourned in *Epitaphium Damonis*. Milton biographies have not pinpointed exactly where Milton was when he received the tragic news of his friend. During his second visit to Florence, before beginning his long return trip to England, Milton took an excursion to Lucca, the Diodatis' ancestral home, perhaps in memory of his friend's death. But it is quite possible that he did not receive the news until he reached Geneva (definitively remapping him 'beyond the bound of the Alps'), where he and the late Diodati's uncle Giovanni met several times in shared grief.[58] The biographical uncertainty as to where Milton received the news of his friend's death might indeed be the result his own unresolved struggle to register the complexly doubled loss of a close friend he would never again see and of the Mediterranean numen of poetic significance to which he never returned.

If *Lycidas* is any indication, then Milton, prior to the Italian tour, was impervious to the kind of cultural melancholia that potentially plagued

---

57 Quoted in Hanford, *John Milton: Englishman* (New York, 1949), 97.
58 This is not to overlook Geneva as also Milton's Protestant safe haven from a prolonged immersion in Catholic Italy. Milton juxtaposes a heroic, Protestant Alps ('the Alpine mountains cold') with 'the triple Tyrant' of Catholic Italy in Sonnet XVIII ('On the Late Massacre in Piedmont').

any humanist-trained early modern English poet writing in the shadow of antiquity's *ultima Britannia*. If the young poet who had not yet traveled to Italy indeed brooded on the ironies of shaping a poetic career on what was, for antiquity, the edges of the world, he left no trace, particularly if we turn to some lines from *Il Penseroso*. Having displayed a virtuosic affinity for the voice of mirth in the companion poem *L'Allegro*, this poem strikes a self-consciously introverted pose, courting the melancholic muse that *L'Allegro* had banished: 'And I with thee will choose to live' (176). In this poem, one of Melancholy's many dwellings is under 'northern' skies. The poet, wrapped in the sable cloak of his muse, composes alone in his study, where he 'may oft outwatch the *Bear*' as it circles the northern sky (87). Melancholy also resides where the poet 'hear[s] the far-off *Curfew* sound, / Over some wide-water'd shore, / Swinging slow with sullen roar' (74–6). And thus does the young poet readily submit to Melancholy's prosodic spell, composing in rhythmic tandem with the lonely sounds of the curfew bell, scarcely audible over the surf's 'sullen roar.'

The Variorum Commentary quotes E.E. Stoll's *Poets and Playwrights* and its perceptive reading of *Il Penseroso*'s shoreline image: 'There the sense of space and distance, with a sight or sound to lure the imagination on, is quite in the vein of the Romantic poets, from Collins to Keats' (322). My requoting Stoll is not by way of continuing to portray Milton as a forerunner of the romantic sublime but rather to gain further purchase on the sophisticated ease with which the young poet wrote in the shadow of *ultima Britannia*. So deeply was Milton accustomed to drawing on what Hanford termed his 'personal reserve' that he breathed new life into the topos, embracing introspection on a lonely coastline under the sign of the Bear, converting a lonely shoreline into a backdrop for the *vita contemplativa*.

In *Il Penseroso*, Milton declared that his home was wherever Melancholy chose to dwell, even (especially?) if the muse chose as her home distant northern shorelines. But on the eve of Milton's return to England following his tour of Italy, one can imagine *Il Penseroso*'s Melancholy as intruding in unpredictable moments to remind the poet that he would be resuming his poetic career not on a proto-Romantic coastline where surf and poetry conjoin but on the shores of an *ultima Britannia* distinctly out of tune with his poetic ambition. To begin unpacking this claim, I return to Milton in Geneva, slowing down the time that elapsed during his brief stay in the city. Geneva was, among other things, a Protestant haven for Milton who had, for two years, immersed himself in Catholic Italy. But it is also the case that even had Diodati not passed away, Geneva would still have been one of Melancholy's homes, all but marking the end of Milton's tour (France being the last stop) before he recrossed the English Channel that, two years earlier, had served as the anticipatory waterway to Italy. In Geneva, the city of Milton's double loss, perhaps not even the poet's 'studied decorum' could have fended off the sad consequences of having to keep such intimate company with loss – the loss of humane learning's home (in the Greece he never saw, as well as in Italy) and the death of a close friend.

While continuing to keep this sad Geneva in focus, let us, for the moment, advance some fifteen years to Milton's account of the reason why he left Italy when he did. Nothing in Milton's career self-presentation, as we have seen, was carelessly worded, least of all how he framed his account of the origin and terminus of his Italian tour in his 1654 *Defensio Secunda* – an account of a moral progression from dilatoriness abroad to heroic action upon returning home. Of the tour's origins he recalled that he had grown desirous, eager (*cupidus*) to visit foreign lands, particularly Italy. Later, he recounted his decision, after almost two years in Italy, to cut short his plans for further travel in the Mediterranean: as he prepared to sail into Sicily and Greece, the sad news he received of civil disturbance in England prompted a change of plans. Responding to a higher purpose thus necessitated the end of his tour, a return to his native England to support the causes of civil liberty and the reformed religion. In short, Milton portrayed himself as progressing from an eagerness for travel to higher-principled preoccupations. Of the other, more deeply personal news he had recently received – i.e., the news of Diodati's death – Milton made no mention. According to *Defensio Secunda*, the Milton who returned to England is a plenitudinous Milton, unburdened by a sadness stemming from the loss of a beloved Italy. Rather, the returning Milton was in the grip of a heroic concern for the fate of his Protestant nation.

When Milton speaks of his once 'cupidinous' need for travel, he speaks less personally than tropically, writing within the constraints of classical topoi. Written years after his return to England, Milton casts the youth who had departed for Italy in the less-than-favorable role of idle traveler. His self-description as, among other things, *cupidus* (afflicted with an excessive eagerness) is a highly calculated gesture of a topos in Roman antiquity that disapproved of unnecessary sea-travel. Seneca used the term *inquieta inertia* to condemn an urge always to be on the move; and in his *Epistles* 1.11, Horace, who (except for a brief stint as a student in Athens) rarely traveled further than between his home in the Sabine hills and Rome, used a similar term *strenua inertia* to frame his critique of travel.[59] Horace's epistle denounces those who pursue the easier option of changing their locus rather than changing their lives.

As it happened, a much younger Milton, just before leaving Geneva, directly quoted Horace's epistle to endow his departure with a ceremonious aura. Ever the strategic allusionist, Milton copied into the autograph album of Count Camillo Cerdogni an echo of Horace's critique of travel: 'I change my sky but not my mind when I cross the sea' (i.11.27).[60] Milton's inscription was an exemplary humanist gesture, turning to antiquity to give voice to his current state of mind, while also testing the album's well-knowing readers' ability to interpret his allusion correctly.

Horace's epistle is replete with Mediterranean place-names; and Milton's echo of Horace is his perceptive decoding of these place-names as sites to be read not so much topographically as tropically, as he was first trained to do as a student at St. Paul's. On the eve of concluding his Italian tour, it is also the case that these coded Horatian loci were not only tropes but actual sites Milton had either finally seen for himself – or would have seen had he extended his itinerary. In passing, Parker summarizes Milton's inscription as 'an appropriate quotation from Horace' (I, 181). To be sure, the inscription is 'appropriate' if we cease focusing on the 'young' Milton of Geneva to focus on a maturing Milton, not only a rising epic poet but also a committed Christian poet preparing for public service. Milton's echo of Horace signals that he had preserved the Reformed faith, even after almost two years in Catholic Italy. But the inscription's appropriateness can be called into question if we remember Geneva's grieving Milton. Milton's self-depiction, in his *Defensio Secunda*, as an over-eager traveler was penned at a time when even some of the more vivid memories of his Italian tour had inevitably faded. But the backdrop of Milton's inscription in Cerdogni's album suggests an admixture of vivid memories of loss (of a friend and the poetry-nourishing Mediterranean) and uncertainty as to

---

59 For this similarity, see Rachel Skalitzky, 'Horace on Travel (*Epist*. 1.11),' *Classical Journal* 68, no. 4 (1973): 320–1. For more on Horace's objections to travel, see E.C. Wickham, *Horace, With a Commentary* (Oxford: Clarendon Press, 1903–12).

60 Quoted in Parker, II, 831n62. Horace's Latin reads: *non locus effuse late maris arbiter aufert, / caelum, non animum, mutant qui trans mare currunt*, 26–7).

whether he was returning to England on his own triumphant terms or as a kind of exile in his own homeland. I propose a reading of Milton's inscription that reveals not only a 'rising poet' but also a grieving poet at odds with himself.

I turn to Horace's epistle, whose moral purpose is to point out to idle travelers that happiness is found not in real places on a map but rather within one's *animus*, or state of mind. Contentedly nestled in his poetic home in the Sabine hills, Horace writes to his friend Bullatius, who has been travelling extensively in Asia Minor and the Grecian isles. Urging his friend to return to Rome, Horace asks Bullatius what he thinks of Lesbos, Samos, Croesus's Sardis, Smyrna, Colophon, and Rhodes – in so doing, all but daring his friend to confirm that these sites are as noteworthy as travelers have customarily made them out to be. Can they really compare favorably, he inquires wryly, to the Campo Martius and the Tiber? Putting further pressure on Bullatius's sea-weariness, Horace asks his friend if he intends to settle in one of the renowned cities of the kingdom of Attalus III, or whether he will seek out the remote, deserted Lebedus on the Ionian coast. Horace ventriloquizes Bullatius's potentially brash reply: 'You know what Lebedus is – a town more desolate than Gabii and Fidenae; yet there would I love to live and, forgetting my friends, and by them forgotten, gaze from the land on Neptune's distant rage' (*scis Lebedus quid sit: Gabiis desertior atque / Fidenis vicus; tamen illic vivere vellem, / oblitusque meorum, obliviscendus et illis, / Neptunum procul e terra spectare furentem*, 7–10).[61] Horace imagines Bullatius insisting he could thrive on a desolate Ionian coast, forgotten by friends and gazing on a stormy sea. Thus does Horace depict Bullatius as a ceaseless wanderer, stretching boundaries so far that he could even settle in isolated Lebedus – with no guarantee that, even there, his restlessness would abate. Horace then points out that if he himself were forced to travel and live overseas, he could just as happily dwell in Ionia's Lebedus as in, say, Ulubrae, some thirty miles from Rome – and, more to the point, a Roman topos of remoteness. In his notes to the epistle, Fairclough observes that Ulubrae was described by Cicero (*Ad fam.* 7.81) as 'a decaying town in the Pomptine marshes, where the frogs were very clamorous' (325). Horace could be content dwelling in Ionian coastal isolation not because, like Bullatius, he is a restless boundary

---

61 The Latin original and the English translation of Horace's epistle are from *Horace: Satires, Epistles and Ars Poetica*, trans. H. Rushton Fairclough, The Loeb Classical Library (Cambridge, MA: Harvard University Press, 1926).

pusher but because the poet is wise enough to enjoy life wherever he may be – even in a marshy, frog-serenaded Ulubrae:

> For if 'tis reason and wisdom that take away cares, and not a site commanding a wide expanse of sea, they change their clime, not their mind, who rush across the sea. 'Tis a busy idleness that is our bane; with yachts and cars we seek to make life happy. What you are seeking is here; it is at Ulubrae, if there fail you not a mind well-balanced.

> (*nam si ratio et prudential curas, / non locus effusi late maris arbiter aufert, / caelum, non animum, mutant, qui trans mare currunt, / strenua nos exercet inertia: navibusque atque / quadrigis petimus bene vivere. Quod petis hic est, / est Ulubris, animus si te non deficit aequus*, 25–30).

Horace claims that for the rational and wise soul, there is no difference between a far-flung, overseas Lebedus and Ulubrae, for the genuinely tranquil mind is equally at ease in both. He argues that change of place – dashing across the ocean – is, in and of itself, a futile exercise that cannot guarantee happiness: the traveler's *inertia* (or idleness) is cured by the faculty of *ratio* (reason).

The epistle's place-names function not as markers of geographical reality but as poetic topoi. The epistle's Lebedus amounts to Horace's critique of restless travel, symbol of the ethical imperative to live a life of reason wherever one happens to reside. And Horace invokes Ulubrae less as a locatable town on a map than as a topos of remoteness – in this case, remoteness-as-contentment. Milton, whose future as a writer of prose and poetry would be shaped as, among other things, a career dedicated to reason, knew all too well how to read Horace's epistle tropically as a rhetorical case for a return 'home' to reason and to a search for a liberty that comes not from without but within. Milton's inscription in Cerdogni's album, then, can be recognized as another example of the English poet's 'studied decorum' – in effect nodding at Horace, strategically presenting his farewell to the Continent as a satisfying return to England-as-Ulubrae: the inscription signals his conviction that he will be far more fulfilled returning to England than he would have been had he continued his travels to Italy – and beyond, to Sicily and Greece.[62]

---

62 This observation offers, I believe, the fullest context for assessing Milton's self-criticism in *Epitaphium Damonis*: 'Alas! What wandering fancy carried me across the skyey cliffs of the snow-bound Alps to unknown shores?' (*Heu! Quis me ignotas traxit*

But at this point, returning to Parker's assessment of Milton's inscription as 'appropriate,' we can ponder the significance of the fact that the young poet marked the end of his Mediterranean travels by paraphrasing the line, 'I change my sky but not my mind when I cross the sea,' rather than, say, *Quod petis hic est, / est Ulubris*, the latter a surer indicator that Milton was fully reconciled with his aborted travels and return to England. Milton's choice of lines to quote from Horace's epistle left unclear whether he was the conveyor or the unwitting target of the epistle's moral critique of travel. Perhaps, upon writing the inscription, Milton imagined himself as Horace, content to compose poetry at home, content with his own 'Ulubrae' as the site of reason. But Horace resided not in Ulubrae but in the Sabine hills (when not in Rome) – not only numinous sites that Milton the traveler took such pleasure in visiting, but also where Horace, one of early modern English humanism's most revered models, had mapped Milton's Ulubrae in antiquity's *ultima Britannia*. Perhaps Milton imagined himself not as Horace but as Bullatius. That is to say, perhaps Milton's inscription signaled that the one-time Mediterranean traveler had now become a reformed Bullatius, ready to return to England and/as a Horatian life of reason, no longer goaded by an urge to travel. But Milton's inscription foregrounds the fact that upon his return to England, he could assure neither himself nor the inscription's future readers that he would not revert to the original Bullatius, gazing into a raging sea, forgotten (*obliviscendus*) by friends. Milton's inscription was no guarantee that he would not feel forgotten by his Italian friends (Buonmattei, Francini, Dati, Salzilli) – or that he would not end up overwhelmed by the permanent loss of the deceased Diodati, with whom he was to have shared his Italian travels and his newly refined epic ambitions.

These are, for sure, only speculations. But however one chooses to respond to them, one outcome was certain: Milton's return to England guaranteed that he would never be the epistle's original Bullatius who, with whatever degree of idleness, *did* get to travel to Lesbos, Samos, Smyrna, and Colophon. Nor could Milton ever, in good faith, have hoped to become a Horace using Rome's Campo Martius and the Tiber as touchstones for Mediterranean sites of 'one's own' – sites of a numinous poetics any rising point would have hesitated to leave behind.

---

vagus error in oras / Ire per aereas rupes, Alpemque nivosam?, 113–14). This self-criticism seems a compensatory gesture, attempting to depict Italy as remoteness itself.

The Milton of the *Defensio Secunda* openly admits that the sad news of England's religious turmoil was the reason he returned to England. But the Milton who, on the eve of his return, wrote the Horatian echo in Cerdogni's album may also have struggled with a less easily articulated sadness, a whirling constellation of Horatian place-names too numerous to process in Geneva, and all conspiring to undermine the plenitude of his 'studied decorum.' The constellation would include Horace's home in the Sabine hills – for the epistle's author a state of mind in the exercise of reason but, for the early modern Milton, hallowed traces of 'the antiquities of Rome' that he must now leave behind; Ulubrae, Horace's symbol of remoteness but far closer to the Roman *axis mundi* than London would ever be; the fact that he will never be a Bullatius asked to compare Rome's Campo Martius to, say, Sardis; the coastal town of Lebedus, a symbol of maritime remoteness but also proximate to the Ionian Homer's Mediterranean. In the final analysis, all of these place-names point to the fact that Horace's building a moral around the shortcomings of travel are close to meaningless for anyone residing outside the bounds of the Mediterranean and the Aegean. Hence, Milton, who never 'crossed the sea' to view Homer's Ionia, is now on the verge of crossing the 'wrong' sea, the English Channel as the gateway to *ultima Britannia*.

I conclude by returning full circle to the Tomitan Ovid whose name Milton had forgotten. The didactic aim of Horace's epistle is how to turn exile into home, precisely accomplished by the *Mare Ovidianum* of the *Tristia*. But Milton, caught in a dialectic between home and exile, and putting himself under pressure to sort through the allusive density of Horace on Mediterranean travel, was surely resistant to imagining himself as a vulnerable *flebilis exul* banished to the remote shorelines of the Roman periphery. And we are now fully positioned to appreciate just how different the *Epitaphium Damonis*, the immediate inheritor of this entangled knot of travel, friendship, exile, and loss of a numinous poetics, might have looked had Milton returned to England predisposed less with Horatian than with Ovidian habits of thought – habits that might have encouraged him to reread Ovid's *ex Ponto* 2.10. This poem was written to Ovid's fellow Roman poet and close friend Macer, reminiscing about their youthful travels through Asia Minor and Sicily. Ovid's easing the boredom and pain of exile with remembrances of Mediterranean travels passed in the company of a close friend warranted at least some allusive attention in *Epitaphium Damonis*. As it stands, we are left to ponder the fact that passing away with Diodati were also any hopes of retracing the Mediterranean trajectory so fondly recorded by the Naso Milton chose to forget.

It mattered, of course, that Milton returned to England to help a revolution; and much would await the returning, more mature Milton. But the full consequences of the loss of Diodati would also await him, exacerbated by his forgetting to 'love his Naso's name.'

Chapter Five

Coda: Exiting the Shadow of *Ultima Britannia* in *Paradise Lost*

Paradise Lost's Raphael 'Sailes between worlds and worlds,' as he makes his way to Adam to warn of impending danger. As scholars have long noted, the mature Milton's *Paradise Lost* was of such expansive scope that, in many ways, it was destined to become the last link in the chain of epic literary history and its inheritances from classical antiquity. As mentioned in my first chapter, Frank Lestringant has remarked on early modernity's 'rupture of scales that changed people's way of viewing the world.' Milton, augmenting his story of the Fall with an incessantly roving cosmographic eye, ruptured any prior sense of epic scale. And thus, *Paradise Lost*, among so many other things, can be viewed as the disappearance of the shadow of *ultima Britannia* in English verse. But before punctuating this claim, we do well, one last time, to pass through the exiled Ovid.

In his epic's first book, Milton uses several similes to depict the '[i]nnumerable' hordes of fallen angels languishing on the sulphurous floors of Hell. One oft-quoted simile is the poet's description of the stunned, fallen angels, 'Thick as Autumnal Leaves that strow the Brooks / in *Vallombrosa*, where th' *Etrurian* shades / High overarch't imbow'r' (1.301–3). Parker foregrounds this passage as deeply autobiographical, Milton's brief postponing of the demands of his epic narrative in order to indulge in lyrical reminiscences of his strolls through the shades of the Arno Valley outside Florence. Here, as Parker writes, the young poet 'enlarged his experience . . . discovering himself . . . storing up memories' – memories that eventually made their way into the epic he earlier anticipated while strolling in the Arno Valley (172).

Editorial commentary has also long offered enriching opportunities to read Milton's autumnal simile through the lens of the poet's impeccable knowledge of epic literary history. Years ago, C.M. Bowra noted similar images in Homer, Virgil, and Tasso, all of whom depict doomed spirits, numerous as fallen autumn leaves, departing on Charon's boat across the Styx.[1] And Merritt Y. Hughes linked the passage to Milton's familiarity with a simile in the third canto of Dante's *Inferno* (219n302–4). Thus does Milton's simile range from the specificity of autobiographical reminiscence to the broader scope of epic literary history. What we do not see, however, is any trace of the exiled Ovid, an absent presence all the more noteworthy given that he, too, had contributed to literary history's autumnal simile in *Tristia* 3.8.

In this elegy, there is little evidence of the *Musa iocasa* that Ovid courted throughout his poetic career. The elegist himself is dying. Ovid ponders the misery of his frozen exile on the shores of the Black Sea by echoing Virgil's famous lines in the *Aeneid* 6 and their account of the dead souls congregating on the banks of Lethe as they await ferrying across the river (*quam multa in silvis autumni frigore primo / lapsa cadunt folia*, 309–10). The simile, where dead souls are as wasted and dispensable as autumnal fallen leaves, is perhaps (as Milton likely judged) epic literary history's most haunting depiction of impending doom. Thus, the moment is intertextually charged when Ovid, observing his withered skin, writes, 'such a hue is in autumn, when the first chill has smitten them, [it] shows on the leaves that young winter has marred' (*quique per autumnum percussis frigore primo / est color in foliis*, 29–30). So severe are the Tomitan winters that Ovid's skin, continually assaulted by the cold, has taken on the dying hue of autumnal leaves. In the metaphorical 'autumn' of his career, Ovid also knows that it will be the all-too-real Tomitan winters, distancing him from Rome as surely as Charon's dead souls were distanced from their former early existences, that will eventually do him in.

In this morbid passage Ovid's *ingenium*, in the form of his intertextual dialogue with Virgil, is nevertheless very much alive. But just five lines later, the poet, with little trace of his characteristic play, anticipates his death: 'Clinging and standing like a visible body before my eyes is the figure of my fate that I must scan' (*haerat et ante oculos veluti spectabile corpus / astat fortunae forma legenda mea*, 35–6). More than fifty years ago, the classicist A.G. Lee praised these lines as 'unparalleled in Latin poetry.'[2] Although such hyperboles are typical of the at-times florid

---

1 *From Virgil to Milton* (London: Macmillan & Co., 1945), 240–1.
2 A.G. Lee, 'An Appreciation of "Tristia" III.viii,' *Greece & Rome* 18, no. 54 (1949): 119.

prose of an earlier scholarly era, what prompted Lee's effusive praise of this passage is worth lingering over, particularly his translational note that '*Spectabilis* usually means not only "visible" but "worth looking at, remarkable," almost "compelling the attention"' (119).

And thus does the exiled Ovid bow out to his rival Virgil, whose path to epic he had rejected earlier in his career. Ovid concedes that he has become one of the dying leaves of the *Aeneid* 6, no longer capable of captivating his readers' attention, awaiting death on a remote shoreline – perhaps also (in this elegy at least) awaiting expulsion from literary history. It can go without saying that Ovid's place in literary history has been long-since secured. But it is also the uncanny case (in light of this book's previous chapter) that both Hughes and Bowra excluded Ovid from the possible sources for *Paradise Lost*'s autumnal simile. The absence of Ovid from their source list suggests that Milton had himself utterly 'forgotten to love his Naso's name' in a simile wholly invested in mastering the epic simile.

Some fifty lines later, Milton deploys another simile to depict the hordes of fallen angels, a simile also hinting at the absent presence of the exiled Ovid in *Paradise Lost*. Milton describes a 'multitude, like which the populous North / Pour'd never from her frozen loins, to pass / *Rhene* or the *Danaw*' (351–3). Milton's 'map consciousness' (to echo David Fletcher's conceptual term) is clearly evident in this passage, where his simile consults not a 'map' of literary history but the proliferating early modern world maps mentioned in my introductory chapter. These maps, among other things, allowed geographers and historians to trace more precisely such migratory patterns as the mass movement of the Vandals on a North-South axis from the Rhine to the Danube – and further south to Libya.[3] Allan H. Gilbert's spare entry on Milton's 'Danaw,' which he lists under 'Danubius,' reads: 'A river rising in southern Germany and flowing southeast into the Black Sea. It was for a long period a boundary of the Roman empire.'[4] Neither Milton's simile nor Gilbert's gloss observes that on the boundary of the Roman empire Ovid established the protocols for how to write poetry where the 'Danaw' estuary empties into the marginal Black Sea. Milton, 'content with these British islands as my world,' was also 'content' to

---

3 It should also be noted, however, that as editors have pointed out, Milton's reference to these migrations was probably taken directly from an anonymous 1674 translation of Machiavelli's *The Florentine History*.

4 *A Geographical Dictionary of Milton* (New York: Russell & Russell, 1919), 98.

forget his Naso's name, consulting not an Ovidian poetic 'map' of the 'Danaw' as it emptied into the Black Sea but rather the detailed maps of an increasingly consolidated early modern 'map consciousness.'

In his preface to Book II of *Reason*, Milton alluded to Aristotle's geohumoural theory that northern races lacked creative intelligence (*Politics*, 7.6.1) to voice concern that 'our climate' might be an obstacle to his goal of becoming a great epic poet. But in the invocation to Book 9 of *Paradise Lost*, Milton, trusting that 'cold / Climate' would not 'damp my intended wing' (44–5), is fully in control of his epic's 'higher Argument' (42). We can even detect traces of the *Londini Milto* of the Italian tour, displaying to the likes of Salzilli and Manso the genius of a poet from *ultima Britannia* where, to be sure, the lungs of winds blow with uncontrollable force, but also nurture *ingenium* on a shoreline far from the Mediterranean.

Throughout *Paradise Lost*, there is much evidence that the mature Milton had indeed achieved his goal of a profound 'content with these British islands as my world.' Taking up residence on what was once antiquity's *ultima Britannia*, Milton wrote an epic so cosmographically expansive that it trivializes any effort to perceive Miltonic distinctions between a much earlier Mediterranean centrality and British Isles marginality. In Book 2, the *apeiron* is found not on the shores of the British Isles but rather in Chaos, an 'Illimitable ocean without bound / Without dimension . . . length, breadth, and highth' (2.892–3), an inchoate stew that is 'neither sea, nor shore' (912). Attempting to build a causeway from Hell to Earth, Sin and Death at one point end up 'shoaling towards the mouth of Hell,' trapped in the 'Solid or slimy' waters of Chaos (10.286–8). And thus Milton's verse, far from shadowed by thoughts of writing on an *apeiron*, instead creates it, *ex nihilo*, from his teeming poetic imagination.

In those moments when his epic does allude to existing shorelines, Milton ranges with equal allusive ease from the Mediterranean to the North Atlantic. At one point, he indulges in a punning coastal etymology when the pre-lapsarian Eve samples the bounty of the Mediterranean's 'middle shores' (5.339), the poet's reminder that the very name 'Mediterranean' never fails to speak poetically, especially when rendered in English vernacular. But at scattered points throughout his epic, Milton does not pay homage to antiquity's *peirar* but rather turns to the Mediterranean and the Hellespont as imagistic repositories for further portraying the formless Chaos through which Satan struggles to reach earth. Chaos is likened to the vast Barca, between the Gulf of

Sidra and Tunis (2.904); to the bottlenecked Bosporus straits, where the *Argo* journeyed 'betwist the justling Rocks' (2.1021); and to the straits of Messina, navigated 'with difficulty and labor hard' by Ulysses (2.1021). In Book 10, Satan, making his way back to Hell, is compared to the Greek-invading Xerxes, attempting to tame the Hellespont's 'indignant waves' (10.311). In these images, the poet dwells not on Mediterranean centrality but rather on an unruly Mediterranean otherness – the Mediterranean, that is, as appropriate for portraying Chaos as an *apeiron*.

Unhampered by the 'cold climate' on the edge of antiquity's *mappae mundi* and unintimidated by the Mediterranean's centrality for antiquity, Milton also ambitiously takes his poetry to 'western' seas. In book 1, the poet turns to Plutarch's *On the Cessation of the Oracles* to trace a trajectory from the Mediterranean to the edges of the western seas. He narrates Plutarch's story of how Saturn, having lost power to Zeus, fled 'over *Adria* to th' *Hesperian* Fieldds, / And o'er the *Celtic* roam'd the utmost Isles' (1.520). With this allusion, a remnant of the classical gods has migrated west from the Adriatic to Anglesey where Saturn slumbers not all that far, relatively speaking, from where Milton composed his epic. At one point, Uriel, on his way to warn Gabriel that an evil spirit has escaped from the infernal depths, descends on a sunbeam that 'Bore him slope downward to the Sun now fall'n / Beneath th' *Azores*' (4.591–2). When Satan lands at the world's outermost orb, his telescopic vision – the same wide-angle lens through which the Satan of *In quantum Novembris* glimpses the wave-beaten cliffs of Albion (*Iamque fluentisonis albentia rupibus arva / Apparent*, 25–6) – espies the constellation Andromeda, 'far off Atlantic Seas / Beyond the Horizon' (3.559–60). Whether espied by an angel or an archfiend, the North Atlantic is eminently mappable within Milton's world geography. All of which is to conclude that nowhere evident in *Paradise Lost* was a poet haunted by the spectral geographies that, as much of this book has argued, haunted any number of prior early modern English humanist inheritances from antiquity. The poet of *Paradise Lost* was disinvested in antiquity's quarantining of the British Isles from the domain of poetry itself; he did not brood on thoughts that he was writing his epic not all that far from a shoreline that Virgil had declared sundered from the world.

In *Areopagitica*, Milton famously praised the poet of *The Faerie Queene* as his 'original.' In his 1630 sonnet 'On Shakespeare,' he praised the bard as 'the great heir of Fame' (5). But the mature Milton followed neither of his esteemed predecessors into the shadow of *ultima Britannia*.

'Sailing,' like Raphael, 'from world to world,' Milton gazed not upon Spenser's Ptolemaic Hebrides; nor Britomart's Thames, remapped by the cynical Paridell on the 'utmost angle' of the world; nor Colin Clout's choppy Irish Sea (so metrically smoothed out in *Lycidas*); nor *Lear*'s ever-receding Dover coastline and Shakespeare's attenuated North Atlantic sublime; nor the cognitive dissonance destabilizing *Cymbeline*'s queen as she approaches the East Anglian shoreline. The late sixteenth-century Samuel Daniel fretted over Guarini's accusation of British 'costs . . . with no measures graced.' But the mature Milton (unlike his younger persona who was the 'last of the Elizabethans') no longer gazed on Tasso's and Manso' Bay of Naples, anxiously measuring the North Atlantic's (poetic) distance from the Mediterranean. Put another way, by the later seventeenth century, early modern English verse had rendered obsolete not only the geographic topos of *ultima Britannia*, but also any impulse to view local shorelines through the mediating lens of antiquity's Mediterranean.

Bibliography

Alpers, Paul. *The Poetry of the 'Faerie Queene.'* Princeton: Princeton University Press, 1967.

Anderson, Judith H. 'The Antiquities of Fairyland and Ireland.' *JEGP* (1987): 199–214.

Ariosto, Ludovico. *Ludovico Ariosto: Orlando Furioso.* Edited by Lanfranco Caretti. Torino: Giulio Einaudi, 1966.

– *Ludovico Ariosto's 'Orlando Furioso,' translated into English Heroical Verse by Sir John Harington.* Edited and with an introduction by Robert McNulty. Oxford: Clarendon Press, 1972.

Armitage, David. 'The Elizabethan Idea of Empire.' *Transactions of the Royal Historical Society* 14 (2004): 269–77.

Arthos, John. *Milton and the Italian Cities.* New York: Barnes and Noble, 1968.

Ascoli, Albert. *Ariosto's Bitter Harmony: Crisis and Evasion in the Italian Renaissance.* Princeton: Princeton University Press, 1987.

Attridge, Derek. *Well-Weighed Syllables: Elizabethan Verse in Classical Metres.* Cambridge: Cambridge University Press, 1974.

Bailyn, Bernard. *Atlantic History: Concept and Contours.* Cambridge, MA: Harvard University Press, 2005.

Baldwin, T.W. *William Shakespeare's Small Latine and Lesse Greeke.* 2 vols. Urbana, IL: University of Illinois Press, 1944.

Baker, David J. *Between Nations: Shakespeare, Spenser, Marvell, and the Question of Britain.* Stanford, CA: Stanford University Press, 1997.

– '"Wildehirissheman": Colonial Representation in Shakespeare's *Henry V.*' *ELR* 22 (1993): 31–67.

Barkan, Leonard. *Nature's Work of Art: The Human Body as Image of the World.* New Haven: Yale University Press, 1975.

Barroll, J.L. 'Shakespeare and Roman History.' *Modern Language Review* 53 (1958): 327–43.

Bates, Catherine. *The Rhetoric of Courtship in Elizabethan Language and Literature.* Cambridge: Cambridge University Press, 1992.

Bede. *History of the English Church and People.* Translated and with an introduction by Leo Sherley-Price. Harmondsworth, Middlesex: Penguin Books, 1955.

Beer, Gillian. 'Discourse of an Island.' In *Literature and Science as Modes of Expression,* edited by Fredrick Amrine. Dordrecht and Borton: Kluwer Academic Publishing, 1989.

Bellamy, Elizabeth Jane, and Rachel Trubowitz. 'A River Runs Through It.' Paper given at the 2006 RSA, Cambridge, England.

Bennett, Josephine Waters. 'Britain Among the Fortunate Isles.' *Studies in Philology* 53 (1956): 114–40.

Benson, Pamela J. 'Florimell at Sea.' *Spenser Studies* 6 (1985): 83–94.

Berger, Harry Jr. *Revisionary Play: Studies in the Spenserian Dynamic.* Introduction by Louis Montrose. Berkeley and Los Angeles: University of California Press, 1988.

Bergeron, David. '*Cymbeline*: Shakespeare's Last Roman Play.' *Shakespeare Quarterly* 31 (1980): 31–41.

Besslich, S. 'Ovid's Winter in Tomis.' *Gymnasium* 79 (1972): 177–91.

Biow, Douglas. '*Mirabile Dictu*': *Representations of the Marvelous in Medieval and Renaissance Epic.* Ann Arbor: University of Michigan Press, 1996.

Blaeu, Willem Janszoon. *The Light of Navigation.* Amsterdam: William Johnson, 1612.

Blissett, William. 'Florimell and Marinell,' *SEL* 5 (1965): 87–104.

Bodin, Jean. *Method for the Easy Comprehension of History.* Translated by Beatrice Reynolds. New York: Octagon, 1966.

Bourne, William. *The Regiment of the Sea.* London: Thomas Hackett, 1574.

Bowra, C.M. *From Virgil to Milton.* London: Macmillan, 1945.

Braden, Gordon. 'Riverrun: An Epic Catalogue in *The Faerie Queene*.' *ELR* 5 (1975): 25–48.

Bradner, Leicester. *Musae Anglicanae: A History of Anglo-Latin Poetry, 1500–1925.* New York: Modern Language Association of America, 1940.

Braudel, Fernand. *Les Memoires de la Mediterranée: Prehistoire et Antiquité.* Paris: Éditions de Fallois, 1998.

– *The Mediterranean and the Mediterranean World in the Age of Philip II.* Translated by Sian Reynolds. New York: Harper & Row, 1972–3.

– *Memory and the Mediterranean.* Translated by Sian Reynolds. New York: Alfred A. Knopf, 2001.

Brockbank, J.P. 'History and Histrionics in *Cymbeline.' Shakespeare Survey* 11 (1958): 42–9.

Browne, William. *Britannia's Pastorals.* London: John Haviland, 1625.

Bruster, Douglas, and Robert Weimann. *Prologue to Shakespeare's Theatre: Performance and Liminality in Early Modern Drama.* New York: Routledge, 2004.

Burrow, Colin. 'Shakespeare and Humanist Culture.' In *Shakespeare and the Classics,* edited by Charles Martindale and A.B. Taylor, 9–27. Cambridge: Cambridge University Press, 2004.

Bush, Douglas, ed. *A Variorum Commentary on the Poems of John Milton.* Vol. 1: The Latin and Greek Poems. New York: Columbia Press, 1970.

Caesar. *Commentaries.* Translated by Arthur Golding. 1565.

Camden, William. *Britain, or a Chorographicall Description of the Most Flourishing Kingdomes, England, Scotland, and Ireland.* Translated by Philemon Holland. London: George Bishop & John Norton, 1610.

– *Britannia.* Translated by Richard Gough. 1607 edition. London: Nichols and Son, 1806.

– 'Poems by William Camden, With Notes and Translations from the Latin.' Edited by George Burke Johnston. Translated by Philemon Holland. *Studies in Philology* 72 (1975).

– *Remains Concerning Britain* (1605). Edited by D.R. Dunn. Toronto: University of Toronto Press, 1984.

Carroll, Clare. 'The Construction of Gender and the Cultural and Political Other in *The Faerie Queene* 5 and *A View of the Present State of Ireland*: The Critics, the Context, and the Case of Radigund.' *Criticism* 32 (1990): 163–91.

Cassano, Franco. 'Southern Thought.' Translated by Sandra Palaich. Edited by Artemis Leontis and Peter Murphy. Special issue, 'The Mediterranean,' *Thesis Eleven* 67 (2001): 4–5.

Catullus. *Catullus.* Edited by Francis Warre Cornish. Cambridge, MA: Cambridge University Press, 1961.

Caxton, William, ed. *Polycronicon.* English translation by John of Trevisa. Westminster, 1482.

Chaucer, Geoffrey. *The Works of Geoffrey Chaucer.* Edited by F.N. Robinson. Boston: Houghton Mifflin, 1957.

Cheney, Patrick. *Marlowe's Counterfeit Profession: Ovid, Spenser, Counter-Nationhood.* Toronto: University of Toronto Press, 1997.

Claassen, Jo-Marie. *Displaced Persons: Literature of Exile from Cicero to Boethius.* Madison, WI: University of Wisconsin Press, 1999.

Coleridge, Samuel Taylor. *Miscellaneous Criticism.* Edited by T.M. Raysor. Cambridge: Harvard University Press, 1936.

Colie, Rosalie. *The Resources of Kind: Genre-Theory in the Renaissance*. Berkeley
    and Los Angeles: University of California Press, 1973.
Condee, R.W. *Structure in Milton's Poetry*. University Park, PA: Penn State
    University Press, 1974.
Conley, Tom. *The Self-Made Map: Cartographic Writing in Early Modern France*.
    Minneapolis: University of Minnesota Press, 1996.
Corbett, Margery, and Ronald Lightbown. *The Comely Frontispiece: The Emblem-
    atic Title-page in England, 1550–1660*. London: Routledge and Kegan Paul,
    1979.
Cormack, Lesley B. *Charting an Empire: Geography of the English Universities,
    1580–1620*.
Chicago: University of Chicago Press, 1997.
Curran, John E. Jr. 'The History Never Was Written: Bards, Druids, and the
    Problem of Antiquarianism in *Polyolbion*.' *Renaissance Quarterly* 51 (1998):
    498–525.
– 'Royalty Unlearned and Honor Untaught: British Savages and Historio-
    graphical Change in *Cymbeline*.' *Comparative Drama* 31, no. 2 (1997):
    277–303.
Curtius, E.R. *European Literature and the Latin Middle Ages*. Translated by
    Willard R. Trask. New York: Harper and Row, 1953.
Daiches, David. 'Some Aspects of Milton's Pastoral Imagery.' In *More Literary
    Essays*, 96–114. Edinburgh and London: Oliver and Boyd, 1968.
Daniel, Samuel. *The Complete Works in Verse and Prose of Samuel Daniel*. Vol. 1.
    Edited by Alexander B. Grossart. London: Spenser Society, 1885–96.
– *Poems and a Defence of Ryme*. Edited by Arthur Colby Sprague. Cambridge,
    MA: Harvard University Press, 1930.
Danson, Lawrence. '*Henry V*: King, Chorus, and Critics.' *Shakespeare Quarterly*
    34, no. 1 (1983): 27–43.
Dee, John. *General and Rare Memorials Pertayning to the Perfect Arte of Naviga-
    tion*. London, 1577. Reprint, Amsterdam: Theatrum Orbis Terrarum, 1968.
Dilke, O.A.W. *Greek and Roman Maps*. Baltimore: The Johns Hopkins Uni-
    versity Press, 1998.
Dodge, R.E. Neil. 'Spenser's Imitations from Ariosto.' *PMLA* 12 (1897).
Dorian, Donald C. *The English Diodatis*. New Brunswick, NJ: Rutgers Univer-
    sity Press, 1950.
– *The Works of Michael Drayton*. Edited by J. William Hebel. Oxford: Shake-
    speare Head Press, 1961.
Dubrow, Heather. 'The Arraignment of Paridell: Tudor Historiography in *The
    Faerie Queene*, III.ix.' *Studies in Philology* 87 (1990): 312–28.

Durling, Robert M. *The Figure of the Poet in Renaissance Epic*. Cambridge, MA: Harvard University Press, 1967.

DuRocher, Richard J. *Milton and Ovid*. Ithaca, NY: Cornell University Press, 1985.

Eccles, Marc. 'Samuel Daniel in France and Italy.' *Studies in Philology* 34, no. 2 (1937): 148–67.

Edwards, Philip. *Sea-Mark: The Metaphorical Voyage, Spenser to Milton*. Liverpool, Liverpool University Press, 1997.

Elton, Oliver. *Michael Drayton: A Critical Study*. London: A. Constable, 1905.

Erickson, Wayne. *Mapping 'The Faerie Queene': Quest Structure and the World of the Poem*. New York: Garland Press, 1996.

Evans, Harry B. 'Winter and Warfare in Ovid's Tomis.' *Classical Journal* 70, no. 3 (1975): 1–9.

Falconer, Alexander Frederick. *Shakespeare and the Sea*. New York: Frederick Ungar Publishing Co., 1964.

Ferguson, Arthur B. *Clio Unbound: Perceptions of the Social and Cultural Past in Renaissance England*. Durham, NC: Duke University Press, 1979.

– *Utter Antiquity: Perceptions of Prehistory in Renaissance England*. Durham, NC: Duke University Press, 1993.

Fichter, Andrew. *Poets Historical: Dynastic Epic in the Renaissance*. New Haven: Yale University Press, 1982.

Finucci, Valeria. *The Lady Vanishes: Subjectivity and Representation in Castiglione and Ariosto*. Stanford, CA: Stanford University Press, 1992.

Fitzpatrick, Joan. *Shakespeare, Spenser and the Contours of Britain*. Hertfordshire: University of Hertfordshire Press, 2004.

Fletcher, Angus. *The Prophetic Moment: An Essay on Spenser*, 106–21. Chicago: University of Chicago Press, 1971.

Fletcher, David. *The Emergence of Estate Maps: Christ Church, Oxford, 1600–1840*. Oxford: Clarendon Press, 1995.

Floyd-Wilson, Mary. *English Ethnicity and Race in Early Modern Drama*. Cambridge: Cambridge University Press, 2006.

Fränkel, Hermann. *Ovid: A Poet Between Two Worlds*. Berkeley and Los Angeles: University of California Press, 1945.

Franson, J. Karl. 'The Fatal Voyage of Edward King, Milton's Lycidas.' *Milton Studies* 25 (1990): 67–88.

Frazer, Sir George James, ed. *Ovid's Fasti*. Cambridge, MA: Harvard University Press, 1951.

Frye, Northrop. *Anatomy of Criticism*. Princeton: Princeton University Press, 1957.

Fussner, F. Smith. *Tudor History and the Historians.* New York and London: Basic Books, Inc., 1970.

Geoffrey of Monmouth. *Geoffrey of Monmouth: Historia Regum Britanniae.* Edited by Jacob Hammer. Cambridge, MA: The Medieval Academy of America, 1951.

Giamatti, A. Bartlett. *Exile and Change in Renaissance Literature.* New Haven: Yale University Press, 1984.

– *Play of Double Senses: Spenser's 'Faerie Queene.'* Prentice-Hall, 1975.

Gibbons, Brian. *Shakespeare and Multiplicity.* Cambridge: Cambridge University Press, 1993.

Gilbert, Allan H. *A Geographical Dictionary of Milton.* New York: Russell & Russell, 1919.

– *Literary Criticism from Plato to Dryden.* New York: American Book Company, 1940.

Giles, J.A., trans. *Six Old English Chronicles.* London: Henry G. Bohn, 1891.

Gillies, John. *Shakespeare and the Geography of Difference.* Cambridge: Cambridge University Press, 1994.

Goldberg, Jonathan. *James I and the Politics of Literature: Jonson, Shakespeare, Donne, and* Gordon, Andrew and Bernhard Klein, eds. *Literature, Mapping, and the Politics of Space in Early Modern Britain.* Cambridge: Cambridge University Press, 2001.

Gottfried, Rudolf B. 'Spenser and the Italian Myth of Locality.' *Studies in Philology* 34, no. 2 (1937): 107–25.

Greenblatt, Stephen. 'Invisible Bullets.' In *Shakespearean Negotiations: The Circulation of Social Energy in Renaissance England,* 21–65. Berkeley and Los Angeles: University of California Press, 1988.

Greene, Jack P. and Philip D. Morgan, eds. *Atlantic History: A Critical Appraisal.* New York: Oxford University Press, 2009.

Greene, Thomas. *The Descent from Heaven: A Study of Epic Continuity.* New Haven: Yale University Press, 1963.

– *The Light in Troy: Imitation and Discovery in Renaissance Poetry.* New Haven: Yale University Press, 1982.

Gross, Kenneth. 'Reflections on the Blatant Beast.' *Spenser Studies* 13 (1999): 101–23.

Guy, John, ed. *The Reign of Elizabeth I: Court and Culture in the Last Decade.* Cambridge: Cambridge University Press, 1995.

Hadfield, Andrew. *Edmund Spenser's Irish Experience: Wilde Fruit and Salvage Soyl.* Oxford: Clarendon Press, 1997.

– *Shakespeare, Spenser, and the Matter of Britain.* Harmondsworth: Palgrave MacMillan, 2004.

Hale, John K. 'Milton's Self-Presentation in *Poems...1645.' Milton Quarterly* 25, no. 2 (1991): 37–48.

Hall, Henry. *Idylls of Fishermen: A History of the Literary Species.* New York: Columbia University Press, 1914.

Hanford, James Holly. *John Milton: Englishman.* New York: Crown Publishers, 1949.

– 'Milton's Italy.' *Annuale Medievale* 5 (1954): 49–63.

– 'The Youth of Milton: An Interpretation of His Early Literary Developments.' In *Studies of Shakespeare, Milton and Donne.* New York: MacMillan, 1925.

Hardie, Philip. *Ovid's Poetics of Illusion.* Cambridge: Cambridge University Press, 2002.

Harding, Davis P. *Milton and the Renaissance Ovid.* Urbana, IL: University of Illinois Press, 1946.

Harper, Carrie Anna. *The Sources of the British Chronicle History in Spenser's 'Faerie Queene.'* Philadelphia: Haskell House, 1964.

Harrison, Stephen. 'Ovid and Genre: Evolutions of an Elegist.' In *The Cambridge Companion to Ovid*, edited by Philip Hardie, 79–94. Cambridge: Cambridge University Press, 2002.

Harrison, William. *William Harrison: The Description of England.* Edited by George Edelen. Ithaca: Cornell University Press, 1968.

Hartog, François. *The Mirror of Herodotus: The Representation of the Other in the Writing of History.* Translated by Janet Lloyd. Berkeley and Los Angeles: University of California Press, 1988.

Harvey, Gabriel. *Pierces Supererogation, or a New Prayse of the old Asse* (1593). In *The Works of Gabriel Harvey*, Vol. 2, edited and with an introduction by Alexander B. Grosart. 1884. Reprint New York: AMS Press, 1966.

Harvey, P.D.A., and R.A. Skelton. Introduction to *Local Maps and Plans from Medieval England.* Oxford: Clarendon Press, 1986.

Hawkes, C.F.C. 'Pythias: Europe and the Greek Explorers.' The Eighth J.L. Myers Memorial Lecture, Oxford University, May 20, 1975.

Helgerson, Richard. *Forms of Nationhood: The Writing of Elizabethan England.* Chicago: University of Chicago Press, 1992.

Herendeen, Wyman. *From Landscapes to Literature: The River and the Myth of Geography.* Pittsburgh, PA: Duquesne University Press, 1986.

Herodotus. *The Famous Hystory of Herodotus.* 1584.

Herron, Thomas. *Spenser's Irish Work: Plantation and Colonial Reform.* Aldershot: Ashgate, 2007.

Hesiod. *Works and Days*, 170–4; Hymn VII, 29. In *Hesiod, The Homeric Hymns and Homerica.* Translated by H.G. Evelyn-White. Cambridge, MA: Harvard University Press, 1936.

Higden, Ranulf. *The English Translation of John Trevisa and of an Unknown Writer of the Fifteenth Century*. Edited by Churchill Babington et al. 9 vols. London, 1865–86.

– *Polycronicon*. English translation by John of Trevisa. 1387. Westminster: Wynkyn de Worde, 1495.

Highley, Christopher. ' "The Cause be not good": *Henry V* and Essex's Irish Campaign.' In *Shakespeare, Spenser, and the Crisis in Ireland*. Cambridge: Cambridge University Press, 1997.

Hoffman, Nancy Jo. *Spenser's Pastorals: 'The Shepheardes Calender' and 'Colin Clout.'* Baltimore: The Johns Hopkins University Press, 1977.

Holderness, Graham. ' "What ish my nation?": Shakespeare and National Identities.' *Textual Practice* (1991): 74–93.

Homer. *Homer: The Odyssey*. Translated by E.V. Rieu. Harmondsworth: Penguin Books, 1946.

Hopkins, Lisa. 'Neighbourhood in *Henry V*.' In *Shakespeare and Ireland: History, Politics, Culture*, edited by Mark Thornton Barnett and Ramona Wray, 9–26. Basingstoke: Palgrave, 1997.

– *Shakespeare on the Edge: Border-Crossing in the Tragedies and in the 'Henriad.'* Aldershot: Ashgate, 2005.

Horace. *Horace: The Odes and Epodes*. Translated by C.E. Bennett. Cambridge, MA: Harvard University Press, 1919.

– *Horace: Satires, Epistles and Ars Poetica*. Translated by H. Rushton Fairclough. Cambridge, MA: Harvard University Press, 1926.

Horden, Peregrine, and Nicholas Purcell. *The Corrupting Sea: A Study of Mediterranean History*. Oxford: Blackwell, 2006.

Hunt, Clay.*'Lycidas' and the Italian Critics*. New Haven: Yale University Press, 1975.

Hunter, G.K. *John Lyly: The Humanist as Courtier*. London: Routledge, 1962.

James I. 'Speech of 1603.' In *The Political Works of James I*. Edited by Charles Howard McIlwain. New York: Russell and Russell, 1965.

James, Heather. *Shakespeare's Troy: Drama, Politics, and the Translation of Empire*. Cambridge: Cambridge University Press, 1997.

Jones, Emrys. 'Stuart *Cymbeline.*' *Essays in Criticism* 11 (1962): 84–99.

Jonson, Ben. *Ben Jonson*. Vol 7. Edited by C.H. Herford and Percy and Evelyn Simpson. Oxford, 1941.

Johnson, Samuel. *Johnson on Shakespeare: The Yale Edition of the Works of Samuel Johnson*. Vol. 8. Edited by Arthur Sherbo. Introduction by Bertrand Bronson. 1968.

Jones, Ivor W. *Shipwrecks of North Wales*. Newton Abbot, Devonshire: David, 1973.

Justa Edouardo King: Reproduced from the Original Edition, 1638, with an Introduction. Introduction by Ernest C. Mossner. New York: Columbia University Press for the Facsimile Text Society, 1939.

Kahn, Charles E. *Anaximander and the Origins of Greek Cosmology*. New York: Columbia Press, 1960.

Kaplan, M. Lindsay. *The Culture of Slander in Early Modern England*. Cambridge: Cambridge University Press, 1997.

Keats, John. *John Keats: Selected Poems and Letters*. Edited and with an introduction Douglas Bush. Boston: Houghton Mifflin, 1959.

Keilen, Sean. *Vulgar Eloquence: On the Renaissance Invention of English Literature*. New Haven: Yale University Press, 2006.

Kendrick, T.D. *British Antiquity*. London: Methuen, 1950.

Kennedy, E.J. 'Ovid.' In *The Cambridge History of Classical Literature*, vol. 2, edited by W. V. Clausen and E.J. Kenney, 420–57. Cambridge: Cambridge University Press, 1982.

Kennedy, William J. *Jacopo Sannazaro and the Uses of Pastoral*. Hanover and London: University Press of New England, 1983.

Kenney, E.J. and Sidney Hinds. 'Elegiac poetry, Latin.' In *The Oxford Classical Dictionary*, 3rd ed. Oxford: Oxford University Press, 1996.

Kilgour, Maggie. 'Writing on Water.' *ELR* 29 (1999): 282–305.

King, John. *Tudor Royal Iconography: Literature and Art in an Age of Religious Crisis*. Princeton: Princeton University Press, 1989.

Kissack, Robert Ashton Jr. 'The Sea in Anglo-Saxon and Middle English Poetry.' *Washington University Studies: Humanities Series* 13 (1926): 371–89.

Klein, Bernhard. *Maps and the Writing of Space in Early Modern England and Ireland*. Basingstroke: Palgrave, 2001.

Knapp, Jeffrey. *An Empire Nowhere: England, America, and Literature from 'Utopia' to 'The Tempest.'* Berkeley and Los Angeles: University of California Press, 1992.

Knight, G. Wilson. *The Crown of Life: Essays on Interpretation of Shakespeare's Final Plays*. London: Methuen, 1958.

Lambarde, William. *Perambulation of Kent*. London: Printed for Matthew Walbancke and Dan. Pakeman, 1656.

Lee, A.G. 'An Appreciation of "Tristia" III.viii.' *Greece and Rome* 18, no. 54 (1949): 113–20.

– *The New Year's Gift*. In *The Itinerary of John Leland*, 9 vols, edited by T. Hearne, 3rd edition. Oxford, 1770.

Lestringant, Frank. *Mapping the Renaissance: The Geographical Imagination in the Age of Discovery*. Cambridge: Polity Press, 1994.

Levin, Harry. *The Myth of the Golden Age in the Renaissance*. New York: Oxford University Press, 1969.

Levy, F.J. *Tudor Historical Thought*. San Marino, CA: The Huntington Library, 1967.

Lipking, Lawrence. 'The Genius of the Shore: Lycidas, Adamastor, and the Poetics of Nationalism.' *PMLA* (1995): 205–21.

Loades, David M. *England's Maritime Empire: Seapower, Commerce, and Policy, 1490–1690* New York: Longman, 2000.

Longinus. *On the Sublime*. In *Critical Theory Since Plato*, rev. ed. Edited by Hazard Adams. New York: Harcourt Brace Jovanovich, Inc., 1992.

Lovejoy, Arthur O., Gilbert Chinard, George Boas, and Ronald S. Crane, eds. *A Documentary History of Primitivism and Related Ideas*. Vol. 1. Baltimore: The Johns Hopkins University Press, 1935.

Low, Anthony. '*Mansus*: In Its Context.' *Milton Studies* 19 (1984): 105–26.

Lucan. '*Pharsalia': Lucan*.Translated and with an introduction by Jane Wilson Joyce. Ithaca: Cornell University Press, 1993.

Luxon, Thomas H. *Single Imperfection: Milton, Marriage and Friendship*. Pittsburgh, PA: Duquesne University Press, 2005.

Lyly, John. *Euphues: The Anatomy of Wit and Euphues and His England by John Lyly*. Edited by Morris William Croll and Harry Clemens. New York: Russell & Russell, Inc., 1964.

MacKellar, Walter. *The Latin Poems of John Milton*. New Haven: Yale University Press, 1930.

MacLean, Gerald M. *Time's Witness: Historical Representations in English Poetry, 1593–1660*. Madison: University of Wisconsin Press, 1990.

MacLeod, Bruce. *The Geography of Empire in English Literature*. Cambridge: Cambridge University Press, 1999.

Maley, Willy. 'Postcolonial Shakespeare: British Identity Formation and *Cymbeline*.' In *Shakespeare's Late Plays: New Readings*, edited by Jennifer Richards and James Knowles. Edinburgh: Edinburgh University Press, 1999. 145–57.

– *Salvaging Spenser: Colonialism, Culture and Identity*. London: Palgrave MacMillan, 1997.

Malkin, Irad. 'Networks and the Emergence of Greek Identity.' In *Mediterranean Paradigms and Classical Antiquity*, edited by Malkin. London and New York: Routledge, 2005.

Marcus, Leah. *Puzzling Shakespeare: Local Reading and Its Discontents*. Berkeley and Los Angeles: University of California Press, 1989.

Marlowe, Christopher. *The Complete Works of Christopher Marlowe*. 4 vols. Edited by Roma Gill. Oxford: Clarendon Press, 1987.

Martz, Louis. *Poet of Exile: A Study of Milton's Poetry*. New Haven: Yale University Press, 1966.

Mason, Eugene, trans. *Arthurian Chronicles: Wace and Layamon*. Toronto: University of Toronto Press, 1996.

Masson, David. *The Life of John Milton*. Vol. 1. London: MacMillan and Co., 1881. McCabe, Richard A. *Spenser's Monstrous Regiment: Elizabethan Ireland and the Poetics of Difference*. New York: Oxford University Press, 2002.

McCrae, Andrew. 'Fluvial Nation: Mobility and Poetry in Early Modern England.' *ELR* 38 (2008): 506–34.

McEachern, Claire. *The Poetics of English Nationhood, 1590–1612*. Cambridge: Cambridge University Press, 1996.

McGowan, Matthew. *Ovid in Exile: Power and Poetic Redress in the 'Tristia' and 'Epistulae ex Ponto.'* Leiden and Boston: Brill, 2009.

McMurphy, Susannah. *Spenser's Use of Ariosto*. Seattle: University of Washington Press, 1924.

Mentz, Steve. *At the Bottom of Shakespeare's Ocean*. Harrisburg, PA: Continuum, 2009.

Milton, John. *The Complete Works of John Milton*. Edited by Don M. Wolfe. New Haven: Yale University Press, 1953–82.

– *John Milton: Complete Poems and Major Prose*. Edited by Merritt Y. Hughes. New York: Odyssey Press, 1957.

– *Poems of Mr. John Milton*. 1645. Facsimile. Menston, York: Scolar, 1973.

– *The Works of John Milton*. Edited by Frank A. Patterson et al. New York: Columbia University Press, 1931–40.

Mikalachki, Jodi. *The Legacy of Boadicea: Gender and Nation in Early Modern England*. New York and London: Routledge, 1998.

Miola, Robert S. '*Cymbeline*: Shakespeare's Validation of Rome.' In *Roman Images: Selected Papers from the English Institute, 1982*, edited by Annabel Patterson, 51–62. Baltimore: The Johns Hopkins University Press, 1984.

– *Shakespeare's Reading (Oxford Shakespeare Topics)*. Oxford: Oxford University Press, 2000.

Momigliano, Arnaldo. 'Ancient History and the Antiquarian.' *Journal of the Warbur and Courtauld Institutes* (1955): 285–315.

Murrin, Michael. 'Spenser's Fairyland.' In *The Allegorical Epic: Essays in Its Rise and Decline*. Chicago: University of Chicago Press, 1980.

Nagle, Betty Rose. *The Poetics of Exile: Program and Polemic in the 'Tristia' and 'Epistulae ex Ponto' of Ovid*. Collection Latomus 170. Brussels, 1980.

Nearing, Homer. 'The Legend of Julius Caesar's British Conquest.' *PMLA* 64, no. 4 (1949), 889–929.

Neill, Michael. 'Broken English and Broken Irish: Nation, Language, and the Optics of Power in Shakespeare's Histories.' *Shakespeare Quarterly* 45 (1994): 1–32.

Nohrnberg, James. *The Analogy of 'The Faerie Queene.'* Princeton: Princeton University Press, 1976.

Norbrook, David. *Poetry and Politics in the English Renaissance*. Revised edition. New York: Oxford University Press, 2002.

O'Connell, Michael. *Mirror and Veil: The Historical Dimension of Spenser's 'Faerie Queene.'* Chapel Hill: University of North Carolina Press, 1977.

Oliensis, Ellen. 'Return to Sender: The Rhetoric of *nomina* in Ovid's *Tristia.'* *Ramus* 26 (1997): 172–93.

Orgel, Stephen. 'Shakespeare Imagines a Theater.' *Poetics Today* 5 (1984), 549–61.

Oruch, Jack B. 'Spenser, Camden, and the Poetic Marriage of Rivers.' *Studies in Philology* 64 (1967): 606–24.

Osgood, Charles G. 'Spenser's English Rivers.' *Transactions of the Connecticut Academy of Arts and Sciences* 23 (1920): 100–6.

Otis, Brooks. *Ovid as an Epic Poet*. Cambridge: Cambridge University Press, 1966.

Ovid. *The Metamorphoses*. 2 vols. Translated by Frank Justus Miller. 3rd edition. Revised by G.P. Goold. Cambridge, MA: Harvard University Press, 1977.

– *Ovid's 'Amores': Book One*. Edited and translated by John A. Barsby. Oxford: Clarendon Press, 1973.

– Ovid's Metamorphoses: Englished by George Sandys. 5th ed. London: Printed by J.F. for Richard Tomlines, 1664.

– *Ovid in Six Volumes, VI: Tristia, Ex Ponto*. Edited and translated by Arthur Leslie Wheeler. Cambridge, MA: Harvard University Press, 1988.

Parker, Patricia. 'Romance and Empire: Anachronistic *Cymbeline.'* In *Unfolded Tales: Essays on Renaissance Romance*, edited by George M. Logan and Gordon Teskey, 189–207. Ithaca: Cornell University Press, 1989.

– 'Uncertain Union: Welsh Leeks in Henry V.' In *British Identities and English Renaissance Literature*, edited by David Baker and Willy Maley, 81–100. Cambridge: Cambridge University Press, 2002.

Parollin, Peter A. 'Anachronistic Italy: Cultural Alliances and National Identity in *Cymbeline.'* *Shakespeare Studies* 30 (2002): 188–215.

Parry, Graham. *The Trophies of Time: English Antiquarians of the Seventeenth Century*. Oxford and New York: Oxford University Press, 1995.

Peckham, Robert Shannon. 'The Uncertain State of Islands: National Identity and the Discourse of Islands in Nineteenth-Century Britain and Greece.' *Journal of History and Geography* 29, no. 4 (2003): 499–515.

Peele, George. *The Araygnment of Paris.* Oxford, The Malone Society: Oxford University Press, 1910.

Piepho, Lee. 'The Latin and English Eclogues.' *Studies in Philology* 81 (1984): 461–72.

Pigman, G.W. III. *Grief and English Renaissance Elegy.* Cambridge: Cambridge University Press, 1985.

Plato. *Plato: The Sophist & The Statesman.* Translated and with an introduction by A.E. Taylor. Edited by Raymond Klibanski and Elizabeth Anscombe. London: Thomas Nelson and Sons, Ltd., 1961.

Pliny. *The History of the World, Commonly Called The Natural History of C. Plinius Secundus*, Translated by Philemon Holland. Introduction by Paul Turner. Carbondale: Southern Illinois University Press, 1962.

Prescott, Anne Lake. 'Drayton's Muse and Selden's "Story": The Interfacing of Poetry and History in *Poly-Olbion.' Studies in Philology* 87 (1990): 128–35.

Prince, F.T. *The Italian Elements of Milton's Verse.* New York: Oxford University Press, 1954.

Ptolemy. *Claudius Ptolemy: The Geography.* Edited and with a translation by Edward Luther Stevenson. New York: Dover Publishing, Inc., 1991.

Quilligan, Maureen. *Milton's Spenser: The Politics of Reading.* Ithaca: Cornell University Press, 1983.

Quint, David. 'Alexander the Pig: Shakespeare on History and Poetry.' *Boundary* 2 10 (1982): 49–68.

– *Origin and Originality in Renaissance Literature: Versions of the Source.* New Haven: Yale University Press, 1983.

Quintilian. *The Institutio Oratoria of Quintilian.* Edited and translated by H.E. Butler. Cambridge, MA: Harvard University Press, 1964.

Rabkin, Norman. *Shakespeare and the Problem of Meaning.* Chicago: University of Chicago Press, 1981.

Rambuss, Richard. *Spenser's Secret Career.* Cambridge: Cambridge University Press, 1993.

Rand, E.K. 'Milton in Rustication.' *Studies in Philology* 19 (1922): 109–35.

Rathborne, Isabel E. *The Meaning of Spenser's Fairyland.* New York: Columbia University Press, 1945.

Raymond, Joad. 'Look Homeward Angel: Guardian Angels and Nationhood in Seventeenth-Century England.' In *Early Modern Nationalism and Milton's England*, edited by David Loewenstein and Paul Stevens, 139–72. Toronto: University of Toronto Press, 2008.

Revard, Stella. *Milton and the Tangles of Neaera's Hair: The Making of the 1645 'Poems.'* Columbia, MO: University of Missouri Press, 1997.

Roche, Thomas P. Jr. *The Kindly Flame: A Study of the Third and Fourth Books of 'The Faerie Queene.'* Princeton: Princeton University Press, 1964.

Romm, James. *The Edges of the Earth in Ancient Thought: Geography, Exploration, and Fiction.* Princeton: Princeton University Press, 1992.

Rossi, Joan Warchol. '*Cymbeline*'s Debt to Holinshed: The Richness of III.1.' In *Shakespeare's Romances Reconsidered,* edited by Carol McGinnis Kay and Henry E. Jacobs, 104–12. Lincoln: University of Nebraska Press, 1978.

Sannazaro. *Jacopo Sannazaro: Latin Poetry.* Translated by Michael C.J. Putnam. Cambridge, MA: Harvard University Press, 2009.

Schwyzer, Philip. *Literature, Nationalism, and Memory in Early Modern England and Ireland.* Cambridge: Cambridge University Press, 2004.

Seneca. *Seneca in Ten Volumes.* Vol. 8: Tragedies. Edited by F.J. Miller. Cambridge, MA and London: Loeb Classical Books, 1917.

Seneca the Elder. *Suasoriae* 1.15. In *The Elder Seneca: Declamations in Two Volumes,* edited and with a translation by Michael Winterbottom. Cambridge, MA: Harvard University Press, 1974.

Serra, Luciano. 'Da Tolomeo alla Garfagnana: La Geografia dell'Ariosto.' In *Ludovico Ariosto: Il suo tempo, la sua terra, la sua gente.* Reggio Emilia: A. Manzoni, 1974.

Shakespeare, William. *Cymbeline.* Edited by J.M. Nosworthy. London and Cambridge, MA: Methuen and Harvard University Press, 1964.

– *The Norton Shakespeare.* Edited by Stephen Greenblatt et al. New York and London: W.W. Norton & Company, 1997.

Shawcross, John. 'Milton and Diodati: An Esssay in Psychodynamic Meaning.' *Milton Studies* 7 (1975): 127–63.

Shawcross, John, and A. Bartlett Giamatti, eds. *Commentary on the Poems of John Milton.* Vol. I. New York: Columbia University Press, 1970.

Sidney, Philip. *An Apology for Poetry.* Edited by Geoffrey Shepherd. London: T. Nelson, 1965.

Simonds, Peggy Muñoz. *Myth, Emblem, and Magic in Shakespeare's 'Cymbeline': An Iconographic Reconstruction.* Newark: University of Delaware Press, 1992.

Skalitzky, Rachel. 'Horace on Travel (*Epist.* 1.11).' *Classical Journal* 68, no. 4 (1973): 316–21.

Sobecki, Sebastian. *The Sea and Medieval English Literature.* Cambridge, UK: Brewer, 2008.

Solinus. *De mirabilibus mundi.* Translated by Arthur Golding. 1587. Speed, John. *Theatre of Great Britaine.* 1611.

Spenser, Edmund. *Edmund Spenser: The Faerie Queene.* Edited by A.C. Hamilton. Text edited by Hiroshi Yamashita and Toshiyuki Suzuki. London: Longman, 2001.

– *Edmund Spenser: A View of the State of Ireland*. Edited by Hadfield, Andrew Maley and Willy Maley. Oxford: Blackwell Publishers, 1997.

– *The Yale Edition of the Shorter Poems of Edmund Spenser*. Edited by W.A. Oram, E. Bjorvand, R. Bond, T.H. Cain, and R. Schell. New Haven: Yale University Press, 1989.

Stern, Virginia F. *Gabriel Harvey: His Life, Marginalia and Library*. Oxford: The Clarendon Press, 1979.

Strabo. *The Geography of Strabo*. Edited and translated by H.L. Jones. Cambridge, MA: Harvard University Press, 1917–32.

Strong, Roy. *Portraits of Queen Elizabeth*. Oxford: Clarendon Press, 1963.

Sullivan, Garrett. *The Drama of Landscape: Land, Property, and Social Relations on the Early Modern Stage*. Stanford, CA: Stanford University Press, 1998.

Suzuki, Mihoko. *Metamorphoses of Helen: Authority, Difference, and the Epic*. Ithaca: Cornell University Press, 1989.

Sylvester, Joshua. *The Devine Weekes and Workes of Guillaume de Salluste, Sieur du Bartas*. Edited by Susan Snyder. 2 vols. Oxford: Clarendon Press, 1979.

Tacitus. *Tacitus: The Germanica*. With an introduction and notes by Duane Reed Stuart. New York: MacMillan Co., 1923.

Taylor, E.G.R. *The Haven-Finding Art: A History of Navigation from Odysseus to Captain Cook*. Foreword by Commodore K.St.B. Collins, R.N. London: Hollins & Carter, 1956.

Tylus, Jane. *Writing and Vulnerability in the Late Renaissance*. Stanford, CA: Stanford University Press, 1993.

Vallans, William. *The Tale of Two Swannes*. Oxford: Printed at the Theater, 1769.

Van Es, Bart. *Spenser's Forms of History*. New York: Oxford University Press, 2002.

Virgil. *The Aeneid of Virgil*. Translated by Rolfe Humphries. New York: Bantam Books, 1982.

Waghenaer, Lucas Janszoon. *The Mariner's Mirrour*. Introduction by R.A. Skelton. Amsterdam: Theatrum Orbis Terrarum, 1966.

Wallace-Hadrill, A. '*Civilis princeps*: Between Citizen and King.' *JRS* 72 (1982): 32–48.

Wallerstein, Ruth. *Studies in Seventeenth Century Poetics*. Madison: University of Wisconsin Press, 1950.

Warren, Michelle. *History on the Edge: Excalibur and the Border of Britain, 1100–1300*. Minneapolis: University of Minnesota Press, 2000.

Waters, David W. *The Art of Navigation in Elizabethan England and Early Stuart Times*. New Haven: Yale University Press, 1958.

Wayne, Valerie. '*Cymbeline*'s Severed Heads and the Stuff of Romance.' Presentation for the 2005 SAA workshop 'Shakespeare and Romance.'

Webbe, William. *A Discourse of Englishe Poetrie.* In *The Renaissance in England: Non-Dramatic Prose and Verse of the Sixteenth Century,* edited by Hyder E. Rollins and Herschel Baker. Lexington, MA: D.C. Heath and Company, 1954.

Weinberg, Bernard. *A History of Literary Criticism in the Italian Renaissance.* 2 vols. Chicago: University of Chicago Press, 1961.

Wickham, E.C. *Horace, With a Commentary.* Oxford: Clarendon Press, 1903–12.

Wilkinson, L.P. *The Georgics of Virgil: A Critical Survey.* Cambridge: Cambridge University Press, 1970.

– *Ovid Recalled.* Cambridge: Cambridge University Press, 1955.

Williams, Gareth D. *Banished Voices: Readings in Ovid's Exile Poetry.* Cambridge: Cambridge University Press, 1994.

Wind, Edgar. *Pagan Mysteries in the Renaissance.* New York and London: W.W. Norton & Co, 1950.

Woodhouse, A.P., and Douglas Bush, eds. *A Variorum Commentary on the Poems of John Milton.* Vol. 3: The Minor English Poems. New York: Columbia University Press, 1970.

Woolf, D.R. *The Idea of History in Early Stuart England: Erudition, Ideology, and 'The Light of Truth' from the Accession of James I to the Civil War.* Toronto: University of Toronto Press, 1990.

Wofford, Susanne Lindgren. 'Britomart's Petrarchan Lament: Allegory and Narrative in *The Faerie Queene* III.iv.' *Comparative Literature* 39, vol. 1 (1987): 28–57.

Yates, Frances A. *Astraea: The Imperial Theme in the Sixteenth Century.* London: ARK, 1985.

– *Shakespeare's Last Plays: A New Approach.* London: Routledge and Kegan Paul, 1975.

Index